Puerto Rican Houses in Sociohistorical Perspective

Puerto Rican Houses
in Sociohistorical Perspective

Carol F. Jopling

The University of Tennessee Press / Knoxville

Copyright © 1988 by The University of Tennessee Press / Knoxville.
All Rights Reserved. Manufactured in the United States of America.
Cloth: 1st printing, 1988.
Paper: 1st printing, 1992.

Frontispiece: Designed Criollo Pueblerino House. Two-opening facade. Ponce.

The paper in this book meets the minimum requirements of the
American National Standard for Permanence of Paper for Printed
Library Materials. ∞ The binding materials have been chosen
for strength and durability.

Library of Congress Cataloging-in-Publication Data

Jopling Carol F.
     Puerto Rican houses in sociohistorical perspective.

  Bibliography: p.
  Includes Index.
  1. Archictecture, Domestic—Puerto Rico—Themes,
motives. 2. Vernacular architecture—Puerto Rico—
Themes, motives. 3. Architecture and society—
Puerto Rico—Themes, motives. I. Title.
NA7283.J67   1988   728'.097295   87–6025
ISBN 0–87049–543–7 (cloth: alk. paper)
ISBN 0–87049–763–4 (pbk.: alk. paper)

Contents

Acknowledgments	xvii
Introduction	xix
CHAPTER 1: The Stylistic Development of Puerto Rican Houses in Historical Context	1
Geography	1
Early People and the Styles of Their Habitations	4
Caribbean and European Influences	27
United States Domination	41
Summary	60
CHAPTER 2: A Typology of Puerto Rican Houses and the Pattern of Residence	63
Materials	64
Formal Organization	67
House Types of the Spanish-Criollo Period, 1780–1880	74
House Types of the Eclectic Period, 1875–1910	131
U.S. Influence Houses, 1920–1940	141
Urbanización Houses, 1950–1980	168
Second Houses	176
Parcela, Jíbaro, and Arrabal Houses	179
Summary of Residence Patterns	190
Social Implications of House Form	192

CHAPTER 3: Messages and Meanings	195
Theoretical Considerations	195
Designed Houses	208
Vernacular Houses	235
Urbanización Houses	251
Conclusions	259
Notes	261
Bibliography	269
Index	289

Illustrations

1.	a. Map of Puerto Rico	2
1.	b. Map of the West Indies, 1794	3
2.	Map of Columbus' Second Voyage	6
3.	Taíno *Caney* and *Bohío*	9
4.	*Bohío* Near Patíllas	10
5.	Colonial Spanish House, Uruguay, 1985	14
6.	Colonial Spanish House, Old San Juan, 1979	16
7.	Aerial View of Martín Peña Canal and Tidal Slums	17
8.	Census Data	18
9.	Former Slave Quarters, Boca Chica Hacienda.	19
10.	*Bohío* and Cooking Shed in "Little Africa"	20
11.	House in Boca de Cangrejos	21
12.	Facade Drawing for #83 Calle Cristo	24
13.	View of San Germán, 1821–23	25
14.	View of Ponce, 1821–23	25
15.	Unoccupied House, Hacienda Esperanza	30
16.	Occupied Hacienda House Near San Germán	31
17.	Worker's House, Hacienda Dos Rios	31
18.	Hacienda House near Ciales	32
19.	Hacienda House, Hormigueras	33
20.	Criollo House, Añasco	33
21.	Typical Criollo Patterns	34
22.	Criollo Neoclassic House, Sábana Grande	35

23. Pueblerino House, Fajardo — 35
24. Early Gothic Revival House, Aguadilla — 36
25. Camelback House, Guayama — 37
26. Tower House, Río Piedras — 37
27. High Victorian Gothic House, Fajardo — 38
28. Queen Anne House, San Germán — 38
29. Pueblerino House with Early Gothic Trim, Naguabo — 39
30. Window Design with Circular Light, Añasco — 41
31. Partially Excavated *Tren Jamaica*, Hacienda Esperanza — 42
32. Living Quarters for Sugar Workers — 43
33. Workers' Houses, Sugar *Central* — 44
34. High Neoclassic House, Utuado — 46
35. Beaux Arts House, Ponce — 47
36. Nechodoma House, Aibonito — 48
37. Vernacular Bungalow, Fajardo — 48
38. Spanish Colonial Revival House, San Juan — 49
39. "El Castillo," Spanish Colonial Revival House, Ponce — 50
40. Art Deco House, Moca — 51
41. Vernacular House with Art Deco Ornamentation, San Juan — 52
42. Country House, La Parguera — 53
43. Jíbaro Kitchen, 1979 — 53
44. a. Site Manufacture of Urbanización Houses, Luquillo   b. Later Stage of Construction — 55
45. Completed Urbanización House, Luquillo — 56
46. "El Fanguito," July 1946 — 57
47. Arrabal House in "La Perla" — 58
48. *Arrabal* House Transformed into Pueblerino House and Tienda — 59
49. View of *Arrabal* "La Perla" — 60
50. Block Study of Old San Juan — 65
51. Schema One: Plans I/1, I/2, I/3 — 67
52. Schema Two: Plans II/1, II/2 — 68
53. Schema Three: Plans III/1, III/2, III/3 — 68
54. Facades: Two, Three, and Four Openings — 69
55. *Balcones*: Full, half-*balcón*, Second-Story, Surrounding — 71
56. Roofs: Gable, Extended Gable, Hip, Flat — 71
57. *Galería* — 73
58. a. Vernacular Criollo House, Arecibo   b. Plan — 75
59. Vernacular Criollo House, Arecibo — 76

60. a. Vernacular Criollo House with
    "Window-Box" *balcón*, Manatí b. Plan   77
61. a. Designed Criollo Neoclassic House, Arecibo b. Plan 79
62. a. Vernacular Pueblerino House, Luquillo b. Plan   80
63. Designed Criollo Pueblerino House, Manatí   81
64. a. Designed Criollo Pueblerino House, Ponce b. Plan   82
65. Small Apartment behind House   83
66. Vernacular Pueblerino House, Ceiba   83
67. a. Grand Criollo House, Guayama b. Plan   85
68. a. Vernacular U.S. Influence House, San Juan b. Plan 86
69. Designed Criollo Neoclassic House, Ponce   87
70. a. Vernacular Pueblerino House, Santurce
    b. Plan c. *Comedor*   88
71. a. Designed Criollo House, Río Grande b. Plan   89
72. Grand Criollo Neoclassic House, San Juan   90
73. a. Colonial Spanish House, Mayaguez b. Plan   91
74. Colonial Spanish *Caminera*, San Germán   92
75. a. Grand Criollo Neoclassic House, Guayama
    b. Plan c. Interior View with *Mediopunto*,
    Scrollwork, and Chandelier   94–5
76. a. Vernacular Early Gothic Revival House,
    Naguabo b. Interior with *Mediopunto*   96
77. a. Designed Criollo House, Aibonito b. Plan   97
78. Designed Criollo House, Lares   98
79. a. Vernacular Criollo House, Moca b. Plan
    c. Interior   100
80. a. Grand High Neoclassic House, Guayama
    b. Plan c. Garden   101
81. Designed Criollo House, Añasco   102
82. Designed Criollo House, San Germán   102
83. Designed Criollo Neoclassic House, Yauco   103
84. a. Designed Criollo Neoclassic House, Juana Díaz
    b. Plan   104
85. Designed Criollo House, Guayama   105
86. Designed Criollo House, Ciales   105
87. a. Designed Criollo House, Juana Díaz b. Plan   106
88. a. Grand Criollo House, Coamo b. Plan   107
89. Grand Criollo House, Ponce   108
90. Vernacular Pueblerino House, Hatillo   109
91. Designed Criollo House, Arroyo   110

92. a. Designed Criollo House, Arroyo   b. Plan
    c. Garden Steps   112–13
93. a. Vernacular Criollo Pueblerino Two-House
    Two-Story, Ponce   b. Upper Level Plan   114
94. Vernacular Criollo Two-House Two-Story, Río Piedras   115
95. a. Designed Criollo Neoclassic House
    and Tienda, Añasco   b. Plan   c. Interior   116
96. Designed Criollo House and Tienda, San Germán   117
97. Designed High Neoclassic Corner House
    and Tienda, Adjuntas   118
98. a. Designed Criollo Hacienda House,
    San Germán   b. Plan   119
99. a. Grand Criollo Neoclassic Hacienda House,
    Sábana Grande   b. Wing Extension   121
100. a. Designed Criollo Hacienda House, Maricao
     b. Plan   122
101. a. Designed Criollo Hacienda House, Maricao
     b. Rear View   123
102. a. Designed Criollo Hacienda House, Near Yauco
     b. Plan   124
103. a. Interior of Santa Clara Arriba   b. Plan   125
104. a. Grand Criollo Neoclassic Hacienda House,
     Maricao   b. Plan   126
105. Characteristics of Spanish
     and Criollo House Residents   130
106. a. Grand Queen Anne Two-Story
     One-Family Mansion, Naguabo   b. Plan   132
107. a. Grand Greek Revival Two-Story
     One-Family Mansion, San Sebastián   b. Plan   133
108. Plans of Partial Second-Story Houses   134
109. a. Vernacular Camelback, Puerto Real   b. Rear View   135
110. Designed Camelback Addition, Mayaguez   136
111. Designed Tower House, Aguadilla   137
112. a. Designed Belvedere House, Juana Díaz   b. Plan   138
113. a. Grand Belvedere House, San Germán   b. Interior
     with *Comedor*   140
114. Characteristics of Eclectic House Residents   142
115. a. Grand Beaux Arts House, Ponce   b. Plan   143
116. a. Designed Criollo Corner Entrance House, Aguadilla
     b. Plan   144

117. a. Designed Criollo Neoclassic House,
Humacao b. Plan c. Hallway — 146
118. Designed Bungaloid Influenced House, Aguadilla — 147
119. Designed Bungaloid Influenced Reinforced
Concrete House, Cayey — 147
120. Vernacular Bungalow, Fajardo — 148
121. Vernacular Bungalow, Ciales — 149
122. a. Vernacular Art Deco, San Juan b. Entry — 150
123. a. Designed Bungaloid House, Barranquitas
b. Plan — 152
124. Designed bungaloid House
with Partial-Second-Story Mirador, San Juan — 153
125. Vernacular U.S. Influence Two-Story
One-Family House, Arroyo — 153
126. Designed U.S. Influence Two-Story
One-Family House, Hatillo — 154
127. a. Designed Nechodoma/Prairie House, Coamo
b. Plan — 155
128. Designed Prairie House, Naguabo — 156
129. Designed Art Deco House, Moca — 157
130. a. Designed Art Deco House, Guayama b. Plan — 158
131. Designed Spanish Colonial Revival House, San Juan — 159
132. Designed Spanish Colonial Revival House, San Juan — 160
133. a. Grand Prairie House, Humacao b. Plan — 161
134. a. Designed Art Deco Two-Story One-Family House,
Humacao b. Plan of First Floor — 162
135. Designed Spanish Colonial Revival Two-Story
One-Family House, San Juan — 163
136. Vernacular Finca House, La Parguera — 164
137. Vernacular Two-Opening House — 165
138. Grand Belvedere House, Outside Mayaguez — 166
139. Designed Engineer's House, Sugar *Central* — 167
140. Designed Engineer's House, Sugar *Central* — 167
141. Characteristics of U.S. Influence House Residents — 169
142. a. Vernacular Urbanización House, Carolina
b. Retaining Wall and Front Garden — 171
143. Designed Urbanización House, Río Piedras — 172
144. Designed Urbanización House, Río Piedras — 173
145. a. Grand International Style House by Henry Klumb,
San Germán b. Tienda on Lower Level — 174

146. Vernacular Farm House of Reinforced Concrete — 176
147. Concrete Vernacular Country House under Construction — 177
148. Vernacular Fisherman's House — 177
149. Characteristics of Urbanización House Residents — 178
150. Water House, La Parguera — 179
151. Parcela Wood House, Luquillo — 181
152. a. Parcela Wood House, Naguabo b. Side View Showing Waterfront Site — 182
153. Parcela Reinforced-Concrete House, La Parguera — 183
154. Jíbaro House, Piñones — 184
155. Old Jíbaro House, near San Germán — 185
156. Jíbaro Building with Yagua Roof, near San Germán — 185
157. a. Jíbaro House with *Balcón*, near Luquillo b. Back view c. Interior — 186
158. "El Fanguito," 1946 — 187
159. Arrabal House and Tienda under Construction, Carolina — 188
160. Characteristics of Parcela, Jíbaro, and Arrabal House Residents — 189
161. Summary of Characteristics of Vernacular, Designed, and Grand House Residents — 191
162. Hotel Francés, Vieques — 199
163. Town Plan of Añasco — 202
164. Sports Store, Ponce — 206
165. Commercial Building, Adjuntas — 207
166. Funeral Home, Arecibo — 208
167. Street of Colonial Spanish Houses, San Juan — 210
168. Street of Criollo Houses, Arecibo — 212
169. Patio Garden of Criollo Neoclassic House, Humacao — 213
170. Patio Garden of Criollo Neoclassic House and Tienda, Añasco — 213
171. Interior of Spanish Colonial House — 215
172. *Mediopunto*, San Germán — 216
173. *Mediopunto*, Mayaguez — 217
174. Doorway, Añasco — 218
175. Doorway Paneling, Arroyo — 219
176. Puerto Rican Nineteenth-Century Furniture — 219
177. Interior, with Painting of Sacred Heart — 220
178. Interior, with Antique Furniture and Oil Paintings — 221

179.	Doorway of Spanish Colonial Revival House, San Juan	224
180.	*Rejas* on Spanish Colonial Revival House, San Juan	226
181.	*Rejas* on Spanish Colonial Revival House, San Juan	227
182.	Informal *Comedor* Sitting Area, Humacao	228
183.	"Maria Teresa" Style Furniture	229
184.	Plaster Moldings, Ponce	229
185.	Interior of Spanish Colonial Revival House, San Juan	230
186.	Street of Criollo Vernacular Houses, Camuy	235
187.	a.–d. Patterns of Decorative Concrete Block for *Balcones*	237
188.	Vernacular Bungaloid House, Camuy	240
189.	Vernacular Art Deco Renovation, Río Piedras	241
190.	Interior, Vernacular Bungaloid House, Camuy	242
191.	Interior, Vernacular Two-Story Two-Family House, Ponce	243
192.	*Arrabal* Settlement Pattern, Hato Rey area, San Juan	247
193.	Interior, Arrabal House, Camuy	248
194.	*Sala*, Arrabal House, Arecibo	249
195.	Front of Urbanización House, Luquillo	252
196.	a.–c. Facade Variation, Three Urbanización Houses with the same plan	254
197.	Front Yard, Urbanización House, Luquillo	256
198.	a.–c. *Rejas*, garden walls, and other modifications made to Urbanización Houses, Boqueron	257
198.	b. Urbanización House, Luquillo	257
198.	c. Urbanización House, Luquillo	257

Mi casa y mi hogar cien dobles val.
>> Juana G. Campos and Ana Barella, *Diccionario de Refranes*

 My house and home are worth a hundredfold.

 Casa propria es un tesoro que no es pagado con oro.
Grande o chica, pobre o rica, casa mía.
>> Luís Martínez Kleiser, *Refranero General Ideológico Español*

 One's own house is a treasure that cannot be bought with gold.
Large or small, poor or rich, my own house.

◼ Acknowledgments

I am indebted to a number of instutitions and individuals for their assistance and support of this investigation. Earthwatch provided funding, and Dr. Gordon R. Willey, Harvard University, initially supported the grant. Dr. Ricardo Alegría, director of the Centro de Estudios Avanzados de Puerto Rico y El Caribe, and his wife, Doña Melia, generously offered every possible assistance. At the School of Architecture, University of Puerto Rico, its acting dean, Dr. Efraín Pérez-Chanis, and Professors Eugene Crommett and Rafael A. Crespo located student assistants, enabled me to use the school's library and other facilities, and provided useful advice. Others who freely gave of their time and expertise include Dan Jones, photographic archivist, Peabody Museum, Harvard University; Thomas Marvel, architect; Jack Delano, Farm Security Administration photographer; Professor Rafael Ramírez, Head, Department of Anthropology, University of Puerto Rico; Professor Eugenio Fernández-Méndez, anthropologist; Ovidio Dávila, archaeologist; Dr. Luis Pumarada, University of Puerto Rico, Mayaguez; and José Dávila, architectural historian. Competent student assistants, Jorge Ortiz Colón and Juan Gómez Véliz, and the unfailingly diligent Earthwatch volunteers who are listed below contributed in large measure. I am particularly indebted to the residents of the houses I investigated; their courtesy and generous welcome were beyond all expectations. I also appreciate the useful criticisms of a previous draft by Dr. Pérez-Chanis, Dr. Pumarada, and Dr. Ramírez, as well as the comments of Dr. Jay Edwards, Louisiana State University; Dr. Juan Pablo Bonta, University of Maryland; and Dr. John Vlach, George Washington University.

Earthwatch Volunteers

Joan Arbeiter, Arnold Coggeshall Sr., Helen Dowdeswell, Anne Gibbons, Celine Marie Larkin, Nora Nixon, Jesse Wheeler, Virginia J. Wheeler, Barbara Zinn.

Credits for Illustrations

Drawings, based on photographs and sketches, were created by: Julio Montañez (figures 3, 12, 13, 14, 20, 22, 23, 24, 25, 26, 27, 28, 30, 34, 35, 36, 37, 38, 39, 40, 41, 42, 45, 67a, 72, 78, 107a, 111, 172, 173, 176, 187), Ernesto Santalla (figures 16, 18, and a number of plans), and José E. Solis (figures 1a, 2, 50, 108, 163, 192, and a majority of the plans).

Unless otherwise indicated, photographs were taken during the survey in 1978–79 by Earthwatch volunteers, student assistants, and the author.

Dennis Kan made the black-and-white prints.

The General Archives of Puerto Rico has granted permission for the use of the following photographs: figures 32 and 33, photographed by Jack Delano; figures 7, 46, and 158, photographed by Charles E. Rotkin; and figures 4 and 10, photographed by Rosskam.

Introduction

This book seeks to answer the question, Why are Puerto Rican houses as they are? Cast in an ethnological framework, it searches for sociocultural explanation of the diverse forms, the intense and colorful decorative elements, and the varied configuration of Puerto Rican houses. A second intent is to comprehend the relationship between Puerto Rican houses and their inhabitants and, ultimately, to understand the articulation of houses with Puerto Rican society. What were the origins of the various styles? In what ways are the residents of diverse house types alike or different? For answers to the book's guiding question and others such as these, the study draws on the sociohistorical background of Puerto Rico, as well as on formal analysis, survey questions, and informal interviews.

This investigation of Puerto Rican houses was inspired by a previous study I made of the adaptative strategies of Puerto Rican immigrants residing in three Boston housing developments in the South End neighborhood. The investigation of their habitations found that the majority had created a spatial order that seemed based on a Puerto Rican model and an intense use of color and pattern which was apparently an idealized or nostalgic evocation of the ambiance of Puerto Rico. The very importance of these habitations to their residents, evinced by the individuality and the proportionately high investment in furnishings and embellishment, recommended the houses of Puerto Rico as attractive subjects for further research.

Above all, the lively diversity of the Puerto Rican built environment, which contrasts sharply with less differentiated, plainer North American settings, invites architectural investigation. In Puerto Rico there are distinctions between the residence areas of rich and poor, but characteristics such as zoning of residential and commercial sections or entire communities composed of houses with uniform architectural styles or of similar value, common in North America, were rare in Puerto Rico, as elsewhere in Latin America until recently. Such differences have been attributed to the greater emphasis put on the outward appearance of individual distinction by people of Spanish heritage, in comparison with North Americans, who are more comfortable with conformity (Boorstin 1958:5–9; Perin 1977). It is not a case of "Every man for himself," but rather, "I am as good as or better than the next man, and it is up to me to display that in my bearing, dress, and dwelling." The ancient Spanish idea that the king owed his power to the support of the populace both peasant and bourgeois, meant that each man "*da la real gana*" (felt himself a king). In Latin America this idea has been transformed into the notion of *dignidad* (dignity), a term that expresses pride and self-worth and is similar to the Spanish term *orgullo* (pride), but without the connotation of arrogance. The concepts of *respeto* (respect) and *dignidad* are pervasive among middle and lower levels of Puerto Rican society. Every person has *dignidad*, which is demonstrated by neat dress, mannerly behavior, and adherence to social standards. A person of *dignidad* expects *respeto*, that is, expects to be treated as a worthy individual of *dignidad* (Landy 1965), and so presents the best possible image—well dressed, well housed, and, these days, possessing a handsome shiny car. A house, therefore, is a vehicle for presenting the owner as a person of *dignidad*.

It has also been pointed out that people of Iberian heritage do not have the idea of progress, of ultimately rising in society, that is fundamental to North Americans (Boorstin 1958:155–58). Instead they expect their present state to continue into the future. Puerto Ricans, once settled in their own house, plan to live in the same neighborhood for the rest of their lives. Consequently they invest proportionately large amounts of energy and income embellishing their houses to express *dignidad* and to establish their position in the community. Diversity of ornamentation and color, among other differentiating features, is the outcome of such individual expression.

Puerto Rico's island situation (itself, as many researchers have noted, conducive to a survey) affords the opportunity of considering comparatively the houses of an entire culture. It was possible to visit all of the island, selecting representative examples of houses in nearly every town and city and in the rural areas of every region.

This book is based on data gathered during a four-month period from December 1978 to April 1979. The six-week survey, funded by Earthwatch, was conducted with the support of three teams of Earthwatch volunteers and assistance from architectural students in the School of Architecture, University of Puerto Rico. Since a principal aim of the investigation was to create a typology of Puerto Rican houses, the immediate goal was to visit, photograph, and record data on at least one example of every type of Puerto Rican house, omitting all multidwelling buildings, such as apartments, condominiums, and housing developments. A second purpose was to obtain demographic information on the residents of every house surveyed.

Selection of the 145 houses included in the survey was based primarily on visual apprehension and also depended on the presence of residents and their willingness to participate. At each house, the following procedures took place. The exterior of the house, the interior *sala* (living room), and, when possible, other rooms were inspected and photographed. Measurements were made of the *sala*; the facade, including distance between openings; the width of the *balcon* (porch or balcony); the height above ground level; and the distance from the street. The orientation of the house was noted. In some cases, sketch plans were made. House residents were interviewed informally to elicit specific data on age, occupation, education, mobility, time or duration of residence, home ownership, and personal and anecdotal information on the house.

To maintain consistency during the survey, a number of questions which might lead to the meanings of houses were kept in mind. These included: What is the relationship of private ownership to house preference, to house decoration, to location? Are the patterns of decoration consistent throughout the island or do they differ from rural to urban, rich to poor? How does the material of construction affect the form of houses? Does it indicate social level? Do colors of houses vary according to social level and urban or rural situation? The data resulting from the survey were later supplemented by consultations with various professionals—archaeologists, architects, artists, anthropologists, and other specialists and nonspecialists—and by library and archival research.

Through the survey method a large amount of data was accumulated that provided insight into the historical associations of developmental changes in houses; into resident preferences for and/or relationships with particular house types, according to social level; and into social meanings related to these issues.

It certainly can be said that houses present an image of a society at a particular moment, constitute a record of change through time, reflect cultural choices—social, economic, religious, aesthetic—and mirror the vision that people have of the ideal life (Rapoport 1969). However, interpretation of house meanings presents difficulties to both insiders and outsiders in any society.[1] Though the inquiry concerning meaning, recurring throughout this book, is grounded in the material and documentary evidence as far as possible, it must be asserted that meanings change according to sociohistoric context and that social codes are easily misconstrued. "Meaning," a term that encompasses multiple aspects of significance, is used here also to specify the broad categories of historical (past), social or societal (present), and personal meaning. Societal and historical meanings are of primary concern, although these always overlap with personal ones. Nevertheless, the many private, personal, sentimental meanings attached to particular houses by their residents and known only to them were not explored. Rather, the focus is on the interpretation of social meanings of houses—that is, those meanings commonly held by the general populace or broad segments of it—through examination of Puerto Rican house forms in their historical and cultural context.

The book proposes (1) to attempt to understand the relationship between Puerto Rican houses and culture through analysis of style, form, spatial order, and ornamentation; (2) to interpret the articulation of houses and society by examining the relationships between house types and social characteristics of residents; and (3) to penetrate the meanings attached to houses by close analysis of the spatial organization and ornament. To address these goals, chapter 1 looks at the stylistic development of houses in the context of history. The drawings used as illustrations are idealized representations intended to accentuate stylistic characteristics. In chapter 2 a typology of house types is offered, and the connections between types and social characteristics of residents are examined. The photographs are records of the houses as they appeared at the time of a visit. The accompanying plans, not to scale, are essentially diagrams intended to show spatial organization and room order. The third chapter, conceived within the framework of nonverbal communication, examines the messages communicated by house forms, in an effort to reach the meanings of houses in present-day society.

Through reliance on information from many individuals and numerous written sources and other documentation, the study attempts to understand the houses from the Puerto Rican standpoint. But in the end it is perforce an outsider's description and analysis. Puerto Rican opinions and beliefs obtained directly from residents or others are so identified.

Why are Puerto Rican houses the way they are? Do certain kinds of people choose to live in certain kinds of houses? What are the relationships of Puerto Rican houses to the society? These are the questions to which answers are sought in the following chapters.

Puerto Rican Houses in Sociohistorical Perspective

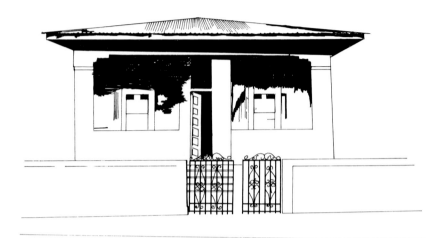

CHAPTER 1

The Stylistic Development of Puerto Rican Houses in Historical Context

A description of the physical reality must be the starting point in understanding the meanings of Puerto Rican houses from the Puerto Rican standpoint. Thus we begin with an examination of the styles of existing houses within a broad historical perspective. It is assumed that indications or clues to meaning will emerge through: (1) identification and analysis of the styles selected by Puerto Ricans, (2) understanding of the development of house forms and their relationship to Puerto Rican culture and other contributing cultures, and (3) assessment of temporal and geographical similarities and differences in houses. Technology of construction, types of materials used, and siting of structures are also essential to the analysis, but are considered here primarily in conjunction with style.

GEOGRAPHY

The geography of Puerto Rico must be considered first, because of its prominent role in the social development and history of the island. But Puerto Rican geography has influenced house structure and style directly as well. Until the mid-twentieth century, the siting of houses and the materials of their construction were closely tied to the terrain and the tropical climate.

The smallest of the Greater Antilles, Puerto Rico lies farthest to

Figure 1a. Map of Contemporary Puerto Rico.

the east, between the Atlantic and the Caribbean. Its territory includes the satellite islands of Vieques and Culebra to the east and Mona to the west. The island of Hispaniola, now Santo Domingo and Haiti, is its nearest Caribbean neighbor.

Measuring 100 by 135 miles, Puerto Rico has an extremely varied landscape for an island of its size. Each of its eleven distinct geographical zones is suitable, because of climate and terrain, for a particular type of cultivation. The mountainous interior, which reaches 4,389 feet at its peak, makes up 40 percent of its land. The surrounding coastal area varies regionally. The broad northern plain rises to a plateau 500 feet above sea level in the west and then slopes to the east, ending in lagoons and lakes near San Juan and the Luquillo sierra, the area of highest rainfall. The southern coastal plain is much narrower, and the drop from the mountain heights is precipitous, in contrast to the more gradual northern incline; this plain, which is particularly fertile between Patillas and Ponce, becomes a hilly landscape in the dry southwest area. Great triangular valleys intersect the mountain ranges at both eastern and western ends of the island. Fifty rivers and numerous small streams provide Puerto Rico with an abundant water supply. The climate is tropical, but the island is cooled by east or southeast tradewinds and frequent showers, particularly in the mountains and to the northeast.

Puerto Rico is rich in tropical vegetation, minerals, and other resources, although they have been badly exploited. Its hardwood forests were stripped for charcoal and furniture manufacture and its

Figure 1b. Detail from a map of the West Indies by J. Russell, 1794. The paucity of place names noted for Puerto Rico is indicative of the island's level of development at the time.

cultivable lands eroded through overcropping and overgrazing. Yet, even though one quarter of the land cannot be cultivated because of its forty-five-degree incline, the rest, with proper management, could provide a greater percentage of the subsistence of its people than is presently the case (Figueroa 1972).

As one would expect, the majority of Puerto Rican houses were built of wood, and until late in the nineteenth century a large proportion had thatched palm roofs. Beginning early in the sixteenth century, however, the intrusion of European culture brought a variety of styles and additional materials.

Early People and the Styles of Their Habitations

The records, both documentary and architectural, are incomplete, but enough remain to permit at least a partial reconstruction of the stylistic development of Puerto Rican houses in their historical context.

Two of the many definitions of style are particularly relevant for our purposes. The first, by an architect, Henri Focillon, emphasizes the constituents of style: "What then constitutes a style? First its formal elements, which have a certain index value, and which make up its repertory, its vocabulary, and occasionally, the very instrument with which it wields its power. Second, although less obviously, its system of relationships, its syntax. The affirmation of a style is found in its measures. In such wise did the Greeks understand a style when they defined it by the relative proportions of its parts" (Stiny 1981:258).[1]

The second, Meyer Schapiro's well-known essay, includes similar ideas but also points out the relationship between style and culture: "Description of a style refers to form elements or motives, form relationships, and qualities (including an all-over quality which we may call the 'expression') (Schapiro 1961:83). Similarities in style arise from cultural norms. As norms change through innovation or the introduction of new elements, style changes. By relating style to specific cultural events, it can be associated with temporal sequence. Styles are manifestations of change over time; but different styles occurring simultaneously within a culture are also expressive of different groups (Schapiro 1961:81–91).

"Style then is [a] means of communication, a language not only as a system of devices for conveying a precise message by representing or symbolizing objects and actions, but as a qualitative whole which is capable of suggesting the diffuse connotations, as well, and intensifying the associated or intrinsic effects" (Schapiro 1961:104). In one sense, Puerto Rican culture history is displayed in the distinctive styles of existing dwellings which were built during various historical periods for people of diverse ethnic backgrounds and social levels.

Puerto Rican society evolved from the merging of different peoples, three of whom were of greatest importance: the Taíno Indians (an Arawak people) who populated the island at the time of first European contact, the Spaniards who conquered the island early in the sixteenth century and the black Africans who were brought as slaves from the sixteenth to the middle of the nineteenth century. Other Europeans, limited in number until their extensive increase in the mid-nineteenth century, also contributed to the population and culture. Their imprint is still visible in some of the houses as well. Since 1898, the major and pervasive influence has come from the United States. The architectural styles of all of these peoples are still identifiable even though they were always modified and adapted so as to become distinctively Puerto Rican. Yet the majority of Puerto Rican houses have changed over time according to function, the aesthetic tastes of owners, and changing fashion. The result is a kind of layering of styles, the elements of which can be uncovered, if at times only with the aid of documentation. This investigation of stylistic-historical development therefore relies on both documentary and architectural evidence. It proceeds chronologically, beginning with the *bohíos* of the Taíno Indians.[2] In each section, historical and architectural descriptive information precedes a brief analytical discussion.

Taíno Indians

In Puerto Rico, the term *bohío*[3], derived from the Taíno term for house, *buhío*, generally signifies a two-room house built of a timber frame, walled with cane or *yagua* (inner bark of palm), roofed with thatch, and with either a dirt floor or a wooden one raised on posts. Throughout most of Puerto Rican history this dwelling in its various versions was the common vernacular house. Today *bohíos* made of cane or *yagua* exist only as folkloric reconstructions; nevertheless, they remain important in cultural memory not only as evocations of Puerto Rican history, but as significant influences on the spatial order and technology of subsequent vernacular houses. Puerto Rican

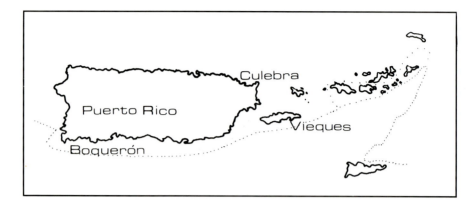

Figure 2. Map of the Second Voyage of Columbus. (Morison 1942.)

bohíos originated with the aboriginal Taíno dwellings first described in the accounts of Columbus's second voyage. He was the first European to visit Puerto Rico, but since his own records of this voyage did not survive, the exact site of his landing on the west coast is still a matter of dispute (Brau 1973; Morison 1939, 1974). Reconstruction of the Puerto Rican visit differs according to recorder, so controversy as to the more accurate version has persisted. However, the descriptions of the houses by Bartolomé de las Casas and Fernando Colón (son of Columbus), who both had access to Christopher Columbus's records and library, are now generally believed to be reliable.[4]

> Some Christians went ashore and went to some houses, all very well made though of straw and wood; they had a plaza with a road from it to the sea, very clean and straight, made like a street; and the walls of cane, crossed or interwoven, and above also with their graceful greens as if they were grapevines or orchards of orange or citron trees like those in Valencia or Barcelona; and next to the sea was a watch tower where ten or twelve persons could fit, well made in the same manner; it must be a summer house of the lord of that island or of that part of it.
> (Las Casas, taken from Pérez Chanis 1976:7, author's translation)

> Then he put into port at the island, which he called San Juan Bautista but the Indians called Boriquen, and the fleet anchored in a channel on the west of it, where they caught many fish, some like ours, and saw falcons and wild grapevines; and more to the

east some Christians went to certain houses of the Indians, which were well built, as was their custom; these houses had a square with an exit toward the sea, a broad street with towers of cane on both sides, which at the top were interwoven with beautiful work of plants and grasses, as in the gardens of Valencia. And at the end toward the sea was a high, well-made wooden platform that could hold ten or twelve people.
(F. Colón 1944:128, author's translation)

Though limited, these descriptions provide the useful information that the houses were well made of cane and wood, that they faced a square or plaza, and that at least one structure was a raised platform, suggesting the use of supporting posts—all characteristics which persisted.

Loven's conclusions about Taíno houses, which were based on Columbus's impressions of Taíno dwellings on Española and elsewhere, and on his own analysis of some South American Arawak houses, seem plausible. He says that the *cacique* (chief) and his wife and concubines lived in a spacious elliptical or polygonal residence on the plaza or *batey*. The townspeople lived in round houses, thirty to forty feet in diameter, which accommodated several families, possibly fifteen men with their wives and children. These houses were bell-shaped, narrow at the top and wide at the bottom, and had no walls or doors; and the floors were of packed leveled earth (Loven 1935:336–44).

Under Spanish influence Taíno houses apparently changed very quickly from round and elliptical or polygonal to rectangular, first those of the *caciques*, who were closely associated with the first Spanish settlers, and later those of the townspeople. On his third voyage, Columbus was already commenting on the form of a large house, the home of a town *cacique*: "una casa grande hecha a dos aguas ... y no redonda, como tienda de campo, de la manera que son las de las islas" [a large house with a roof of two slopes ... and not round like indigenous houses in the islands] (Loven 1935:339).

Oviedo, a seventeenth century observer, is responsible for the most complete description of Taíno houses, including drawings and details of their construction. He recorded the building of a *caney* (round house) in Haiti, where, evidently, unmodified indigenous house types persisted longer.

> They sunk into the ground a number of round posts of good wood (and convenient diameter) in a circle with a distance of four to five paces, or whatever distance they wished, between posts. And after they were set in the ground higher than a man's head, they put stringpieces [wall plates] on top, and on them in turn place[d] roundabout the ribs [truss system] which form the template for the thatch [cover], with the butts or thick part of the ribs [rafters] on the stringpieces [wall plates] with the thinner part towards the top where all the ends come together in a peak, in the manner of a tent [pavilion].
>
> And on the ribs [rafters] they place crossways canes, or lathes, just an inch apart or closer, either double or single, and over these a covering of long fine grass. Others cover them with the leaves of the *bihao* (calathea insignis); others with the shoots of cane; others palm leaves, and also with other things. And below, instead of walls between the crossbeams and the earth, they put thick canes, sunk into the earth and as close together as the fingers of a hand. And with one next to another they make a wall, and they fasten them very well with *bejucos*, which are vines or rounded creepers that grow twined about the trees (and also hanging from them) like small rope. These *bejucos* are very good for fastening, because they are pliant and flexible, and don't rot, and they take the place of cords and nails to fasten one piece of wood to another, and likewise to tie the canes.
>
> The *buhío* built in such fashion is called a *caney*.
> (Daymond Turner 1975:100, translator; bracketed architectural terms added by author)[5]

As Oviedo illustrated, the *caney* was supported by a central mast or post to which the rafters of the roof were tied. He encountered another type of house, the dwelling of the "principal men and chiefs, 935" which manifested the hispanification of Taíno dwellings (Loven 1935:340–41); and Oviedo noted the details of the technology involved in the transition from polygonal to four-cornered houses:

> Instead of placing the posts in a cornered circle, they are arranged in a rectangle. In place of an upright stick of timber to support the roof at the central point, this was sustained by a row of "horcones que acá llamamos haytinales que llegan a la cumbrera e caballete alto" (ridge posts called here *haytinales*, reach the ridgepole and top gable) that extended the whole length of the house. The insertion of walls between the posts remained the same. Instead of the roof-beams being united as in the round house to the cen-

Figure 3. Copies of Oviedo's drawings of a Taíno *caney* and *bohío*. (Fernández de Oviedo y Valdés 1959:138.)

tral post that supported the entire roof, they were now fastened at an angle and opposite to each other to the ridge-piece which lay on forked posts (Oviedo, quoted in Loven 1935:340–41 Author's paraphrase of Loven's text.)

A further modification was the porch, which "they set . . . to serve as entryway or reception room, covered with thatch" (Turner 1975: 102). Oviedo observed that "the Christians are already building this kind of house . . . with attics and lofty rooms and windows, because, since they have nails and make very good boards and know how to build better than Indians, they make of these houses so well that any lord could lodge in one of them" (Turner 1975:102).

The house, as modified and adapted by the Spaniards, resembled more closely the *bohío* that persisted over the next few centuries than the dwellings described by Las Casas and Fernando Colón [Columbus]. However, Puerto Rican *bohíos*, evolving still further, soon departed from the elegant structure depicted and described by Oviedo. Becoming dwellings primarily of the lower class and the poor, they were built for practicality with familiar materials and lost whatever their original import as Taíno houses had been (figure 4). Thus the principal contributions of the Taíno *bohío* to Puerto Rican vernacular houses were the use of certain materials, the technology of construction, and some aspects of spatial order.

Figure 4.
Bohío near Patillas, 1946.
(Archivo General de Puerto Rico, No. 1476.)

Taíno subsistence and settlement pattern also affected the development of Puerto Rican culture and, in consequence, its architecture. With a population estimated to have been 60,000 to 85,000 at the time of contact, (Brau 1973:67; Fernández-Méndez 1971:47–48; Rouse 1941:360–61), families of Taínos lived in small groups, each with its local *cacique,* in caves and rock shelters as well as in open villages. These dwelling sites were scattered throughout the mountainous interior and along the coast, reflecting the Taíno's agricultural subsistence, based primarily on the cultivation of corn, manioc, and tobacco. The distribution of settlement persisted, in part because of the mode of exploitation pursued by the Spanish. A number of Puerto Rican cities—Guanica, Utuado, and Caguas, among them—are located on the sites of Indian villages and still bear the names of their *caciques.*

After Columbus's voyage further exploration took place, but actual colonization by the Spaniards did not begin until Ponce de León established a settlement in 1509 at an inland site, afterwards named Caparra. He came with a handful of men to develop the gold-mining industry. Following practices previously established in Santo Domingo, he enlisted the labor of the Taíno *naborías,* the lowest and worker class, through their *caciques*. Later, the Spanish government granted to loyal colonizers *estancias* or *conucos* (ranches or farms), each comprised of the lands and *naboría* of a Taíno *cacique*, as well as plots in towns. The system was easily adopted because the Taíno and Spanish societies were similarly stratified, but it deprived the Indians of their lands and ultimately destroyed the power of the *caciques*. The Indians eventually rebelled as a result of this and other maltreatment, but the Spanish, with their superior arms, subdued them, thereby increasing their own power. Indian captives were enslaved in accordance with Spanish law, and others, free men, were converted to Catholicism.

The Taíno gradually became less important in Puerto Rican political and economic development as mining operations decreased. Their numbers were depleted in part by migration to other islands, where they joined the supposedly more bellicose Carib to raid the coastal settlements of the Spanish in the West of the island. But a greater loss, caused by a devastating smallpox epidemic in 1518 which was introduced by the first importation of slaves from Africa, reduced the Taíno population by a third. Many continued to survive in Puerto Rico, however. They withdrew into the mountains as the Spanish took over the coastal lands. Later intermarrying with escaped black slaves and deserting Spanish soldiers, they eventually became the rural proletariat (Silva 1975:681). Indeed, their imprint is still visible in the faces and stature of many Puerto Ricans as well as in the island's language (Mintz 1974:84).

Spaniards

After the initial conquest and gold-mining period, Puerto Rico was for Spain little more than a military outpost, maintained primarily to protect its hegemony in the Caribbean. There was a transfer of people to support this base, but for the most part they were soldiers and lesser functionaries. Thus, although many social customs, laws of governance, and technological innovations were introduced into Puerto Rico, the architecture during the first centuries of occupancy, apart from Spanish adaptations of Taíno dwellings, consisted primarily of military fortifications and an occasional church and governor's residence. Yet in spite of these inauspicious beginnings, the Spanish conquest had an enormous and lasting effect on Puerto Rican society and thus ultimately on the house structures that emerged.

During the first hundred years of colonization, the Spanish established the lineaments of Puerto Rican social, economic, and political life by transplanting their form of government, with some adjustments to local situations. Power was concentrated in Seville in Spain, in the Consejo Real y Supremo de las Indias, to which the colonial *audiencias* (tribunals) were responsible. The Spanish government, under Philip II, promulgated documents and orders—the Laws of the Indies—which eventually governed nearly every phase of life in the Puerto Rican colony. There were rules for the establishment of population centers, for granting lands, and for the treatment of laborers and slaves. The centers were classified as cities (San Juan), villas (San Germán), and towns and places of Spanish peoples. The categories of lands were *hatos* (cattle ranches), *corrales* (farms for raising hogs), *estancias* (farms for fruits or vegetables), and *solares* (residential plots in towns). At first, the waters and mountains were held in common, but many disputes ensued among rich landholders, so common lands eventually comprised only barren and inaccessible areas.

Local government was vested in the *Cabildo* (town hall), with four *regidores* (councilmen), who were rich men named to the post by the Spanish government; an accountant; a treasurer; and a bailiff. The *regidores* elected the ordinary mayors for each town. Public officials and large landholders had to prove their *limpieza de sangre* (hereditary purity—they had to be white people, without Jewish, Moorish, black, or mulatto ancestry). During the sixteenth and seventeenth centuries this concept prevailed in Spain, and consequently had a major effect on Puerto Rican social development.

From the beginning, the Laws of the Indies created a ruling oligarchy of privileged Spanish landholders who were separated from the artisans, workers, Indian *naborías*, and Indian and black slaves. It was a basically capitalistic system organized to exploit the resources of the colonies.

After the gold-mining industry lost its viability, the Spanish government supported an agricultural economy based primarily on cattle raising and the initial attempts to produce sugar—still a luxury product during the sixteenth century. Yet the situation of the Puerto Rican settlers was precarious, since the island was under constant siege by Dutch, English, and French pirates who attacked the coasts. The French burned San Germán in 1538 and again in 1559. The English pirate Drake occupied San Juan in 1595, and three years later

Cumberland sacked the city. These assaults accelerated the building of fortifications, but despite them, the Dutch invaded and burned San Juan in 1625. By this time the Spanish government was ascribing greater importance to Puerto Rico considering it not only a military post but also a commercial center and a location for the deposit of slaves. The San Juan forts were supported by special assignments from Mexico, which, however, were often prevented by pirate ships from reaching their destination—once for eleven years. The Puerto Ricans therefore resorted to trading their crops of ginger, pigs, and tobacco for contraband brought by the buccaneers.

The slave traffic, ceded by Spain to German, English, French, Dutch, Italian, and Portuguese ships, provided further opportunity for contraband transactions. When slaves were brought from Africa, the ships carried provisions and gifts for Spanish officials as well. The illicit traffic permeated all levels of Puerto Rican society, including the military, clergy, and lower government officials as well as the landowners whose livelihood depended on it. When a new bishop came to San Juan in 1644, he reported a small impoverished island with poorly maintained fortifications, a population less than that of Seville's jail, few houses resided in by many *caballeros* (gentlemen, the class of people who do not work with their hands) trading in ginger and pigs, and a cathedral with few priests.

Between 1640 and 1750 Puerto Rico remained an agricultural country with the majority of the population living on *hatos* or *estancias*, although increasingly oriented toward the centers and ports of San Juan, Guayama, Arecibo, Mayaguez, Cabo Rojo, San Germán, and its port of Guadianilla. The owners of sugar mills, *hatos*, and large *estancias*; mayors; councilmen; and military officials formed the upper class. Below them were small landowners and free black peasants; and below these, the *agregados* (those without title to land they occupied) and slaves. The people worked, but they also entertained themselves with *fiestas patronales* (celebrations on patron saint's days), horseracing and other activities. Puerto Rico was a closed society with a populace of about 69,000, composed mostly of lower-class Spanish from Andalusia, Estremadura, and the Canary Islands; some Portuguese soldiers; and mixed populations of Spanish, Indians and blacks. There were few foreigners except for occasional deserters from the trading ships.

The spectacular military fortifications of El Morro and San Cristóbal are the best-known examples of colonial architecture, but glimp-

Figure 5. Colonial Spanish house, 1985. This early house, preserved in the town of Colonia, Uruguay, (original roof replaced by zinc) suggests what Puerto Rican dwellings of the seventeenth and early eighteenth centuries were like, since the Spanish populations of both places were quite similar.

ses of early dwellings can be found in the records. Indeed, the first permanent Spanish structure, built by Ponce de León for himself, combined a fort and a dwelling. It was an average house, constructed of *mampostería* (brick and rubble) with cornices of worked and dressed stone and further ornamented with bright polychrome Sevillian tiles. The interior was whitewashed (Fernández-Méndez 1971; Pérez-Chanis 1976:11). For many years, this simple one-story structure with high ceilings and thick rubble walls was a principal model for urban upper-class dwellings. Another was Casa Blanca, which was completed in 1523 as the residence of Ponce de León in the new capital of San Juan, but never occupied by him. It became the residence of the Spanish governor in the eighteenth century.

By 1529 San Juan had 120 houses, most of them built of wood and *yagua*.[6] These first dwellings were subsequently destroyed by a hurricane and replaced in 1590 with 200 houses, in some cases built of stone and in others of adobe and wood, and an additional 100 *bohíos* on the outskirts (Brau 1973:97). The stone and adobe houses were probably not very different in plan and configuration from those found in Spain at the same period.[7] Their most common characteristics were simple walls, low roofs, roof tiles, grilles, balconies of *ausubo* wood (a native tree of the *sapodilla* family), and gates and cornices decorated with Spanish Renaissance motifs (Morales 1943).

The plan of the city followed the ordinance issued by Philip II in 1576, which decreed that parallel streets should bound the four sides of a central plaza of sufficient size to allow for population growth. "The four corners of the plaza must look to the four principal winds, so the streets would not be exposed to them" (Pérez-Chanis 1976:32, quoting from the document). At this time, San Juan had a rural aspect, with houses separated by large patios or shaded corrals, grass growing in the streets, and a common pasture (Brau 1973:98).

By 1646, San Juan was reported to have 500 residents living in 400 houses of stone and some of boards. The town was described as a happy, shady, walled city surrounded on three sides by the sea. Another account characterized the houses as strong one-story buildings with flat tiled roofs and cisterns. Mulattos lived in houses of boards and beams, blacks and the poor in huts made of canes supported by stakes (Fernández-Méndez 1971:142).

The second city, San Germán, had a population of 200 residents, but in 1606 its church was still built of *yagua* for lack of funds (Brau 1973).

Puerto Rican houses of the early colonial period, with occasional exceptions, were principally utilitarian—*yagua*, wood, adobe, and stone adaptations of Spanish vernacular houses and Taíno *bohíos* built for shelter. Besides the rare governor's house, fine architecture was reserved for religious buildings. But these, by providing technical experience to artisans and by serving as models, were very influential in the subsequent architectural design and construction of houses. The style of the early Spanish colonial house consisted of a simple, austere one-story structure built of *mampostería* at curb height, enhanced only by such restrained details as repeating straight lines of shallow relief, dentils below the soffit of the cornice, and horizontal molding (see figure 6). The style is characterized by a feeling of solidity and weight, conveyed by the materials, the thickness

Figure 6.
Colonial Spanish House,
Old San Juan, 1979.

of the walls, and the horizontal lines. Obviously, in the early years such Spanish houses were typically the dwellings of the more affluent Spanish members of Puerto Rican society.

Africans

Spanish culture was the predominant influence in the development of Puerto Rican society after 1500, but important contributions by African slaves, who first arrived with the earliest Spanish settlers and continued to come thereafter, must also be taken into account. In 1518 a change in regulations permitted the importation of larger numbers of blacks to work in the gold mines. But their greatest impact on Puerto Rican economic and social development came later with their productive work in the sugar industry, which could not have been sustained without their labor in the cane fields and refineries.

The first sugar mill was established in the San Germán part of the island in 1524. Four others came to the San Juan area by 1540, and by 1582 there were eleven mills on the island. Further growth of the industry was then slowed because a limit was imposed on the number of slaves allowed to be imported. Out of fear of rebellion, the royal officials in 1532 restricted the proportion of black slaves, requiring that one Christian must enter with every five blacks—a regulation that created a class of white peons. Moreover, the slave trade, controlled by the English, Dutch, and Portuguese in the seventeenth and eighteenth centuries, fluctuated according to the European political situation. After 1640, the sugar industry declined until 1765–94, when slaves were obtained as contraband and their population increased 300 percent. The introduction of steam mills and the industrialization of the sugar industry in the nineteenth century increased the demand for slaves, and their population rose to 21,000 in 1820

Figure 7. Aerial view of Martín Peña Canal and Tidal Slums. Hato Rey, Puerto Rico, March 1948. (Archivo General of Puerto Rico, No. 6609.)

Figure 8. Census Data.

Year	1530	1787	1834
WHITES	369	46,756	
Spanish Property Owners	71		
Married to Whites	57		
Married to Indians	14		
Propertyless, Single	298		
FREEMEN			315,268
PARDOS LIBRES*		34,867	
MULATTO SLAVES		4,657	
SOLDIERS AND PRISONERS			1,750
INDIAN	1,148	2,302**	
Free *Encomendados*	473		
Slaves	675		
BLACKS	1,523	6,603	41,810
African Males	1,168		
African Females	355		
Free Blacks		7,866	
Totals	3,040	103,051	358,836

*Not classifiable as white or black (Mintz 1974:87)
**A specific population near San Germán
Source of Data: Brau 1973: 52–53; 173; 212.

and reached 50,000 in 1843. Several rebellions took place, probably as a result of inhumane conditions, although they were attributed to the instigation of Haitian slaves who were brought with their fleeing masters during the Haitian revolt of 1797. Slaves came primarily from the Guinea coast of Africa, but during the late eighteenth and the nineteenth century others arrived with their masters not only from Haiti, but also from such new republics of South America as Venezuela and from many other places. Slaves were obtained from the North American colonies when the English were prohibited from trade with them during the American Revolution.

Not all Puerto Rican blacks were slaves (Mintz 1974:141). Free black African refugees arrived from St. Croix in 1664 and again in 1714. They were allowed to form a colony apart at San Mateo de Cangrejos

(Santurce) and to organize militarily. Each man received a plot of land in usufruct, on which he could build a house. This settlement later moved to the area of the Martín Peña channel, where the land was more fertile, near a section that became notorious in the 1930s as the site of "El Fanguito" (the mud) *arrabal* (squatter settlement).

Census data from different time periods indicate the increase in Puerto Rico's population; the changing proportions of Indians, blacks, and Spaniards; and the changing categories of ethnicity and class. By 1834 racial categories had dropped out, and the population was defined as freemen, slaves, soldiers, and prisoners. Except when otherwise indicated, only males were counted (Brau 1973:52–53, 173, 212).

Africans, valued as commodities and as labor, figure in economic history, but records of their culture—aside from the music and dance which were part of *hacienda* (working plantation) life—or complete descriptions of their dwellings have not been found. Generally, slaves were housed separately from their masters. According to a 1532 ac-

Figure 9. Former Slave Quarters, Boca Chica Hacienda. Each section measures 12 by 16 feet. The building may have housed as many as 125 slaves.

count, a sugar plantation resembled an *alcaría* (small Spanish village), with a great house for the owner, a church or chapel, and overseers and blacks living apart, each in his house (Fernández-Méndez (1971:136). By the eighteenth century, the blacks lived in buildings called slave quarters, some of which still exist as ruins or warehouses (see figure 9). Here the blacks were locked up at night to sleep for a few hours after working in the fields during the day and in the mills at night. These L-shaped or straight buildings, consisting of small rooms with individual doors, were devised by Spanish slave owners and give no evidence of an African concept of a house. But certain characteristics which synthesize African and European concepts are manifested in a few houses. A 1946 photograph (figure 10) shows a *bohío* and cooking shed at Boca de Cangrejos, a place

Figure 10. *Bohío* and Cooking Shed in the Northeastern Coastal Area Known as "Little Africa," 1946. (Archivo General de Puerto Rico, No. 1223.)

Figure 11. House in the Northeastern Coastal Area of Boca de Cangrejos. There were originally two doors, but one was converted to a window. The house is painted blue with pink trim.

known as "Little Africa" because it has always been occupied by descendants of free blacks or freed black slaves. Today in this same area, houses (see figure 11) are built on or close to the ground and bear some resemblance to the African-inspired houses found elsewhere in the Caribbean (Vlach 1977). Probably more important in their effect on Puerto Rican architecture were the subtle influences exerted by the craft and workmanship of black carpenters and artisans whose skills were employed in the construction of hacienda and town houses for the upper classes (see also Lockhart 1974: 171–77). Other Africanisms—though still undefined—entered more directly into the construction of *jíbaro* houses.

Jíbaro is the Puerto Rican folk term for the country rustic of mixed Indian, black and Spanish ancestry who lived in the mountainous interior.[8] By 1800, a substantial portion of the population practiced subsistence farming in the highlands; at that time the *jíbaros* exceeded the number of slaves (Mintz 1974:88). *Jíbaro* dwellings, generally called *bohíos*, were variants on the Taíno house. Differing from urban *bohíos*, the majority were raised on *zocos* (posts) above the ground due to the periodic flooding that occurs in mountain regions.

An eighteenth-century *Jíbaro* house was described by Ledru:

> About 12 or 20 posts are driven into the ground and united by transversals. At two meters a floor about 15–16 meters square is formed of boards. This is surrounded by poles attached to the basic structure and the whole is covered with *yaguas*. The roof similarly is covered with *yaguas* or dry sugar cane leaves. The lower edges of the roof extend out from the house to protect it from rain, heat and wind. This type of house is divided inside into three sections; the front, which is more open, serves as a place for the children, for performing household tasks; in the second, which has large doors, the furniture and cooking utensils are located; and the last, very narrow and closed, serves as a warehouse and sleeping room for the family. Curtains, shutters or gratings are used instead of windows. Ordinarily, they sleep on cots lined with cloth; the rich cover themselves with a large gauze canopy to keep out the mosquitoes but to permit the air to circulate.
> (Pérez-Chanis 1976:37)

Fray Iñigo Abbad's account adds further details:

> The houses that are on the island today are the same construction as that used by the Indians ... they are constructed on posts which are driven into the ground. They are small; one room called a *soberado* and another that serves as a bedroom occupy the same floor which is of boards. The [people] usually sleep in hammocks which are arranged between posts that hold up the roof.
> (Rosario 1975:673)

The plan of the house seems similar to Oviedo's pictured two-room *bohío*, with overhanging *zaguán* roof. And, as previously noted, a Taíno building constructed on posts was observed by Columbus.

According to a study of Cuban vernacular houses, one African modification was the incorporation of the kitchen into the house (Pérez de la Riva 1952:44–45). In Africa, cooking was done in the center of the house, but among the Taíno, outside or in a separate structure. In Puerto Rico cooking continued to take place in separate kitchens or attached lean-tos, but the *jíbaro* adopted the Spanish *fogón* (stove). A more probable Africanism was the changed and increased use of the *batey*, originally a ceremonial plaza for the Taíno. Most Jíbaro houses were dispersed in mountain areas, each on its land. This land typically included a *batey*, consisting of a yard with gardens and fruit trees (Mintz 1974:225-50). But some houses were grouped around a *batey*. The term *batey* itself retained a certain emotional significance, but the land came to function more as a "commons" suitable for every kind of social and political activity during the first three centuries after conquest (Pérez de la Riva 1952:35).[9] The major African contribution, however, was technical knowledge, which brought to house construction an increased use of wood in place of cane as well as other such innovations (Pérez de la Riva 1952:45–46).

Later Trends

Throughout the first three centuries of Puerto Rico's colonial history, house styles changed very little, and then only gradually, from those established at contact. Toward the end of the eighteenth century, however, the island became less of a military outpost and lost some of its frontier quality. As the society stabilized, the urban houses of the upper class became more refined than earlier models. Moreover, by this time Hispanic buildings had acquired their own Puerto Rican character, influenced by local conditions and by such constructions as the Dominican Convent. The convent's central cloister, bordered by arches, was adopted as a central patio, or located at the east side when space was insufficient. Large windows suitable to the Puerto Rican climate were protected by *persianas* (louvered shutters) devised specifically to protect against the northwest winds. However, a possibly earlier observer reported that the beauty of San Juan "is greatly diminished by the canvas, or wooden lattice that they use instead of glass windows" (Jeffreys 1762:97; see note 10 for further description of the island at this time). Yet Spanish influence was still evident in the designs of doorways and cornices, which were characteristic of simplified classic eighteenth-century Spanish Renaissance style (Morales 1975:1030; Pérez-Chanis 1976:35). According to an account of the time by José Luis Vivas, the majority of San Juan houses were one-story structures built of stone, brick, rubble, cane, bamboo, and thatch. The houses of the rich were spacious with broad flat roofs, balconies, and large cisterns. Those of lower economic po-

Figure 12. Facade Drawing for #83 Calle Cristo, Old San Juan. One of many similar drawings submitted to the government with requests for permission to improve the facade. (Archivo General de Puerto Rico, No. 1864.)

Figure 13.
View of San Germán, Copied from Drawing by Augusto Plée, 1821–23. (Alegría 1975: figure 16.)

Figure 14.
View of Ponce, Copied from Drawing by Augusto Plée, 1821–23. (Alegría 1975: figure 7.)

sition were small and built of rubble; and those of the poor were merely shanties (from Pérez-Chanis 1976:38). The houses of the rich could be classified as European Neoclassic. This style is exemplified by one-story residential buildings or two-story structures that combined commercial and residential uses. The buildings are ornamented with pilasters and occasionally also by rustication, iron railings, and other classical details such as pediments, cornices, and moldings. This style relies for interest on simple proportions, refined details, and rhythmic repetition of doorways and windows. Examples of these Neoclassic residences still can be seen, especially in Old San Juan, though modified through restoration or conversion into apartments, shops, and museums (figure 12).

Early nineteenth-century drawings by Augusto Plée (1821–32) illustrate the small size of the towns and the basic simplicity of the houses (Alegría 1975:20–41) (figures 13 and 14). At this time San Juan's population had increased to about 9,000, out of a total of 103,000 for the entire island. A much smaller Ponce is reported to have had seventy houses in the plaza area, and in the neighborhoods, more than four hundred houses built very close together in comparison to other towns (Fernández-Méndez 1971:194).

Discussion

In the early post-contact period, the simple utilitarian aspect of the houses suggests little meaning beyond the fundamental one of shelter. For the Spanish, at least at first, the house was probably also a fortress. Built of strong materials like its Spanish predecessors the colonial dwelling indeed offered better protection from hurricanes and raiding pirates than lower-class wood and cane adaptations of Taíno *bohíos*. Display of status distinction also was notable from first contact, though chiefly in the size and materials of construction: stone and rubble for upper socioeconomic levels, wood for the less affluent, and cane for the lower class. Rural houses differed structurally, since most—especially those in the mountain regions—were raised on posts. Rural houses and the urban houses of the poor, devised primarily for shelter, were adapted to the tropical Puerto Rican climate. Conversely, the style of the less adjusted stone houses signified Spanishness as well as affluence and was a means of uniting Spaniards as well as distinguishing them from the rest of the populace (Norberg-Schultz, in Whitten 1969:viii). Spaniards considered themselves *gente de razón* (people of reason) (Wolf 1982:131), and it was important to them not only to maintain but also to manifest their superiority over Indians and blacks. Moreover, the persistence of Spanish houses implies that people of Spanish descent long continued to regard themselves as citizens of Spain. By the end of the period, however, modifications and refinements of upper-class residences reveal a growing identity with Puerto Rico, a greater sense of security, and probably increasing wealth.

Manifestations of status differences became magnified during the nineteenth century, and styles diversified increasingly with the growing variation and affluence of the society.

Caribbean and European Influences

1800–1875 Period

Puerto Rico's economic development and social order changed radically as a result of reforms initiated in the late eighteenth century by the Bourbon King Carlos III of Spain. The reforms were instigated as a result of a report by Field Marshall O'Reylly, who was sent by the Crown in 1765 to investigate Puerto Rico's defenses and the state of its residents. In his observations, O'Reylly estimated a population of 44,833 inhabitants of whom, 5,000 were slaves. He remarked that the towns were no more than villages, occupied only by a curate, with the residents of neighboring haciendas coming on fiesta and market days; that, because of lack of commercial opportunity, the people worked principally to satisfy their needs; that contraband trade exceeded legitimate trade with Spain by 300,000 pesos annually; that the forts were in ruined condition and the soldiers impoverished. Among the reforms that ensued, several were of greatest consequence. First, permission was granted to merchant companies in Barcelona and Venezuela to trade directly in Puerto Rico, and Catholic foreigners versed in sugar technology were allowed to immigrate. Second, land reforms were instituted.

During the late eighteenth and early nineteenth centuries, Puerto Rico was gradually transformed from a cattle-raising country dependent on contraband to a monocultivation economy with sugar in the coastal areas and coffee and tobacco in the interior mountain regions. The commercial crops, sold directly in foreign markets, required increasing amounts of capital investment in slaves, other labor, lands, and machinery. The raising of tobacco (called the poor man's crop) continued to be a family operation. But whereas previously small landholders had predominated, monocultivation accelerated the concentration of landholdings, as the small farmer was pushed off his lands and forced to work as part of a mass of laborers. The wealth thus garnered by the major landowners was usually spent on imported products, European travel, and European education for the children (Centrón and Levine 1972:928).

Throughout the nineteenth century, Puerto Rico continued to grow in population, wealth, and freedom. Immigration of deposed royalists or their sympathizers—Spanish, Dominicans, Venezuelans, French, and English, many of them knowledgeable in sugar production—was stimulated by the Latin American independence movements that were inspired by the American and French Revolutions. Catalans, who arrived in rising numbers, monopolized the financing and marketing of sugar and coffee. The intensification of commercial activity led to the establishment of new cities: Vega Baja, Rincón, Moca, Cangrejos, Cayey, Aguadilla. But in spite of increasing prosperity, a number of the problems continued that had existed since Ponce de León's time. The British attacked Mayaguez and Aguadilla; hurricanes periodically destroyed crops and houses; occasionally smallpox epidemics occurred, although to a lesser degree after vaccination was introduced in 1802; and piracy plagued the western coasts until 1824. During this period most Latin American countries achieved independence from Spain. Although Puerto Rico's revolutionary movement was unsuccessful at Lares in 1868, it still gained the right to hold elections for local offices in 1871 and ultimately attained autonomy under Muñoz Rivera in 1891.

Haciendas

Economic success was dependent on sugar and coffee, with first one and then the other taking ascendancy. Their production encouraged distinctive social systems, and haciendas, rather than towns, were the centers of life on the island at this time. Sugar had its *hacendados* (plantation owners), slaves, and *jornaleros* (day laborers or unsalaried proletariat).[11] The division between worker and owner, characteristic of a typical sugar hacienda, was reflected in the architecture and the siting of buildings. The *hacendado* lived in his great house, apart from the slaves in their quarters and the *jornaleros* in their shacks. This capitalistic enterprise involved the buying and selling of slaves, land, and equipment, and the acquisition of great riches through the labor of wage workers and slaves. The hacienda was of necessity self-sufficient, since poor transportation limited contact with the towns. Artisans of the city, such as masons, carpenters, shoemakers, and tailors, provided special services, and peddlers supplied cloth and personal items. The diversions observed by Fray Iñigo Abbad in the early eighteenth century—dances, chicken fights and horseracing—continued throughout the nineteenth century, although dancing was the favorite. The completely separate worlds of master and slave were manifested not only by the difference between their respective dwellings, but also by the difference between the European dances of the great house and the *baile de bomba* performed in front of the slaves quarters.

From its beginning in the sixteenth century as a simple system, sugar production developed into an elaborate one of large coastal landholdings, intensive use of labor, and a complex administration. In 1898, Puerto Rico had about twenty small *factorías centrales* (central processing plants) and about four hundred *trapiches* (mills) on haciendas. The requirements of the former resulted in an increase in the number and variety of hacienda buildings to include processing plants, warehouses, and houses for superintendents and mechanics as well as workers (see Mintz 1974:95–130 for a full discussion of the historical development of the Puerto Rican sugar industry).

The styles of hacienda houses varied, but great houses generally fall into the *Criollo* (creole) category. Applied to people, the term *criollo* signifies those of European ancestry who are born in the Western hemisphere. Similarly, *Criollo* is a Puerto Rican style with regional variations. Such houses adapted and incorporated various specific, mostly European architectural elements, such as hip roofs and wrought-iron balustrades, which were selected for their appropriateness to the Puerto Rican situation and their resonance with the historical background of their owners. The similarity of plantation architecture throughout the Caribbean sugar-producing areas reflects also the interchange of ideas and people that resulted from trade and the commonality of economic interests. The architectural designs that evolved were eminently suited to the climate and hence were widely adopted. Architectural forms and motifs were available through builders' handbooks, among other sources, and were introduced and adopted randomly, so that an exact sequence of stylistic development cannot be determined (Gosner 1982:19–21). Stylistic distinction was concentrated on the great houses, which differed from each other largely in size and in amount and type of ornamentation. Usually they were two-story structures with stores and offices at ground level and a residence above. An imposing central stair leading to the second-story entrance was a common feature. Nineteenth-century immigrants to Puerto Rico from Corsica, Mallorca, the Canary Islands and other European and Caribbean areas tended to settle in the South and West of the island, while those from Spain (Galicia, Asturias, Andalusia) chose the East and the vicinity of San Juan. The architecture of the period reflects these different backgrounds;

Figure 15. Unoccupied House on Hacienda Esperanza. Working hacienda near San Juan.

thus Esperanza, located not far from San Juan, looks more Hispanic, and a house near San Germán, more French—although what has been termed "French" style is actually of West Indian and possibly Spanish origin (Whiffen 1969:16).

Coffee, introduced into Puerto Rico as a crop in 1736 (commercial planting began in 1755), surpassed sugar in economic importance toward the end of the nineteenth century. Though as complex as sugar production, coffee is more sporadic in its labor requirements. Moreover, the hilly lands where it grows and the nature of the crop itself led to smaller holdings. Coffee cultivation encouraged a semifeudal social organization, with some labor hired intermittently when necessary. This system was eminently suited to the independent *jíbaro* who lived in the coffee-producing mountain areas. He picked and sorted beans when the crop was ripe but otherwise continued his self-reliant existence (Pico 1983:1). The coffee *hacendado*, therefore, had a somewhat familial, reciprocal relationship with his workers, in contrast to the sugar *hacendado*'s total control over his slaves and *jornaleros*.

THE HISTORICAL CONTEXT 31

Figure 16.
Occupied House on Working
Hacienda near San Germán.

A large coffee hacienda had a sizable owner's house, two warehouses with adjacent machine house, a manger, milk house, *mayordomo*'s (steward's) house, migrant laborers' houses, and the houses of *agregados* (landless workers). The harvest of coffee centered around the drying yard near the main house. The machinery that removed the hull from the bean was situated in or next to the warehouse where the harvest was stored. The beans were prepared and sacked, then transported by mule to buyers. The workers' houses were some-

Figure 17. Worker's House on Hacienda Dos Ríos, Maricao. Working hacienda.

times separate buildings but often consisted of several sleeping rooms in a line, with a narrow connecting balcony. In either case, they were raised on short posts above the ground.

The one-story main house was constructed of native ironwood or other hardwood, with the central living area bounded either front and back or on all sides by balconies. As the house was often situated on a slope, the space below was used for stores or occasionally for the hulling machinery. Usually the style of these coffee hacienda residences is Criollo Pueblerino, which like Criollo combines various elements but is more obviously utilitarian and less refined. Decoration is minimal, but the climatically advantageous high hip roof is present. Later, as the coffee industry prospered, some hacienda residences had two stories, and their ornamentation was elaborated (Pérez-Chanis 1976:37).

Town Houses

The stylistic diversity of Criollo and Criollo Pueblerino, more visible in the towns, contrasted with the relative homogeneity that had persisted for several centuries. These new styles did not always displace those of previous periods where the latter were well established, but the Corsicans and Catalans who dominated the trading of coffee, sugar, and needed imports also dominated stylistic taste in the southern and western towns they settled—Ponce, Guayama, Yauco, Arroyo, San Germán. Here wood houses exhibit many features reminiscent

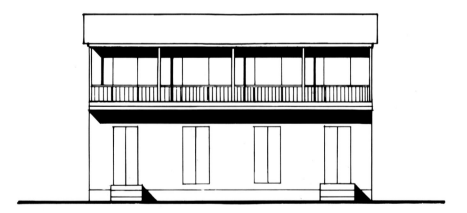

Figure 18. Unoccupied Criollo Pueblerino House on Working Hacienda near Ciales. Built 1885.

Figure 19. Occupied Two-Story House on Working Hacienda, Hormigueras.

of Victorian Europe, New Orleans Creole, and Art Nouveau styles: pierced wood fanlights, balconies with wrought iron railings in arabesque designs, slanting high-pitched roofs, and wood jalousies. In the San Juan area, the more stolid Mediterranean architecture of the previous period continued, with plain walls solidly constructed of brick as often as *mampostería*, well-proportioned facades, wood or

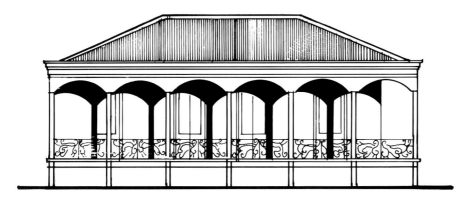

Figure 20. Criollo House, Painted White, Añasco.

Figure 21.
Typical Criollo Patterns. Note the carved pierced fanlight above the window, and the curvilinear wrought-iron balustrade of a second-story *balcón*, Ciales.

cast-iron balustrades, and logical plans that included interior patios (Pérez-Chanis 1976:32).

As the century progressed and wealth increased, a Criollo Neoclassic style appeared which essentially augmented and elaborated classical decorative motifs. Criollo Neoclassic houses were generally built of *mampostería* and had such neoclassic details as window arches with *mediopunto* (half-circle) transoms, sometimes with mother-of-pearl or stained glass panes, pilasters intercalated between the arches, and double jalousied doors. Houses built of wood incorporating these elements and exhibiting equally refined execution are included in this category as well.

The gradual development of a middle class brought about the appearance of a style called *Pueblerino* (vernacular). The term, in effect implying absence of style, is applied to simple, usually owner-built wood houses that incorporate elements of Criollo and Criollo Pueblerino styles. Although these buildings were conceived as units, their various Criollo-derived architectural features and decorative

Figure 22. Criollo Neoclassic House, Sábana Grande. Painted white with gray trim.

elements appear to have been accrued separately rather than as part of a total style. Most of the existing examples are now also painted in bright colors, particularly light green and aqua, and have been further ornamented with various decorations patently North American in inspiration.

The 1875–1898 Period

Eclectic Styles. Growing affluence toward the end of the nineteenth century led to the construction of ostentatious mansions in the towns, many of them in styles then prevalent in Europe and North America. The romantic eclecticism of the Victorian period is manifested

Figure 23. Pueblerino House, Fajardo. Aqua with white trim.

Figure 24.
Early Gothic Revival House, Aguadilla. Aqua with white trim.

in Victorian architecture, which was composed of various architectural stylistic features characteristic of earlier periods such as Gothic, Romanesque, and Classic. In Puerto Rico, as elsewhere, the adoption and florescence of these varied styles enlarged the decorative and structural vocabularies of the architecture. Puerto Ricans acquired ideas for their houses either in travel to Europe or from pattern books. Therefore some houses closely resemble European or American prototypes, while others incorporate only particular elements. The choice of styles and features was often based on practical and climatic as well as display considerations.

Numerous styles can be identified, sometimes within a single house. The following are included because their occurence is sufficiently frequent to permit assumption of patterned rather than idiosyncratic adoption.

Early Gothic Revival is an English style that became popular and spread throughout the United States, where it was usually characterized by steep roofs, a dominant central pointed gable, gingerbread bargeboards, and spacious verandas. In Puerto Rico a striking example can be seen in Aguadilla (figure 24). The gingerbread edging alone, often replicated in cast iron, became widespread.

Two styles seem to have inspired Puerto Rican house types having a partial second story. A Puerto Rican version of the New Orleans Camelback house combined a shotgun-type house in front with a

Figure 25.
Camelback House, Guayama.
Mustard yellow with
White trim.

one-room, two-story structure in back (Kirk 1977). Italian Villa style, or possibly the Mission tower introduced by the architect Pedro de Castro (Pérez-Chanis 1976:79–80), appears to underlie a tower-like unit at the front of houses with a variant style. Besides the off-center square tower, many other elements were derived from Italian Villa style, such as balustraded balconies, cupolas, glazed belvederes, gabled roofs with eaves supported by brackets, and loggias (figure 26).

High Victorian Gothic, which combines Gothic elements from England, Italy, and France, in contrast to the English-derived Early

Figure 26.
Tower House, Río Piedras.
Rose with white trim.

Figure 27. High Victorian Gothic House, Fajardo. Aqua with white trim.

Figure 28. Queen Anne House, San Germán. White.

Gothic Revival style, is noted for complex roof lines and heavy or large-scale details. Disregarding the coherence of true Gothic, this eclectic style replicated only certain features, often incorporating them into buildings in combination with elements from other stylistic periods. A grandiose projecting loggia tacked on to a rather simple house is a case in point (figure 27).

Irregularity of plan and massing and variety of color and texture characterize the Queen Anne style. Windows, usually glazed, are of many forms, including bay. Roofs are high and multiple, their ridges meeting at right angles, and a round or polygonal turret is a common feature. Elements of Eastlake style, which became very popular in California, also reached Puerto Rico. It adds to Queen Anne a distinctive type of carpentered ornament consisting of curved brackets and turned columns which resemble furniture legs (figure 28).

Only a few large, elaborate houses were built which exemplified these styles in a form close to their European or American models. But such decorative elements as Early Gothic gingerbread were quickly taken up and added as lacy embellishment to numerous Pueblerino houses (figure 29). Other architectural features such as the two-story tower and the belvedere were also widely adopted.

Figure 29. Pueblerino House, Naguabo. Painted dark green with white Early Gothic-like trim.

Discussion

During the period after 1850, Puerto Rican houses lost much of their provincialism and narrow affinity with Spain and became more closely allied with the architecture of Europe, other areas of the Caribbean, and the United States. Though specifically recognizable styles were adopted by Puerto Ricans, in the houses based on these, materials often differed from those of the originals, and designs were further adapted to the tropical climate and different social milieu. The distinctive, picturesque charm of many houses that remain from this period results from the imaginative adaptation, recombination, and application of ornament and architectural feature. Their diversity implies a broadening of interests as well as cultural pluralism. Moreover, certain Criollo and Criollo Neoclassic houses have particular characteristics that identify them with specific towns. A special style of window, for example, is seen more commonly in Añasco (figure 30). Stylistic idiosyncracies were, of course, indicative of artisan as well as cultural and ethnic differences and preferences. Taken together, the houses reveal greater individualism as well as pride in property. No longer a fortress, the upper-class house showed an increased investment in aesthetic display, probably for its own sake as well as to manifest status and economic and ethnic distinctiveness. Distinctions between the houses of rich and poor were also clearly visible, but, except at the two extremes, a general similarity in scale, proportion, and ornamentation between Criollo and Pueblerino, for example, implies a community of interests and a familial society. Carrying the analysis further, one could surmise that respectability was linked with property ownership and conformity to social norms.

Toward the end of the century, differences became more pronounced and more clearly based on class, as the houses of the most affluent increased in size and ostentation. Such houses stand out markedly from their neighbors, since only rarely was more than a single example of a particular style of grand house built in the same town. Display of wealth and probably power was apparently an important attribute of certain houses at this time.

In the contrast between the elaborate mansions of wealthy plantation owners and the simple houses of small farmers, rural dwellings show even stronger evidence of class differences in both town and country, the plain dwellings of the rural *jíbaro* and his town counterpart, still relatively unchanged since contact, remained primarily

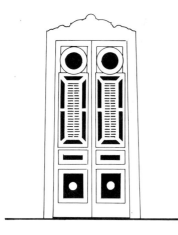

Figure 30.
Window Design with Circular Light.
Rarely seen except in Añasco.

shelters, almost unaffected by the stylistic innovations of the nineteenth century.

Class distinction and display of wealth were important to upper- and middle-class Puerto Ricans during the late nineteenth century. Yet even though the houses of the very rich are conspicuous in scale and ostentatious elaboration, overall, the Puerto Rican houses of this period still appear related to each other because of a general similarity of materials, range of decorative motifs, and architectural features.

UNITED STATES DOMINATION

On the verge of separating from Spain after four hundred years of rule, Puerto Rico experienced a prosperous and optimistic period during the 1890's. But in 1898, the year after Puerto Rico had achieved autonomy, the United States took over the island. The ensuing changes in Puerto Rican society were the most drastic since the arrival of the Spaniards.

Puerto Ricans expected to be freed but instead found themselves under military rule. A series of governors appointed by the United States followed. Puerto Rico's nineteenth-century agricultural society was rapidly destroyed as the island became an integral part of the North American system of production and consumption.

The transformation was first apparent in increased mechanization and centralization of sugar production. From an essentially paternalistic system based on owner-managed properties, each with its own *trapiche* (sugar mill) and *tren Jamaica* (processing system) (figure 31), the industry was consolidated by American corporations into three *factorías centrales* (processing plants). One fourth of the land— 30,000 acres—was administered by salaried employees who were concerned with converting products of the soil into wealth for sugar companies. Dotting Puerto Rico's landscape are the ruined chimneys of once-productive haciendas that testify to this transformation.

As a result of the system of piecework wages and company credit, plantation workers became a rural proletariat dependent first on consolidated *haciendas,* then on the *centrales* (Mintz 1974:122). Many were forbidden to grow their own food and were forced to live in workers' houses (Centrón and Levine 1972:9–28) (figures 32 and 33). Later in the 1930s and 1940s, hundreds who were without work and facing starvation migrated to the city to become the urban proletariat.

Because of U.S. influence, other changes subsequently were intro-

Figure 31. Partially-Excavated *Tren Jamaica,* Hacienda Esperanza. Building where sugar cane syrup was processed by boiling in large vats. The close quarters and amount of space allocated to cooking fires are vivid reminders of the working conditions of slaves.

Figure 32. Barracks-Like Living Quarters for Sugar Workers, 1946. (Archivo General de Puerto Rico, No. 2986.)

duced or evolved. These included new forms of political administration; the rise of a professional class involved with commercial and industrial interests; an increase in entrepreneurial middlemen; the development of transportation—roads, motor vehicles, air and sea transport; mandatory public education; sanitary hygiene; separation of church and state; the introduction of Protestant religion; segregation of large amounts of property for military purposes; urbanization; and, since 1946, the investment of capital in the development of industry.

In 1952, under Muñoz Marín, Puerto Rico acquired a somewhat more autonomous political system, though major decisions are still subject to the approval of the United States Congress and the econ-

Figure 33. Workers Houses in "Colonia Carolina," 1946. (Archivo General de Puerto Rico, No. 2696.)

omy is basically dependent on investments made by North American government and industry.

Although the *criollo* society that had evolved in opposition to Spain, especially during the nineteenth century, was ostensibly greatly modified by the impact of U.S. culture, the underlying structure of dependency persisted. Long-established dependent relationships on the landlord, the church, and the Spanish government were shifted to the Federal bureaucracy of the United States and its host of intermediaries (Ramírez 1976:iv, 10). At first, the U.S. presence was welcomed, but disillusionment soon followed, with the forced use of English in the schools and the economic deprivation and dislocation that resulted from the exploitation of Puerto Rico's resources. The experience of U.S. domination, in place of Spanish, varied according to social class but was negative for most Puerto Ricans except those who profited economically and politically. Therefore, there was a renewed emphasis on Hispanicism in opposition to Americanization, analogous to the creolization that had taken place in opposition to Spain.

In the 1940s, the United States made a concerted effort to alleviate the serious poverty that had resulted from its economic policies. It instituted social programs to improve the housing, education, and health of the rural proletariat in particular, which had moved to *arrabales* (squatter settlements) in the cities. These goals have not been entirely fulfilled, since *agregados* (the landless poor), though urbanized and culturally integrated, are economically marginal and still live in *arrabales* (Ramírez 1977). However, these reforms and others led to even greater fundamental changes in the social fabric. The social levels of the Spanish period—first, upper and lower; and later, upper, middle, and lower—became less clear-cut, and the boundaries between them are now more permeable. Since the 1940s the middle class has opened and expanded to include a wide range of occupations: banking, commerce, real estate, the professions, business, transportation, services, construction, miscellaneous small industries, and, at the lower level, independent workers. The working class, which is sometimes combined with the middle class because of ideological congruence, now resembles its North American counterpart and includes industrial workers in manufacturing, heavy industry, and construction (Centro 1976:80–99). Today, Puerto Rico's fragmented and complex society has lost the coherent unity that existed in the past. Yet, in spite of divisiveness and U.S. dominance, Puerto Rican culture, though experienced differentially by various segments of the society, continues to be a recognizable entity which binds Puerto Ricans together.

The infusion of U.S. political and social influence had a major affect on Puerto Rican houses. Moreover, certain technological innovations—reinforced concrete, metal roofing, glass windows—although unsuitable for the Puerto Rican climate, have transformed the architecture in the last eighty-five years. Originally appearing in government and commercial buildings, they were eventually incorporated into Puerto Rican dwellings.

The 1898–1920 Period

After 1898, U.S. architectural influence was initially gradual. The High Neoclassic style, which appeared first in public buildings, was subsequently adopted for upper-class residences. High Neoclassic did

Figure 34. High Neoclassic House, Utuado. Painted white.

not depart markedly from the equally pretentious styles immediately preceding. Combining Neoclassic elements with such Adamsesque details as garlands and swags, the style is generally rather austere, with plain flat walls enhanced by pilasters as illustrated by an Utuado example (figure 34), and also colonnades of Corinthian columns.

Beaux Arts, a more lively style of the period, is characterized by such features as arched and linteled openings between columns or pilasters, facades with advancing and receding planes, sometimes supporting double columns, and colonnaded upper stories, many with statuary or sculpture. A Ponce house (figure 35) exemplifies several of these characteristics.

The 1920–1938 Period

After 1920, the effect of the United States on Puerto Rican domestic architecture, though more direct, was still not revolutionary. Frank Lloyd Wright was a primary influence, not only through his own architectural designs but also through those of Puerto Rican architects who studied his work in the United States. A theory promoted by Wright and other architects of the time—that architecture must fit its cultural and natural environment—led to more radical stylistic developments. Wright's designs or his philosophy shaped three of the four major styles of the period.

Prairie is marked by its horizontal quality. It usually consists of a broad one-story structure, sometimes with a hip roof reaching out over wide porches or verandas. Other features included ribbon windows with wood casements and rectangular piers, supporting the porch roofs. Antonín Nechodoma, a Puerto Rican architect strongly influenced by Wright, brought his version of this style to Puerto Rico, where it became the model for many houses. Wide flat urns on either side of the entrance steps are a Nechodoma hallmark (figure 36).

Bungaloid incorporates various elements of a true bungalow, which is a small single-story house, sometimes with a dormer or windows in the gables. Two flattened broad gables face the street; the roof line of the front porch gable is repeated by the main house roof behind and slightly to one side. A porch-veranda, used as outdoor living space, is part of the design (figure 37). Through working drawings and illustrated pattern books, Bungaloid became widespread. Popular because of its practicality and suitability to the climate, it was widely adopted in Puerto Rico. A California version with a patio as part of the plan was also adopted.

Spanish Colonial Revival, influenced by Wright's philosophy that ar-

Figure 35. Beaux Arts House, Ponce. Cream with white trim.

Figure 36. Nechodoma-style House, Aibonito. Cream with red roof.

chitecture should be in harmony with its cultural and natural environment, includes a somewhat self-consciously nostalgic use of a Spanish vocabulary derived from the Mexican Spanish styles of California and Florida. The style is identified by low-pitched red tile roofs or flat roofs with tiled parapets; arches, sometimes Mudejar; white plaster walls with few openings; carved or tiled ornaments; flanking columns or pilasters around doors; arcaded or post-and-lintel portals; balconies with railings of wrought iron or wood; window *rejas* (grilles) of wood with turned spindles. In contrast to the two-dimensionality of Criollo house styles, Spanish Colonial Revival houses are usually conceived three-dimensionally; their facades are often asymmetrically ordered with windows of different sizes. They rarely have inte-

Figure 37. Vernacular Bungalow, Fajardo. Aqua with white trim.

Figure 38. Spanish Colonial Revival, San Juan. White.

rior patios. Spanish Colonial Revival is a style very popular in Puerto Rico; its arches and red tile, in particular, are common decorative features on many contemporary houses (figure 39).

The stylistic characteristics of Art Deco, also termed Art Moderne or Modernistic, which originated in Europe, were widely disseminated during the 1920s and 1930s. Primarily a decorative style, its vocabulary was used in a variety of buildings, including movie theatres in particular and office and governmental buildings. Art Deco emphasizes verticality. Also typical are geometric curves; fluting around doors or windows or forming horizontal bands; chevrons; frets; square or oblong blocks around entrances; and piers ornamented only at the top. The facades feature curving corners, glass brick, casement ribbon windows. An architect-designed house (figure 40) is an excellent example of this style.

Styles displaying American influence were at first adopted by upper- or upper-middle-class urban Puerto Ricans, but the lower middle class soon incorporated certain stylistic features and motifs into their Pueblerino zinc-roofed wood houses, in the same way they had acquired late Victorian architectural details. Middle-class urban houses of the early twentieth century, rectangular with the narrow end facing the street, variously incorporate a front-porch type of *balcón*, Bungaloid roof construction, Art Deco frets, and Spanish roof-tile decorative elements, all clearly derived from the foregoing styles (figure 40).

Figure 39. "El Castillo," Spanish Colonial Revival House, on Hill Overlooking Ponce. White.

Country dwellings were also affected by these U.S. styles, but more by U.S. materials, since for the most part they were plain, unadorned buildings. Thus, although characteristic surrounding verandas and spreading roofs seem related to Wright and Bungaloid styles, the connection is more likely one of affinity rather than influence (figure 42).

The *bohío* of the *jíbaro*, still retaining evidence of its Taíno heritage as late as 1937, showed U.S. influence also, but again more in the adoption of such materials as metal roofing and siding than in styles. The following excerpts describe two *bohíos* of the time:

> The *bohío* of the peasant alternates in the fields with small one-story houses of wood, roofed with zinc, with the same proportions. Almost all have a cleared space around them called a *batey*, like the space in front of the *caneyes* used for the ball game....
> At times, the country houses, if they are located in the middle of crops, limit the space to that immediately surrounding the house. Here the peasant farmer grows flowers and ornamental and medicinal plants....

There are two types of construction: that of the native and of the common carpenter. The first builds the framework of the house with interlaced poles or lathes covered with dry cane leaves or with *yaguas* from the royal palm. The carpenter constructs the framework similarly, but with posts which are covered with boards and a roof of zinc sheets. The distance from the floor to the ground is from two to five feet. The space formed by this is used to store household objects like the coffee grinding mortar, the laundry tub, etc. The doors and windows, except for the best wood houses—are built of one panel which are closed inside with a rustic latch. Those of wood have bolts, crossbars, and even locks. . . .

The sala in the front of the house is entered by the door. Behind it is the bedroom (few houses have more than one) and adjacent to one of the walls, a lean-to that serves as a kitchen.

(Cadilla de Martínez 1975:660).

The *bohío* was constructed on the ground or on thick *zocos*. Other pieces joined the *zocos* and sustained the floor beams. Cross beams reinforced the principal walls. The framework of the roof was formed by stringers that made triangles which supported the ridge at their vertex. Tin plates or lathes were nailed to the triangles, to which palm, or straw thatch was tied. The roofs had two or four *aguas* (slopes) with bamboo channels at their edges to collect rain water which drained into a barrel waterproofed with tar. These buildings were small and had few windows, but usually

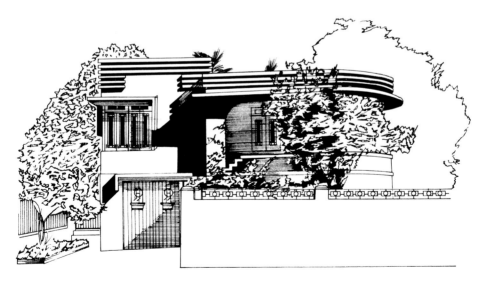

Figure 40. Art Deco House, Moca. White

Figure 41. Vernacular House Ornamented with Art Deco Frets on Columns, San Juan. White with bright blue trim. Following a Puerto Rican tradition, this house was freshly painted for Christmas.

two entrances, one in front and the other in back, which opened into the corral or patio. In the coastal region, the *bohíos* were lower to the ground, at a height of six or seven feet. When they were constructed close to the beach, they were built on the ground mixed with clay. In the plains, the *bohíos* were built near roads or highways, or near a *barranca* on posts or walls of stone, or sometimes were located near arroyos or rivers. . . .

In addition to the kitchen, other outbuildings included a *tormentera* (a triangular-shaped hurricane shelter), and a *rancho* for keeping old things, wood, tools, and implements.
(Canino 1976:3–20).

Besides specific styles, Puerto Rican architecture manifested evidence of other United States influence. By 1920–30 the houses of the upper and upper middle classes had acquired a certain exterior informality, with greater emphasis on commodity and less on form and embellishment in comparison with those of the turn of the century. A tendency toward equalization between upper- and middle-class houses, in both scale and general appearance, also occurred. Such evidence of U.S. democratizing influence probably also reflects economic reality, since many formerly rich Puerto Ricans had lost much of their wealth. Paradoxically, these trends toward Americani-

Figure 42. Country House, La Parguera. White

Figure 43. Jíbaro Kitchen. Inside, a "stove" made of a large flat stone raised on three smaller ones in on the right, a *fogón* on the left. The wood for both is piled nearby. A woman claiming to be a hundred years old was still using this kitchen in 1979.

zation persisted alongside nostalgic references to Spain. Spanish Colonial Revival stylistic elements multiplied, apparently in concert with disillusionment in U.S. policy. Moreover, diversity of styles replaced earlier conformity, so that the individual tastes and needs of a wide range of homeowners could be met. The occurrence of the same styles throughout the island implies greater individual choice and less loyalty to region or town. But the adaptations and adjustments that are reflected in these architectural changes contrast sharply with the seriously worsening housing conditions at the lowest level, especially among the rural poor. Their plight became so severe that reforms in U.S. policy were finally instituted around 1938.[12]

After 1938

In the foregoing period, changes brought to house styles through U.S. influence, though radical in retrospect, emerged gradually. In contrast, the Urbanización/International styles of houses built around 1940 and afterwards reveal the immediate revolutionary effect of U.S. policy reforms.

In 1938 serious efforts were made by the U.S. government to alleviate miserable existing housing conditions by supporting the construction of dwellings through government and private programs. The International style of architecture, then in its ascendancy, was the principal inspiration for the Puerto Rican Urbanización (suburban residential development) style which emerged,[13] but the major impetus came from several *urbanizaciones* constructed in the 1940s, including one financed by IBEC (International Basic Economy Corporation), a Rockefeller corporation. However, the assembly-line production methods of Levitt, who constructed the first Puerto Rican Levittown around 1950, had an even greater impact. His revolutionary mass-construction method of building reinforced concrete houses, with plans determined by modular forms, set the pattern for subsequent house-building. The construction of Urbanización houses has proliferated throughout the island. Results range from developments on large tracts of land which are part of every city and town, to owner-constructed dwellings along streets and highways in towns and in the countryside. The majority of houses in *urbanizaciones* are mass-manufactured at their sites; construction is government-supported (FHA—Federal Housing Agency) if lower- or lower-middle-class dwellings, privately developed if middle-class or above. Though built singly, upper-class International style houses, designed individually by architects, are usually also constructed of reinforced concrete.

The Urbanización style house, inseparable from its reinforced-concrete building material and method of construction, is generally a rectangular, one-story, flat-roofed, box-like structure. In most cases,

THE HISTORICAL CONTEXT 55

Figure 44a. Site Manufacture of Urbanización Houses, Luquillo.

Figure 44b. Later Stage of Construction, Urbanización Houses.

Figure 45. Completed Urbanización House, Luquillo.

its principal distinguishing feature is the facade which serves as a display panel for the attachment of many varieties of commercially produced decorative materials. These are sometimes applied by builders, but often by owners to individualize the house. They consist of red Spanish tiles, imitation stone panels, *rejas* (grilles) for enclosing the balcony or carport, a variety of small ornaments and figures, and bright-colored plastic panels, among many other manufactured items. Paint is sometimes applied decoratively in blocks or panels of color. Urbanización houses and others built of concrete and cement have been adopted widely because of their multiple economic advantages. Actual and prospective owners frequently cite their greater durability in comparison with wood structures, which are always under threat of insect or hurricane destruction. The aesthetic and social preferences that are involved are discussed below.

During the twentieth century, as Puerto Rican society has become increasingly democratized and urbanized and has displayed greater evidence of social mobility and permeable social classes, houses have tended to become more alike in scale and technology, compared with those of the nineteenth and early twentieth centuries. The majority of houses built since 1950 partakes of a common vocabulary of forms, features, decorative elements, and construction materials. But the distinction between the houses of the poor and the rest of society that have existed since early Spanish colonial days still persists. As there were then *bohíos* on the periphery of San Juan, there are now houses in *arrabales* (squatter settlements) at the margins of many towns and cities.

Modern *arrabales* evolved in the 1920s when rural workers began to be displaced from their lands and grew enormously in the 1930s. At that time *agregados* (landless peasants), who had formerly settled on rural haciendas or been provided housing as they worked as *jornaleros* in sugar cane fields, were forced to seek survival in urban areas. Joined by former landed peasants in mounting numbers, they established themselves on unclaimed or undesirable lands usually on the outskirts of cities. The most infamous of these *arrabales*, "El Fanguito" (the mud), arose near and upon Martín Peña caño, a tidal estuary that is now part of the metropolitan area of San Juan. Such settlements were opposed by the government but continued to multiply for lack of alternatives. A still-existing law, passed with the intent of alleviating the situation of homeless *agregados*, prevented their eviction without compensation if they resided in a completed house—four walls, a roof, and a floor. *Agregados* therefore took to constructing rudimentary huts out of packing cases and scraps of metal or wood, surreptitiously at night, and occupying them. Large areas were

Figure 46. "El Fanguito," July 1946. (Archivo General de Puerto Rico, No. 5117.)

rapidly colonized as a result of these tactics, which still continue in spite of many government programs designed to move inhabitants of *arrabales* into various types of government-supported housing. Newly constructed present-day *arrabales* are apt to be situated in the country, along roadsides or *barrancas* (ravines), but those long established in urban sections are still growing.

The Arrabal house is an urbanized version of the Jíbaro house. Often situated near or above bodies of water, it is raised on posts to protect against flooding. It is built somewhat like a *bohío*, first raising a floor on posts, then placing a roof above on other posts or extensions of the first, and finally adding screening walls made of scraps of metal and wood. Depending on their location, the fortunes of their owners, and other factors, Arrabal houses are usually improved gradually over time. Rooms, balconies, and sometimes a second story are added, then the whole house is reconstructed piecemeal in concrete. Several long-established houses in "La Perla" (the site of Oscar Lewis's *La Vida*) are now concrete structures which resemble Pueblerino houses elsewhere (figure 49).

The stylistic characteristics of Arrabal houses, wherever their location, are primarily their assembly and accrual mode of construction and secondarily their brightly-painted colors. Highly individu-

Figure 47. Arrabal House in "La Perla."

Figure 48. House in *Arrabal*, transformed into Pueblerino House and Tienda.

alized and personalized, they are extremely variable within their genre yet similar in their vivid colors and constant renovation. The overall impression is one of great vitality and restless change.

Discussion

Because of their economic accessibility, practicality, and durability, Urbanización style houses have received wide acceptance. Moreover, standardization of structure has challenged rather than stultified individual expressiveness. As every house formerly was embellished with the motifs and features of particular architectural styles, now each is ornamented with a selection of commercial decorative elements. Yet, in contrast to the expression of community loyalty through conformity to particular styles that obtained among Criollo houses, these dwellings are intended as individual personal statements of ownership and status. Upper-class houses are designed by architects as personal statements of architect and owner; at middle and lower social levels, homeowners personalize their developer-built houses with ornament and paint. The Arrabal house is a personal creation like its predecessor the Jíbaro house, but goes beyond it in aesthetic in-

Figure 49. View of "La Perla," from the Grounds of El Morro. Note the *arrabal*'s situation on a narrow ledge between the sea and the city wall of Old San Juan.

vestment. While the general intent is to express individualism through the use of a variety of decorative materials, accessibility to manufactured construction and decorative items sets limits on diversity.

Summary

The foregoing chronology of style is not visible in any one locality in Puerto Rico. Rather, intermingled arrays of styles are clustered differentially in various places and, in some cases, obscured by layers of modifications. Particular styles come to the fore in specific areas where houses are marked for preservation and restoration— eighteenth-century in Old San Juan, nineteenth- in San Germán and Guayama. Here and there architectural gems are being saved, but like the *bohío*, Pueblerino houses may disappear.

This examination has related the styles of Puerto Rican houses to history. Defined by social change, each period had its own quality. In the early years, houses were designed primarily for shelter. The later refinement of simple, austere stone buildings implies greater emphasis on the house as a vehicle for expressing social and economic status, but a restrained Spanish mode prevailed until the nineteenth century, when Puerto Rico was opened to European, Caribbean, and South American migrants. The florescence of styles that ensued matched Puerto Rico's increasing wealth. Exuberant lacy gingerbread trim, pastel colors, and a structural lightness achieved through increased use of wood—these contrasted with the sombre weight of earlier styles. The varied aesthetic investment suggests a rise in fortunes as well as greater social freedom. Moreover, during this time the coherence of style, characteristic of each town, gave its architecture a unity indicative of regional identity.

Toward the end of the nineteenth century, by contrast, ostentatious houses of the late Victorian period, implying great wealth concentrated among a few, emphasized class distinction. This trend continued during the initial stage of U.S. domination at the turn of the century. Then, houses of the 1920s and 1930s became simplified and more informal, a democratic tendency which accelerated with the introduction of mass-manufactured Urbanización houses. The standardization produced by that technology has been somewhat masked, as every homeowner strives to individualize his dwelling with multiple decorative forms. Yet regional variation has faded, as easy access and intensification of communications bring a sameness to the entire society. The variability and individuality that homeowners aspire to and often achieve in their houses is their counteraction.

Despite their differences, a consistent pattern runs through all the historical periods. There has always been a disparity between the houses of the poor and those of the rest of society, and though less marked, a division between rural and urban houses. The houses of both rural and urban poor appear more closely tied to Puerto Rican geography and environment, the houses of upper social levels to foreign or outside influences. Yet the houses of each group have been influenced by the other; there is no direct line from Taíno *bohío* on the one hand, or from Spanish colonial house on the other.

Today all existing historical styles are compressed into a variable mixture of multiple shapes, forms, and colors which is further intensified by the bright floral colors and vistas of the tropical setting. Together, the styles and architectural forms selected and modified by Puerto Ricans add up to a Puerto Rican style. Though this style draws on the past, it is of the present. However chaotic it may appear to a North American accustomed to a tradition of planned orderliness (Perin 1977), it is not random, but rises out of Puerto Rican history, culture, and geography.

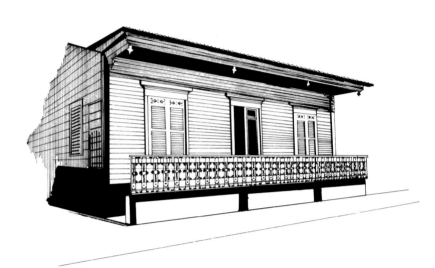

CHAPTER 2

A Typology of Puerto Rican Houses and the Pattern of Residence

In this chapter, the formal organization of Puerto Rican houses and the social characteristics of their inhabitants are examined in order to: (1) establish a typology of the houses; (2) determine the relationships between the social characteristics of residents and house forms; and (3) interpret the meanings that emerge from these findings.

The typology that follows is not intended to represent a classification of the houses according to Puerto Rican perceptions, but as far as possible, it aims to avoid arbitrary categories unrelated to context (Deetz 1977:51). It relies, therefore, not only on observations of house forms but also on data collected directly from house residents through survey questions and informal interviews.

Typologies are created by grouping objects by certain inherent structural similarities (Moneo, "On Typology 1978," quoted in Brown-Manrique 1980:129). Although every Puerto Rican house is as unique as its residents, this typology emphasizes similarity in order to underscore forms and themes held in common. Classification of the 145 houses surveyed is based primarily on plan, the least variable and most fundamental component; and secondarily on the differential applications of certain changeable features such as *balcones*, roofs, and number of stories. One house has been chosen to represent each type, but significant variants are also presented in order to illustrate the rich architectural diversity that is characteristic of Puerto Rico. Each house is described and depicted as a unit, with specific reference to plan, style, material, and general appearance of the exterior and interior.

Since commonality is also based on the social aspects of the houses as habitations, houses are grouped according to additional criteria:

1. Complexity—proceeding from the simplest and most common.
2. Context, by:
    a. Period—houses built before 1930 precede those that followed. The sequential order is, of course, a distortion of the actuality since certain older house types not only exist but continue to be built along with more recent or contemporary models.
    b. Location—urban houses are constrasted with rural.
    c. Social level—Jíbaro and Arrabal houses are considered together, for example, to emphasize their similarities as well as their difference from habitations of the middle and upper social levels in both urban and rural areas.
3. Technical knowledge—Designed (architect/builder) houses are distinguished from Vernacular (owner/carpenter-built) houses. These two categories could be divided further into popular and polite types of architecture, but the designations Designed and Vernacular seem sufficiently representative of the Puerto Rican situation until the arrival of twentieth-century Urbanización houses.

Materials

Building materials do not determine the form of houses but are among the major factors affecting their structure and appearance. Houses with similar plans can be constructed of different materials, yet the technology and materials of construction influence the conception of a house. The *bohío* and the early Spanish house are cases in point. Both now exist only rarely except in modified or restored form, so they are not included in the typology. Of interest, however, is the persistence of elements of their differing technologies of construction and the articulation of these technologies with particular formal structures.

The *bohío* was primarily a post-and-beam structure built of wood, with screening walls made of a bamboo (or similar material) frame to which cane or *yagua* were attached. Unable to bear weight or even to support themselves, the walls were hung on the post-and-beam frame and braced against the floor or ground. The *bohío* and its successors have an open plan with screening walls separating the interior from the exterior. Interior walls can be located variously and are easily penetrated since they are not structurally necessary. The essential core of a *bohío* seems to have been conceived as the basic rectangle formed by the exterior walls.

In contrast, Spanish houses were constructed of solid walls built by piling stone on stone or by using a combination of brick and rubble. Occasionally adobe blocks were also used. Both self-supporting and weight-bearing, the fixed walls with few openings separated in-

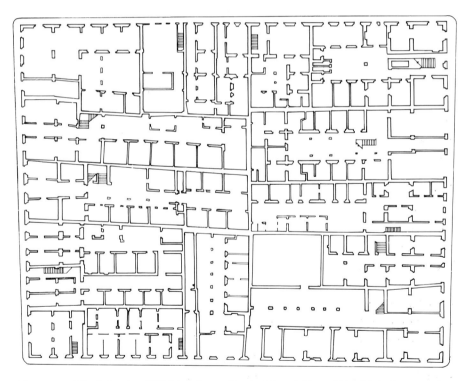

Figure 50. Block Study of Old San Juan, Ground Level Plan, 1966. Note the common walls, continuous facades, and adjoining interior patios typical of Colonial Spanish seventeenth- and eighteenth-century houses. (Adapted from survey no. PR 61, sheet 2 by HABS [Historic American Buildings Survey]).

terior from exterior space, and divided interior space. They were spanned by wood beams which supported the roof. The core of the Spanish house was apparently conceived as a series of adjoining cells surrounding or along two side of an interior patio. These two different types of construction and related concepts of house form endured throughout most of Puerto Rican history. Wood houses generally follow the *bohío* mode; *mampostería* and brick, the Spanish. However, many houses, regardless of material, seem to combine elements of both.

Native hardwood and *mampostería* were the principal materials of construction during the late eighteenth and the nineteenth centuries. Wood houses were built of wide boards of *ausubo* (ironwood) and mahogany, which are long enduring and resistant to termites. Floors were also of hardwood, and roofs were tiled or thatched. Late in the nineteenth century, metal roofing was introduced and gradually replaced thatched roofs. Twentieth-century wood housing is often constructed of United States pine, tongue and groove lumber which was introduced in the late nineteenth century. Such wood is particularly susceptible to termite and carpenter beetle infestation, so many houses built of this material are currently in poorer condition than some earlier ones that have been well maintained. Contemporary wood houses of all kinds are now usually roofed with sheet metal, generally called zinc. Although it attracts heat, with sufficient air space and adequate ventilation, zinc is preferable to thatch because it does not provide a haven for insects and rodents, and if kept painted is more durable. For similar practical reasons, concrete floors covered with modern tile have taken the place of wood floors.

Mampostería was a common building material for houses built in the Spanish mode. It consists of a mixture of clay, lime, and sandstone or limestone, with a line of bricks introduced at intervals for reinforcement. Rows of bricks surround window and door openings also (see figure 74). Toward the end of the nineteenth century, when numbers of brick kilns existed (Morales 1975: 1030), brick replaced *mampostería* as building material. Interior walls were also built of masonry, but more often of native hardwoods in later periods. At first roofs were thatched or tiled with imported Spanish tiles, but later Puerto Rican tiles were used. Spanish tiles were used on floors also, and many still exist in their original state.

Quality and type of materials account in part for the survival of certain houses and the disintegration of others. Old Spanish tiles,

TYPOLOGY OF HOUSES 67

handhewn boards and beams, and strong *mampostería* walls contribute to the overall worth of a house and its endurance. Some houses which lack such quality are disintegrating, but others, well maintained and deeply valued, survive through care. In the following typology, examples of *bohío* and Spanish house spatial order and the various materials of construction are illustrated in conjunction with specific types.

Formal Organization

House forms comprise such variable architectural elements as plan, roof, façade, *balcón*, and height above the ground. Each of these elements has specific social as well as architectural significance.

Schema

Pre-1930 wood houses follow two major patterns of spatial organization and room order or schema.[1] There is also a third schema which is far less frequent. The term "schema" is used to indicate conceptual similarity in room order pattern despite specific differences in plan. For example, all three schemas differ in plan, but have in common the order of certain rooms: the *sala* (living room) at the front, the *cocina* (kitchen) and *baño* (bathroom) at the back, and the *comedor* (dining room) in the center.

The basic unit or core of Schema One, the least common throughout the island, is a rectangle. Within the exterior rectangle, the organization of the interior is variable except for the order noted above (see figure 51).

In the majority of houses within Schema Two, the basic rectangular plan is bisected through the long dimension. Within this schema, plans usually show a *sala* and *comedor* on one side, *dormitorios* (bed-

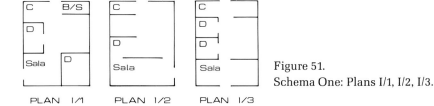

Figure 51.
Schema One: Plans I/1, I/2, I/3.

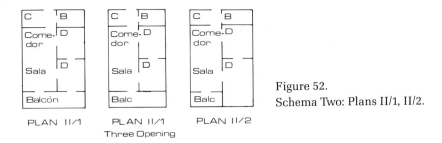

Figure 52.
Schema Two: Plans II/1, II/2.

rooms) on the other, with the *cocina* and *baño* on each side at the back (see figure 52).

The core rectangle of Schema Three (figure 53) often approximates a square. Its front-to-back dimension divides into three interior sections. The *sala* and *comedor* are in the center section, *dormitorios* in the two sections on both sides, and the *cocina* and *baño*, again, are on each side at the back.

Within each schema, plans vary according to presence and place-

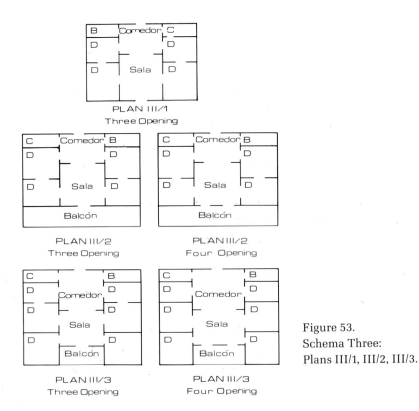

Figure 53.
Schema Three:
Plans III/1, III/2, III/3.

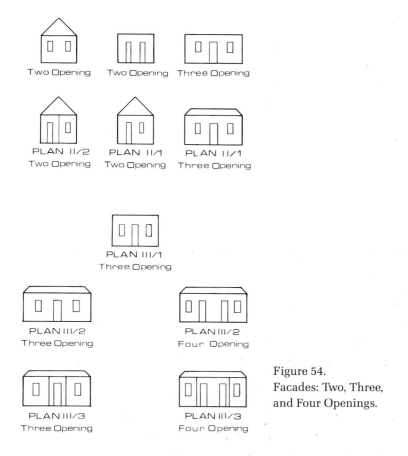

Figure 54.
Facades: Two, Three, and Four Openings.

ment of variable architectural elements such as *balcones*. Houses within these schemas also differ in appearance because of diverse facades and roof structures, which in most cases vary according to style. The styles generally associated with them are Criollo, Criollo Pueblerino, Criollo Neoclassic, Pueblerino, and Bungaloid.

Architectural Elements

Facade

Facades are usually stylistically defined by form and ornament. They relate formally to house plans in number and placement of door and window openings (figure 54). Schema One houses have two and three openings; Schema Two, two and three; and Schema Three, three, four, and sometimes five. Entrance stairways are linked with the height of the house above ground level. A facade is often conceived as an entity in itself, not separate from the house but a focus of attention, a concentration point for all decorative motifs and paint. Tightly constrained and formalized in these latter cases, it takes on a theatrical aspect like a stage set or mask and thus can only reveal significant meaning with more fundamental analysis (Hubka 1980: 67). The facade presents to the world the owner/builder's definition of his house.

Balcón

Balcones (entrance porches), frequently conceived as specific entities in themselves apart from facades, are an important feature of the majority of Puerto Rican houses. Although they are generally prevalent in Caribbean architecture, their antecedent is believed by some to have been the Canary Island *balcón* which was of Arab derivation (Gamble and Puig O. 1978:223–34). Puerto Rican *balcones* vary in configuration, ranging from a small corner space marked by a rail to a broad veranda surrounding three sides of a house. They also differ in materials. Some are built of wood, but even on wood houses, many are of concrete. Their balustrades are made of wrought iron, wood, and concrete block. Style, the placement of the *balcón* within or outside of the core rectangle, the height of the house above ground level, and other factors, affect *balcón* design.

Among many Puerto Ricans, the presence of a *balcón* is a mark of respectability and worth. Additions of *balcones* are usually the first improvements made to Arrabal and Vernacular houses. They are often built of concrete, mainly for practical reasons but also possibly as a further indication of worth. They are usually integral to the style of Designed houses. Most *balcones* are conceived as intermediate to exterior and interior space, and serve as a reception area, especially in small houses lacking interior foyers. Unless a bell or knocker is present, visitors are expected to await invitation before entering onto a *balón* (see also Buitrago Ortiz 1973:23–24). Formal visitors, tradespeople, and strangers seldom proceed further. In this respect, second-story *balcones*, which are not entrances, differ functionally from those on the first floor. Some *balcones* also function as front porches, places from which to view and relate to the outside world.

TYPOLOGY OF HOUSES 71

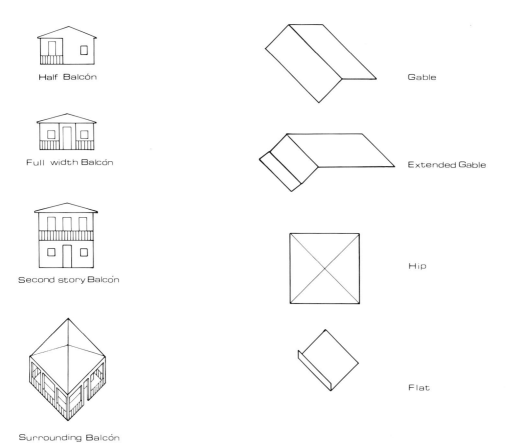

Figure 55.
Balcones: Full-Width, Half-*Balcon*,
Second-Story, Surrounding.

Figure 56.
Roofs: Gable, Extended Gable,
Hip, Flat.

Roofs

Each of the two major types of roofs—pitched, with two or more slopes; and flat—has its advantages. Pitched roofs built with metal sheets or tiles are resistant to storms and promote good ventilation. Flat concrete roofs can be used as outdoor living areas and also allow for the relatively easy addition of a second story.

There are two major types of pitched roofs: gable and hip. These are called *dos aguas* (two slopes) and *cuatro aguas* (four slopes), respectively, by Puerto Ricans. The two types are modified according to their relationship to particular houses. The ridge of the gable roof sometimes runs perpendicular to the facade of the house, with the gable facing the street; in other cases it runs parallel to the facade. In the latter case, more common throughout the island, the roof often has an extension added to the basic gable, in front, in back or both. Sometimes the pitch is quite shallow and hidden by the parapet above the facade. Perpendicular and parallel gable sections are often combined in the roofing of large houses.

The four slopes of a hip roof usually come together at the top in a peak, but sometimes there is a central ridge. Hip roofs more often are associated with particular styles. They also occur on some Vernacular houses irrespective of style because their greater strength is believed to provide better protection. Requiring more material, they are more costly and thus may be a mark of status as well.

Height Above Ground Level

The height of the house above ground level has environmental, economic, and social implications. It is an extremely variable dimension, but three general categories can account for significant differences:

1. Ground level. This category includes Urbanización houses, houses with dirt floors, and Spanish type houses, among others.
2. One to four feet above ground level. Wood houses generally fall into this height range. Some in the southern and southwestern areas of the island are five feet above the ground, and a few have basements.
3. More than five feet above ground level. Houses in rural and mountainous areas are usually built on *zocos* (posts), often six to eight feet above ground level, to protect against occasional flooding and insect and rodent invasion, and to permit air circulation. The resulting space between the ground and the floor serves as a place for storing goods, machinery, and domestic animals, and for hanging laundry.

Galería

A line of rooms with a roofed but open connecting passage which forms an L along two sides of a walled patio is a typical Spanish architectural element (Palm 1974:19–20). *Galería* extensions often occur in larger Schema Two and Three houses, the degree of the extension depending on size of house and economic circumstances.

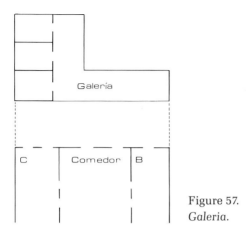

Figure 57.
Galería.

Different versions of nineteenth-century Puerto Rican house types were created by differentially combining the above elements with various plans, styles, and materials.

Plans

The few examples of Schema One houses differ in plan. Their similarity rests on the absence of a *balcón*, and, except for the *sala*, the relatively unorganized character of the rest of the interior. The examples illustrated here, of Schema 1, Plans 1–3 (hereafter coded as I/1, I/2, I/3), are explained below in connection with each house.

Schema Two houses fall into two main categories, each of which has less significant deviations. Schema II, Plan 1 (II/1), has a *balcón* that runs across the full width of the front and sometimes extends to one or more sides. The *balcón* is included under the roof, or within the core rectangle, of some houses (Plan II/1 W [within]) but is attached on the outside of others (Plan II/1 O [outside]).

Schema II, Plan 2, includes a half-*balcón* within the core rectangle (Plan II/2 W). Plan II/2 O is similar, but the *balcón* is outside the roof line and thus outside the core rectangle.

Plans of Schema Two generally show regularity of room placement, but room size and number of rooms vary according to the size of the house. The interior walls are usually penetrated by door openings, permitting circulation from room to room. Only the *baño* has a single entrance. Interior walls amount to visual screens, which are often only partial since they frequently do not reach the ceiling and doorways are sometimes only curtained. Indeed, in larger houses, a division between *sala* and *comedor* called a *mediopunto* (semicircle), is merely a decorative archway or partial wall. In contrast, the exterior wall effectively separates inside from outside; front and back door openings are usually closed, and shuttered or jalousied windows are slanted for privacy or protection against the sun. Designed for maximum cross-ventilation, plans reflect close familial ties within and formal external relationships.

Schema Three plans divide into three main categories. Plan III/1 lacks a *balcón*. Plan III/2 has a *balcón* across the full width of the front, and when this is included in the core rectangle, the plan is termed Plan III/2 W. It is called Plan III/2 O when the *balcón* is outside of it. Plan III/3 has a *balcón*, which, when included in the core rectangle, appears recessed between the two front *dormitorios*, which extend forward into the *balcón* area on either side (Plan III/3 W). On some houses the *balcón* looks the same on the plan, but is outside the basic rectangle of the house (Plan III/3 O). Schema Three houses are somewhat more formal but exhibit many of the characteristics of Schema Two, such as free-flowing interior circulation between rooms and a *mediopunto* dividing *sala* and *comedor*.

Additional specific differences among these plans are described in the discussion of each house. Other plans that occur with other types of houses, composed of additional, sometimes novel components, are considered in relation to specific examples.[2]

House Types of the Spanish-Criollo Period, 1780–1880[3]

Schema One

Schema One houses are rare and the few extant are quite old. Presumably outmoded, they are no longer constructed.

Plan I/1: Two-Opening Facade, Vernacular

In *arrables* the omission of a *balcón* usually indicates lack of ability or resources to build one. In figure 58a, however the exterior of a rare type of house without *balcón*, seen primarily in the northern part of the island, seems partially derived from Spanish-type masonry houses, which similarly lack *balcones*. The interior seems more closely allied with the *bohío*. The house has two front windows with protect-

TYPOLOGY OF HOUSES 75

Figure 58a. Vernacular Criollo (Plan I/2). Extended gable roof. Arecibo.

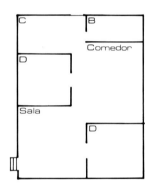

Figure 58b.
Plan of Arecibo House.

ing balustrades and a side entrance into the *sala*. The front extension of its extended gable roof is supported by decorative brackets. Its Plan I/1, with *dormitorio* occupying one side and *sala* the other, is similar to Schema Two in the front part of the house. But in back, the room order is reversed, with the *comedor* behind the *dormitorio* and the second *dormitorio* behind the *sala*. The *baño*/storage area is clearly separated, but the separation of *cocina* and *comedor* space is not well defined.

A second example with the gable ridge of its roof perpendicular to the facade, stands close by the first house (figure 59).

Plan I/2: Two-Opening Facade, Vernacular

The *sala* of a house in Manatí (figures 60a and 60b) extends across the front. Walls and curtains partially separate the *dormitorio* and *cocina* areas in back, but the space is not clearly defined. This house has a very unusual windowbox-like *balcon*, a recent addition. Otherwise it resembles an African-inspired house in its general configuration. Before improvements it probably was like the house adjacent at right, except for its roof orientation. This dwelling is raised above the ground more than the other examples.

Plan I/3: Three-Opening Facade, Designed

A Criollo Neoclassic house, with flat or shallow extended gable roof hidden by the stylistically inspired parapet of its three-opening fa-

Figure 59.
Vernacular Criollo (Plan I/1).
Gable roof. Arecibo.

TYPOLOGY OF HOUSES 77

Figure 60a. Left: Vernacular Criollo House with "Windox-Box" *Balcón*. It was similar to house at right before improvements. Manatí.

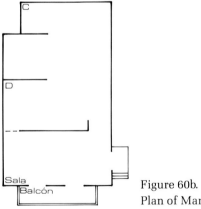

Figure 60b.
Plan of Manatí House.

cade, is more closely related to earlier Spanish type houses (figures 61a and 61b). The entrance at center front leads directly into the *sala*, which extends the full width of the house. In back the plan approximates Schema Two, with *comedor* and *cocina* on the right and two *dormitorios* and *baño*/storage on the left.

Schema Two

Schema Two plans further divide into subtypes with facades of two and three openings. Additional differences such as flat or pitched roofs, or the presence of a *galería*, are categorized as accessory to structures; they modify but do not create subtypes.

The prevalence of Schema Two houses and their manifest adaptability to many styles and sizes demonstrates that this spatial configuration was compatible with a broad spectrum of Puerto Ricans. Plan II/1 with full-width *balcón*, somewhat more adaptable and probably more fundamental, is associated with many different styles. The popularity of the chiefly Vernacular and probably more recent Plan II/2 with half-*balcón* may stem from its compact and economical use of space.

Plan II/1 W: Two-Opening Facade, Vernacular

A Luquillo house (figures 62a and 62b) exemplifies the fundamental two-opening (two doors in this case) house with full-width *balcón* included in the core rectangle. The gable roof is extended on both sides to include *balcón* in front and the *dormitorio* and *cocina* in the back part of the house. The entire house measures 18 by 25 feet and has five rooms, including *sala/comedor*, two *dormitorios*, a *cocina* and storage room. As in many older houses of this type, the owner himself constructed the concrete *balcón* sometime during the last ten years to replace a previous wood structure. Though this one appears to be appended as an afterthought, a *balcón* has always been part of the house plan.

Plan II/1 W: Two-Opening Facade, Designed

A *balcón* on two sides of a Manatí Criollo Pueblerino house (figure 63) is also integral to the house plan, although on the gable side a connecting roof section is required. The Criollo *balcón* illustrated on

TYPOLOGY OF HOUSES 79

Figure 61a. Designed Criollo Neoclassic (Plan I/3). Three-opening facade. Arecibo.

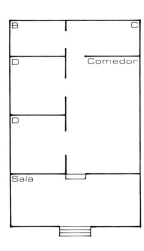

Figure 61b.
Plan of Arecibo House.

80 PUERTO RICAN HOUSES

Figure 62a. Vernacular Pueblerino (Plan II/1 W). Two-opening facade. Luquillo.

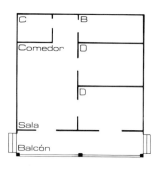

Figure 62b.
Plan of Luquillo House.

Figure 63. Designed Criollo Pueblerino (Plan II/1 W). Two-opening facade.

this example was probably a major inspiration for the Vernacular *balcón*, but the zaguán of the *bohío* should not be discounted as a possible underlying source.

At the front, a Criollo Pueblerino wood house in Ponce (figures 64a and 64b) rests on a 44-inch-high *mampostería* foundation. But in back, the wood floors are supported on short (two-foot) concrete posts. The front openings of the facade consist of a window and door. The *balcón*, integral to the core rectangle, is enhanced by an attractive wood balustrade. Narrow, the house occupies less than the full width of its lot, the remainder being taken up by a driveway on the right and a walkway and drying yard on the left. In back, there is a small paved patio and a tiny apartment against the back wall consisting of *sala/comedor*, *dormitorio*, and *baño* (figure 65). The plan of the main house (figure 64b) includes *sala/comedor* on the right with a *baño* behind, then the *cocina*. Because of its four *dormitorios* the main house looks extensive, but the rooms are very small. Still, the *sala/comedor*, though only 12 by 10 feet, with a 12-foot ceiling, is divided by a *mediopunto* of decorative grillwork. In this house, the single entrance to each *dormitorio* has a door.

Figure 64a. Designed Criollo Pueblerino (Plan II/1 W). Two-opening facade. Ponce.

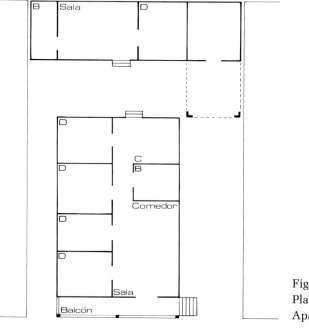

Figure 64b.
Plan of Ponce House and Apartment.

TYPOLOGY OF HOUSES 83

Figure 65.
Small Apartment Behind
Ponce House in Figure 64.

Figure 66. Vernacular Pueblerino (Plan II/1 O). Two-opening facade. Ceiba.

Plan II/1 O: Two-Opening Facade, Vernacular

A concrete *balcón* added to the two-door facade (one converted to a window) of a Ceiba Vernacular house (figure 66) exemplifies very well the difference in type of a *balcón* outside the basic core rectangle. Within, its Schema Two plan is clearly defined.

Plan II/1 O: Two-Opening Facade, Grand[4]

A large Criollo house in Guayama (figures 67a and 67b) has a simple, restrained exterior design. Though part of the original plan, its *balcón* is outside of its core rectangle. The house extends surprisingly far to the back where it is supported by *zocos* rising ten to twelve feet above ground level. It has five *dormitorios* and a *galería* area, now transformed into a family room, overlooking an extensive garden. Except for the intrusion of a *dormitorio* between the *sala* and *comedor* on the left, the house plan fits within Schema Two order.

Plan II/1 W: Three-Opening Facade, Vernacular

This fairly rare type occurs primarily in urban settings. The example here (figures 68a and 68b), set back from the sidewalk behind a concrete wall, has been reconstructed of concrete over the original wood. Its hip roof adds to its substantial appearance. In the interior it follows the conventions of Schema Two, with three *dormitorios*, a *sala/comedor*, and *cocina*.

Plan II/1 O: Three-Opening Facade, Designed

A Criollo Neoclassic house in Ponce (figure 69) presents a totally different appearance. As in figure 67 the *balcón* is part of the plan but lies outside the core rectangle. This house is particularly notable for the fine detailing around the windows, and the handsome wrought-iron posts and balustrades. It has a long *galería* extension in back.

Plan II/2 W: Two-Opening Facade, Vernacular

Defined by its half-*balcón* and Schema Two, this example of a very common type (figures 70a and 70b) includes the *balcón* within the

TYPOLOGY OF HOUSES 85

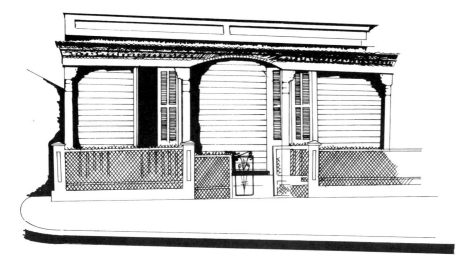

Figure 67a. Grand Criollo (Plan II/1 O). Two-opening facade. Guayama.

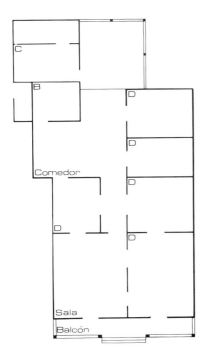

Figure 67b.
Plan of Guayama House.

Figure 68a. Vernacular U.S. Influence (Plan II/1 W). Three-opening facade. San Juan.

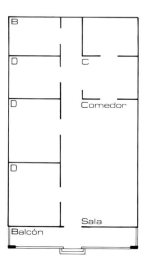

Figure 68b.
Plan of San Juan House.

core. Most houses of this type have a gable rather than a hip roof like this example. The interior (figure 70c) is typical, however, and includes two *dormitorios* and a storage area/*baño* on the right, a *sala/comedor* and a *cocina* on the left. Interior walls are penetrated by doorways, except for one wall separating the *cocina* from the *sala/comedor*, which has an unused pass-through, and the *baño/dormitorio* wall. All doorways are curtained.

Figure 69. Designed Criollo Neoclassic (Plan II/1 O). Three-opening facade. Ponce.

The *sala/comedor*, too small for a *mediopunto*, functions as hallway as well as living, work, and eating room. The tiny *cocina*, usable for minimal food preparation, cooking, and washing up, has little storage space. In consequence, a refrigerator is located in the *comedor*—a common and probably necessary practice, though display of property is probably also involved.

Plan II/2 W: Three-Opening Facade, Designed

The majority of half-*balcón* houses are Vernacular, but the plan is also found in a few Designed houses. The plan of a fairly spacious Criollo house in Rio Grande (figures 71a and 71b) differs in the placement of the *sala/comedor*, which occupies the space usually taken by the front *dormitorio*. The *sala* is entered from the side of the *balcón*.

The house was built on the plaza in the nineteenth century by a prominent citizen who left it to his servant, the grandmother of

Figure 70a. Vernacular Pueblerino (Plan II/2 W). Two-opening facade. Santurce.

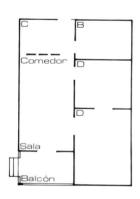

Figure 70b.
Plan of Santurce House.

Figure 70c. Interior View of Santurce House. *Comedor* area. The resident is pointing out *polillo* (carpenter beetle or termite) damage.

TYPOLOGY OF HOUSES 89

Figure 71a. Designed Criollo (Plan II/2 W). Three-opening facade. Río Grande.

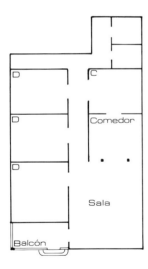

Figure 71b.
Plan of Río Grande House.

the present owner. The former wood siding was covered by brick-patterned embossed metal, possibly in the 1920s, but original cast-iron water tanks are still in use.

Plan II/2 O: Six-Opening Facade, Grand

A Criollo Neoclassic example, grander in design and somewhat larger in scale (figure 72), is one of three houses built in a row around the turn of the century by an *ingeniero* (engineer or technical expert). The house is set back behind a balustraded wall and a small formal garden. Constructed of concrete made to resemble wood, it is painted sky blue with white trim, and has stained glass in the semicircular lights above three of its six front windows. A front entrance stairway leads to a formal half-*balcón* at left, which is clearly part of the original plan but outside the basic core of the house. Moreover, the *balcón* seems to function primarily as an entrance, without the connotations of conventional *balcones*. The front wall at the right has been elaborated into a curve. According to the present occupants, who are not the original owners, the interior plan consists of three *dormitorios*, a *baño*, a storage room on the right, and a *sala/comedor* and a *cocina* on the left.

Schema Three

Schema Three houses have two antecedents: the Spanish Renaissance and the European Central Hall house. Both of these were derived

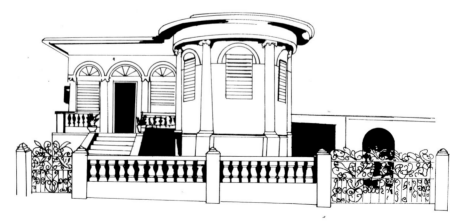

Figure 72. Grand Criollo Neoclassic (Plan II/2 O). Six-opening facade. San Juan.

from the Greek, or more specifically the Roman, house (Oliveira Marquez 1971:98; Palm 1974:13–19). These influences are present in most houses with Schema Three three-section plans. The central core, consisting of *sala, comedor,* and four or more *dormitorios,* is closely related to the European Central Hall plan, while the often-present *galería* extension came from Spain.[5] Masonry structures appear to have greater affinity with earlier Spanish architecture, and wood structures with Caribbean architecture.

Figure 73a. Colonial Spanish (Plan III/1). Three-opening facade. Mayaguez.

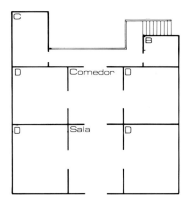

Figure 73b.
Plan of Mayaguez House.

Only Designed examples constructed of masonry were seen of Plan III/1. It is apparently unsuited to Vernacular.

Plan III/1: Three-Opening Facade, Designed

A late eighteenth-century Colonial Spanish *mampostería* house in Mayaguez exemplifies Spanish influence. The plain front wall, close to the street and without *balcón*, is characteristically Spanish. Also Spanish is the *galería*, a feature believed to have been derived from an Andalusian house which had a central patio with a line of rooms forming an L along two sides (Palm 1974:19–20). The house illustrated (figures 73a and 73b) has a central *sala/comedor* with two *dormitorios* on each side, the defining characteristic of Schema Three. In back, the *galería* leading to the *cocina* and other rooms overlooks a small patio below, which is reached by a flight of stairs. Below the *cocina* is a *sótano* (cellar), one of the few in Puerto Rico.

Figure 74. Colonial Spanish Caminera. San Germán.

A related structure (figure 74) is the *Caminera*, a road-tender's house built of *mampostería*. In the nineteenth century, these were built every ten miles along major roads. A few remain. This example still serves to store road-tending materials but is no longer a dwelling. Its original plan was related to Schema Three.

Plan III/1: Three-Opening Facade, Grand

A house built of *mampostería* in 1875 (figures 75a, 75b, and 75c) shows greater Caribbean influence. One of three sisters, who live on adjoining properties in Guayama, owns this handsome Criollo Neoclassic house. The plan is conventional, with central *sala/comedor* and two *dormitorios* on either side. A room on the left at the back has been converted into an interior garden room. Though not "grand" in size, this house earns that characterization because of its refinement and scale. Both exterior and interior have very fine detailing. The *sala* is 15 by 10 feet, with a 12-foot ceiling. Its *mediopunto* is graced with Mozarabic arches.

Plan III/2 W: Three-Opening Facade, Vernacular

Vernacular examples of Schema Three are less common than Designed ones, but a Naguabo house (figures 76a and 76b) with Early Gothic trim, built of United States pine, belongs to Plan III/2 W with *balcón* included within the basic core. Because of greater breadth across the front, even small-sized Vernacular versions of Schema Three appear larger than Schema Two houses. The interior follows a conventional plan with central *sala/comedor* and two *dormitorios* on each side. A rudimentary *mediopunto* is illustrated.

Plan III/2 W: Three-Opening Facade, Designed

U.S. influence is manifested in a pleasingly detailed Criollo house in Aibonito (figures 77a and 77b) which was built in 1918, with ventilators designed to resemble dormers, and a front-porch-like *balcón*. The plan originally followed Plan III/2 W, with *balcón* included within the central core and a standard three-section division. It has been modified by eliminating one *dormitorio* at right to create a larger, separate *comedor* and by enlarging a second *dormitorio* at left.

Figure 75a. Grand Criollo Neoclassic (Plan III/1). Three-opening facade. Guayama.

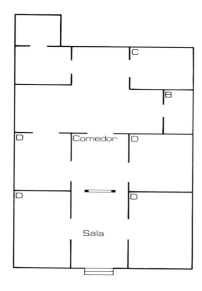

Figure 75b.
Plan of Guayama House.

Figure 75c. Interior of Guayama House. View toward *comedor*, showing Mudejar arches of the *mediopunto*, scrollwork in doorway transoms, and chandelier imported from France.

Figure 76a. Vernacular Early Gothic Revival (Plan III/2 W). Three-opening facade. Naguabo.

Figure 76b. Interior of Naguabo House. Note vestigial *mediopunto*.

TYPOLOGY OF HOUSES 97

Figure 77a. Designed Criollo (Plan III/2 W). Three-opening facade. Aibonito.

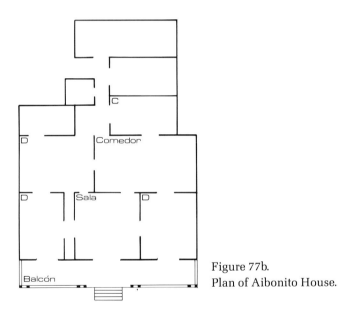

Figure 77b.
Plan of Aibonito House.

Plan III/2 O: Three-Opening Facade, Designed

A Criollo house in Lares (figure 78) has an unusual *balcón*. Although the *balcón* is covered by an overhanging roof and bounded by a handsome, stylistically related wrought-iron balustrade, because of the lack of posts supporting the roof, the *balcón* appears to be outside

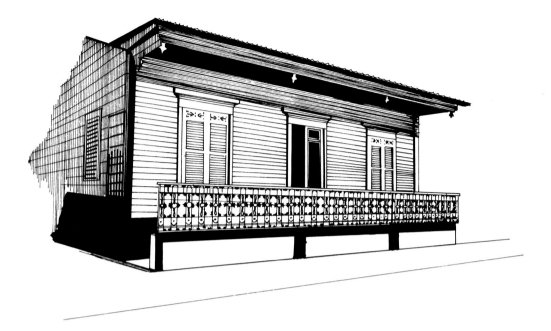

Figure 78. Designed Criollo (Plan III/2 O). Three-opening facade. Lares.

the core rectangle. On the interior, the house's conventional plan consists of two *dormitorios* on either side of a *sala/comedor* which is divided by a *mediopunto*.

Plan III/2: Four-Opening Facade

Four-opening facade houses resemble each other in spatial organization but differ in style. To a greater extent than other house types, four-opening facade Plans III/2 manifest regional stylistic variation, although this is usually an attribute only of their facades on the exterior, and of the *sala/comedor* on the interior. The treatment of fenestration differs markedly. The *balcón*, a prominent feature of the facade, sometimes appears to be integral to the house but in other cases seems an entity in itself. However, there seems to be no difference in function or meaning in the two cases. Roofs vary, but most are extended gable. Wood houses are usually raised two to four feet above street level. Some have front steps at the side of the *balcón*, leading to the entrance. Four-opening facade Plan III/2 houses are also noteworthy for their attractive interiors; some have been restored and others modernized, typically by creating a family room on the back *galería* overlooking the patio.

Plan III/2 W: Four-Opening Facade, Vernacular

A house in Moca (figures 79a, 79b, 79c) is a rare Vernacular example of this type. It has clapboard-like siding, and inside, tongue-and-groove walls and ceiling. In contrast to Designed examples, it is a very plain house, with a minimum of decorative details inside and out. The house contains the basic *sala/comedor*, four *dormitorios*, and a *cocina*. Each doorway into the *dormitorios* has been decorated with a valance. Although one is blocked by the sofa, the two central doors enter into the *sala*. There is no *galería* and only a small patio in back.

Plan III/2 W: Four-Opening Facade, Grand

A High Neoclassic house (figures 80a, 80b, 80c) owned by another of the Guayama sisters illustrates certain of the most common remodeling changes. Two *dormitorios* on the right have been replaced by an office area for both husband and wife, but six *dormitorios* remain. A *galería* at the back of the house has been transformed into a *comedor* with an adjacent enlarged and modernized kitchen. As a result, the *sala* space has been enlarged and seems more hall-like. In back, the garden patio adjoins that of the sister's house described above. An intervening house was torn down, and fruit trees and flowers are now planted in the space. The siting of these two houses and a third belonging to another sister also illustrates the traditional Spanish convention of creating an informal family compound on adjoining properties behind formal facades presented to the street.

Plan III/2 W: Four-Opening Facade, Designed

The exteriors of three other houses show the variability of styles. The French quality created by the height and form of the hip roof of an Añasco example (figure 81) is striking. Its interior plan is more conventional than the previous example. One Criollo Neoclassic house in San Germán (figure 82) has been completely restored, and another in Yauco (figure 83) has been modified on the interior to fit family needs.

Figure 79a. Vernacular Criollo (Plan III/2 W). Four-opening facade. Moca.

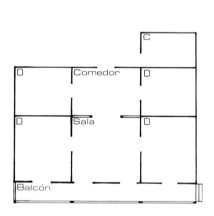

Figure 79b. Plan of Moca House.

Figure 79c. Interior of Moca House.

TYPOLOGY OF HOUSES 101

Figure 80a. Grand High Neoclassic (Plan III/2 W). Four-opening facade. Guayama.

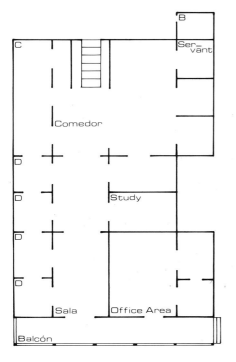

Figure 80c. Garden of Guayama House.

Figure 80b.
Plan of Guayama House.

102 PUERTO RICAN HOUSES

Figure 81. Designed Criollo (Plan III/2 W). Four-opening facade. Añasco.

Figure 82. Designed Criollo (Plan III/2 W). Four-opening facade. San Germán.

Figure 83. Designed Criollo Neoclassic (Plan III/2 W). Four-opening facade.

Plan III/2 O: Four-Opening Facade, Designed

The plan of a Criollo Neoclassic style house in Juana Díaz (figures 84a and 84b) also includes the standard four *dormitorio* arrangement in the front, but the former *comedor* was transformed into an *antesala* (here, informal sitting room), and the *comedor* is now conveniently situated in the *galería* area near the *cocina*. Other Criollo houses of this type are notable for the quality of their architectural detailing. A pale pink Guayama example (figure 85) exhibits an interesting herringbone treatment of the front siding. The windows of a Ciales Criollo Neoclassic house (figure 86) are particularly fine. The gable-shaped ventilators on the roof give added height to the design.

Plan III/2 O: Four-Opening Facade, Grand

An unostentatious Criollo house in Juana Díaz (figures 87a and 87b) has retained much of the original character of Criollo. It has an expanded plan, with seven *dormitorios* and a *galería* that leads to a separate building for the *cocina*.[6] The refinement of its equally modest interior is very pleasing.

Figure 84a. Designed Criollo Neoclassic (Plan III/2 O). Four-opening facade. Juana Díaz.

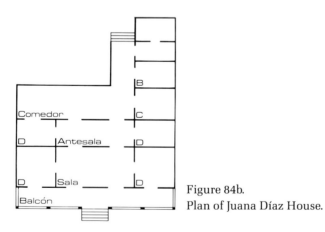

Figure 84b. Plan of Juana Díaz House.

TYPOLOGY OF HOUSES 105

Figure 85. Designed Criollo (Plan III/2 O). Four-opening facade. Guayama.

Figure 86. Designed Criollo (Plan III/2 O). Four-opening facade. Ciales.

Figure 87a. Grand Criollo (Plan III/2 O). Four-opening facade. Juana Díaz.

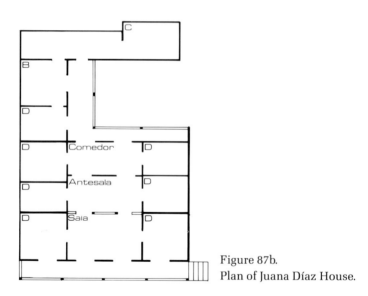

Figure 87b.
Plan of Juana Díaz House.

Two large and more elaborate houses, though related, fall outside the scale of these houses. Their projecting porticos and double stairway entrances to the *balcón* are similar, but the Criollo wood house in Coamo (figures 88a and 88b) is related to Plan III/2 W, while the Criollo Neoclassic *mampostería* house in Ponce is more akin to Plan III/2 O. The front area of the Coamo house is organized according

TYPOLOGY OF HOUSES 107

Figure 88a. Grand Criollo (Plan III/2 W). Four-opening facade. Coamo.

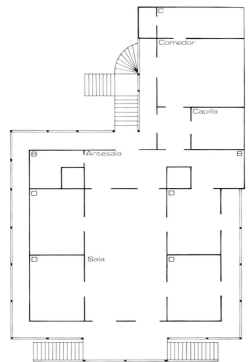

Figure 88b.
Plan of Coamo House.

Figure 89. Grand Criollo Neoclassic (Plan III/2 O). Four-opening facade. Ponce.

to Schema Three, with four *dormitorios* on either side of a very large *sala*. Back of it there are an *antesala*, two baths, and a passage to a former chapel and a large separate *comedor*. A *galería* leading to a string of smaller rooms continues along one side of the large interior court.

Plan III/3

This type, with *balcón* seemingly recessed between two projecting *dormitorios*, is far less common than Plan III/2 houses and occurs only sporadically throughout the island.

Plan III/3 W: Three-Opening Facade, Vernacular

There are a number of Vernacular examples like the one illustrated. The derivation of its distinctive partially-enclosed *balcón* has been attributed to Catalan influence (Gamble and Puig O. 1978), a plausible explanation considering the influx of Catalans to Puerto Rico in the second half of the nineteenth century. The illustrated house (fig-

Figure 90. Vernacular Pueblerino (Plan III/3 W). Three-opening facade. Hatillo.

ure 90) has the usual arrangement of Schema Three, with four *dormitorios*, *sala/comedor*, and *cocina*, but the left front *dormitorio* currently serves as a radio/television repair shop.

Plan III/3 O: Four-Opening Facade, Designed

Two adjacent Criollo houses appear to have been constructed by the same builder. The detailing on both is quite fine. One (figure 91) has herringbone front siding and a painting on its front gable. The second (figures 92a, 92b, and 92c) now carefully restored and maintained, has four *dormitorios*, *sala*, *antesala*, and *comedor* in front, and in the back *cocina* and *baño* reached by a *galería*, which overlooks a spacious patio and sizable lot. As in the majority of Schema Three houses, a decorative *mediopunto* divides *sala* and *comedor*.

Two-Story Houses

All of the houses discussed above make up a family of types unified by the general similarity of their plans, use of materials, and range

Figure 91. Designed Criollo (Plan III/3 O). Four-opening facade. Arroyo.

of styles. The examples given are one-story, primarily urban houses. Some closely related two-story houses also fit into Schema Two and Schema Three.

Although differing in some aspects, certain two-story houses are conceptually and formally related. The House and Tienda (store) consists of a dwelling above and a shop or other business enterprise on the ground floor. Most of these buildings comprise a Schema Three house above and stores beneath. The model for the largest and oldest of these buildings came from Spain. Though usually modified, several early *mampostería* House and Tienda buildings can be seen in Old San Juan. Indeed, the House and Tienda, as a type of town residence, is believed by some to have preceded separate residences in the southwestern region of the island (Alfonso 1975).

Similarly, the rural Hacienda house usually has a Schema Three dwelling above and a space below for stores and machinery. More elaborate Hacienda houses were constructed as two-story dwellings, with offices, storerooms, warehouses, and sometimes machinery on the ground level and a family dwelling above. The styles of both

House and Tienda and Hacienda houses are similar to Designed urban houses, with those of Criollo Pueblerino, Criollo, and Criollo Neoclassic predominating.

Two-story Vernacular habitations, sometimes related in function to the House and Tienda, have a simpler formal organization. Usually they are composed of two Schema Two houses stacked one above the other. This type is often constructed as a dwelling for two families and then later converted to house and *tienda*, or vice versa. Most are Pueblerino in style.

As the following examples illustrate, these two-story types vary in the articulation of upper and lower stories.

Two-House Two-Story Buildings, Vernacular

Two Vernacular buildings comprise two identical Plan II/1 W units built one above the other. The Ponce house with outside stairway (figures 93a and 93b) is the residence of two separate families. A house in Río Piedras (Plan II/1 O), built as a two-family habitation, is occupied by one family that uses the second-story rooms as *dormitorios* (figure 94). The stairway in the house is enclosed at the right side. When the ground floor of this type of building is converted to a *tienda*, the *sala* and often the front *dormitorio* serve as the store area.

House and Tienda

Depending on their size, the lower floor of traditional House and Tienda buildings had three or five openings, with the central one leading into a *zaguán* (arcade)[7] with small one-room shops on either side. From this hallway, a central or side stairway, often elaborately decorated with Spanish tiles, led to the family residence above. The location of the stairway area was related to the residential plan and size of the building. Some buildings follow Schema Two, Plan II/1 W, but the majority are Schema Three, Plan III/2 W.

Plan II/1 W: Three-Opening Facade, Designed. Numerous medium-sized Criollo buildings were constructed as Three-Opening Facade Plan II/1 W dwellings, with three-opening-facade *tiendas* below. An example seen in Arecibo belonging to a former teacher had an outside entrance stairway on the right, and two *tiendas* below, both now converted to rental apartments.

112   PUERTO RICAN HOUSES

Figure 92a. Designed Criollo (Plan III/3 O). Four-opening facade. Arroyo.

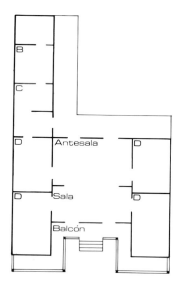

Figure 92b.
Plan of Arroyo House.

Figure 92c. Garden Steps of Arroyo House.

Figure 93a. Vernacular Criollo Pueblerino Two-House Two-Story Two-Opening (Plan II/1 W). Ponce.

Figure 93b. Upper Level Plan. Lower level has same room order, but bar divides *sala* and *comedor*. See Figure 191.

Plan III/2 W: Four-Opening Facade, Designed. A large building on the Añasco town square (figures 95a, 95b, 95c) manifests a number of characteristics typical of the genre. Built of *mampostería* below and wood above, it has five openings at the ground level in front, although the central one, now altered, is no longer a *zaguán* entrance. Above, four front openings lead onto the *balcón*, which typically overhangs the sidewalk below. Dormer-like ventilators are attributed to French as well as U.S. influence (Buissert 1980:6). At the back of the residence there is a *galería* L. The front of the house, with central *sala* and *dormitorios* on each side, follows Plan III/2, but the arrangement at the back is not known. The interior of the *sala* is handsomely appointed with mahogany trim around the doorways. A richly furnished master bedroom occupies a prominent position off the *sala*.

The House and Tienda type has a number of variations besides plan and facade openings. An enclosed side entrance stairway like the one at the left of a Criollo example (figure 96) is associated with Plan II/1 W dwellings. This one has an auto mechanic's shop on the lower level. The facades of many Vernacular and Arrabal buildings are crossed diagonally by second-story entrance stairways. A strik-

Figure 94.
Vernacular Criollo Two-House Two-Story Two-Opening (Plan II/1 O). Río Piedras.

Figure 95a. Designed Criollo Neoclassic House and Tienda (Plan III/2 W). Four-opening facade. Añasco.

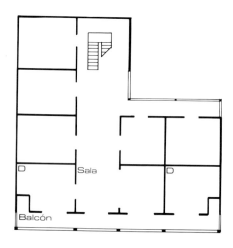

Figure 95b. Plan of Añasco House.

Figure 95c. Interior of Añasco House. Entrance into master bedroom off *sala*.

ing type (figure 97) designed for a corner situation has an elaborate pediment above a corner entrance to the principal shop. The stairway entrance to the Plan II/1 dwelling above is at the far right of the corner. One or more examples of this corner type exist in many island towns.

Hacienda Houses

Hacienda houses on sugar plantations are designed for level land, those on coffee plantations for mountainous terrain. But the two sorts are similar in their Plan III/2 W designs and many other features. Hacienda houses on sugar plantations are most often complete two-story buildings, constructed variously of *mampostería* or wood on the ground floor, and wood above. Hacienda houses in the

Figure 96. Designed Criollo House and Tienda (Plan II/1 W). Four-opening facade. San Germán.

Figure 97. Designed High Neoclassic Corner House and Tienda (Plan II/1). Adjuntas.

coffee areas usually are one story in front but two stories in back, where the ground level drops off.

Sugar Plantation Hacienda House, Designed. This example (figures 98a and 98b) retains its form although it no longer serves its original purpose as the master's house on an operating sugar plantation. The area below, once devoted to stores, machinery, and hacienda activities, has been converted to a garage warehouse. The front of the dwelling above has three doors leading onto the *balcón*. The front part of the house—which apparently consists of four rooms, a *sala* and three *dormitorios* partially separated by curtains—bears some relation to Schema Two. It is closer to Plan II/1 O, since its *balcón* roof is outside the hip roof. A *galería* leads past an open porch to the *comedor* and *cocina* in the back.

Figure 98a. Designed Criollo Hacienda House (Plan II/1 O). Three-opening facade. San Germán.

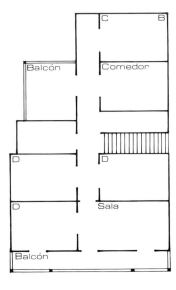

Figure 98b.
Plan of San Germán House.

Sugar Plantation Hacienda House, Grand. A more pretentious Criollo Neoclassic Hacienda house (figures 99a and 99b) on a still-operating sugar plantation, in addition to ground-level stores and offices, has a traditional Plan III/2 W residence. An imposing front stairway leads to the second-story entrance, and in back is a very large *galería* and L extension.

Coffee Area Hacienda Houses, Designed. Hacienda houses in the coffee areas, commonly less elaborate, are often as simple as Vernacular buildings. The five openings of Delfina's facade (figures 100a and 100b) are somewhat unusual, but otherwise the house follows the standards of Plan III/2 W. One of the four *dormitorios* is used as an office. The *balcón* traverses the front and continues around one side; a *galería* or second *balcón* extends across the back and leads to the *cocina*. The house is supported in the back by *zocos* extending to ground level, twelve or more feet below. The partially open space underneath, with dirt floor, is used for stores, machinery, farming equipment, and supplies.

At Hacienda Delicias, the Criollo master's house (figures 101a and 101b), attractively painted pale yellow with white trim, is still a simple design. In back, though more formally organized than Delfina, it is a utilitarian building.

Santa Clara Abajo (the lower) is now a separate property managed and run by its owner, who resides in the house (figures 102a and 102b). Its facade has three openings, and its *balcón*, clearly conceived as integral to the core of the house, surrounds the central rooms on three sides. A *galería* leads to the *cocina* and *baño* and is sometimes used as *comedor*.

Santa Clara Arriba (the upper), with a similar distinctively shaped extended gable roof, is situated on a working hacienda but is no longer occupied (figures 103a and 103b). It has an idiosyncratic plan which takes advantage of the site. The *sala* overlooks a valley below, and the *dormitorios* are configured to fit the space adjacent to a road. Both houses were built in the nineteenth century of native hardwoods.

Coffee Area Hacienda House, Grand. In their refinement and more elaborate construction, Dos Ríos, a Criollo Neoclassic house (figures 104a and 104b), and a complete two-story house on a coffee hacienda at Hormigueras (figure 19) are somewhat comparable to the master's

Figure 99a. Grand Criollo Neoclassic Hacienda House (Plan III/2 W). Four-opening facade. Sábana Grande.

Figure 99b. Wing Extension of Sábana Grand House.

Figure 100a. Designed Criollo Hacienda House (Plan III/2 W). Five-opening facade. Hacienda Delfina, Maricao.

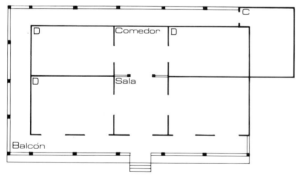

Figure 100b. Plan of Hacienda Delfina House.

TYPOLOGY OF HOUSES 123

Figure 101a. Designed Criollo Hacienda House (plan III/2 W). Four-opening facade. Hacienda Delicias, Maricao.

Figure 101b. Rear View of Hacienda Delicias House.

Figure 102a. Designed Criollo Hacienda House (Plan III/2 W). Three-Opening facade. Hacienda Santa Clara Abajo, near Yauco.

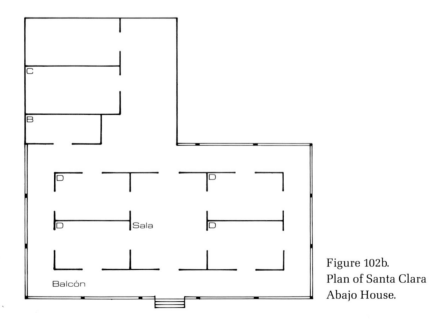

Figure 102b. Plan of Santa Clara Abajo House.

TYPOLOGY OF HOUSES 125

Figure 103a.
View of Santa Clara Arriba.
Note wide boards of
native wood.

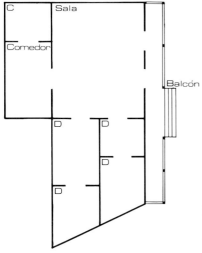

Figure 103b.
Plan of Santa Clara Arriba
House.

126 PUERTO RICAN HOUSES

Figure 104a. Grand Criollo Neoclassic Hacienda House (Plan III/2 W). Four-opening facade. Hacienda Dos Ríos, Maricao.

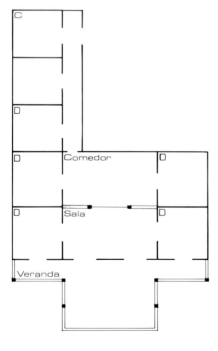

Figure 104b.
Plan of Dos Ríos House.

house on the sugar plantation, Hacienda San Francisco (see figure 99). Despite variation in style, scale, and degree of refinement, the formal organization of all these Hacienda houses is generally similar.

Summary

A few general meanings emerge from the foregoing typology. Regardless of the actual time of their construction, these Spanish-Criollo Period houses follow a nineteenth-century schema, with the *sala/comedor* as focal point. Combined with easy communication and circulation from room to room, such organization indicates close family relationships. Such relationships appear to outweigh personal privacy in importance, especially in Vernacular houses.

The differentiation and elaboration of facades imply that distinguishing oneself from one's neighbors as well as formal relations with outsiders were important to house owners. Taking their measure from their neighbors, urban houses are made distinctive mainly through style, color or materials, and size. That so much was invested in elaborating Criollo houses to distinguish them from each other suggests the significance to each family of its identity and status.

There is also evidence that preference for certain formal arrangements correlates with social level. Presupposing that social stratification is reflected in the range of Vernacular to Grand house types, with the exceptions noted Schema One and Two are chiefly Vernacular, while Schema Three is Designed. This difference has some economic basis, but diverse attitudes may also underlie it.

Houses in rural areas, conceived in relation to other buildings on the hacienda or property, are less refined than urban ones. The general simplicity of country houses expresses their utilitarian function; urban houses more often also signify socioeconomic status. The greater elaboration of Hacienda houses on sugar, as compared to coffee, plantations can be partially explained by a difference in owner residence patterns. Coffee hacienda owners were also entrepreneurs whose principal residence was in town near the place of trade. Sugar plantation owners more commonly resided in the grand mansion on the hacienda; the town house was secondary.

One of the goals of this study is to test the validity of such assumptions by correlating demographic information on house residents with types of houses. A brief digression is necessary to explain not only the background of the survey of house residents but also the graphs that represent the results.

Residence Pattern

Currently, Puerto Ricans select from a range of housing options depending on their economic circumstances and the strategies they use to meet their needs.[8] At the lower end of the social scale, the choices include: rental of a unit in a government subsidized multifamily building (the least favored), rental of a rundown older urban house, and purchase of an Urbanización house in a government financed *urbanización*. One must hold a job to qualify for the last. More affluent people can also choose to buy a privately constructed Urbanización house, older city dwelling, condominium, or build an architect-designed house. The numerous opportunities for choice raise questions. Is there a predictable pattern of relationship between type of dwelling and type of resident? Analysis of the form and style of Puerto Rican houses provides general clues to the social character of residents, but do the inferences reached on this basis actually fit? Indeed, are the general appearance and configuration of a house sufficient evidence for predicting the nature of its residents? The categories of Vernacular, Designed, and Grand describe houses, but do they correlate with resident social level? These questions underlay the decision to seek quantifiable data from house residents on age, time or duration of residence, occupation, education, and amount of travel. Occupation, education, and amount of travel were assumed to be indicators of social level, and together with age, of aesthetic preference as well. Time of residence discloses stability/mobility. A large amount of supporting anecdotal data was obtained in open-ended interviews, but the above categories were sufficient to show correlation of types of houses with resident social level.

Owing to particular Puerto Rican circumstances, some of the categories employed involve multiple issues. For example, not only is age a measure of chronology, but, since before 1940 school attendance was not required of all Puerto Rican children, age also relates to degree of education. As a group, older people tend to have less education and therefore less specialized or technically sophisticated occupations than younger ones. Occupation, though related to education, identifies social status more precisely.

Employment opportunities for Puerto Ricans exist in numerous fields, including industry, agriculture, commerce, government, and the professions. But jobs are scarce, and as there are fewer jobs for the untrained and unschooled, the unemployment rate is very high (Sánchez Vilella 1984). In their responses to questions, unemployed and underemployed persons tended to give type of occupation rather than employment status and therefore are not represented accurately in the survey.

Time of residence often correlates with age of resident and, of course, with age of house. Houses are usually acquired at marriage or shortly thereafter and lived in until the children are grown or longer (see also Mintz 1974). In many cases, however, they are inherited, so inception of residence coincides with birth.

Degree and kind of travel are social indicators. They show type and amount of outside contact, along with a host of other stimulating or motivating factors.

The graphs (figure 105), organized according to the classification established in the text, show only proportional relationships within categories. The first set of graphs based on data taken from occupants of Spanish and Criollo houses reveals that in each category residents are predominantly middle-aged or older. The average time of residence is more than ten years, an indication of stability and possibly of an age-related preference for older house types. Residents of Designed houses are more often professionals, merchants, and managers with six or more years of education who have traveled in Europe and the United States. Though unsurprising, these findings confirm a correlation between house type and social level. Vernacular houses and lower- to middle-class status are correlated; while Designed houses and upper-middle- to upper-class status are correlated. (Because of minimal difference, Grand is lumped with Designed to simplify discussion.) The data reaffirm the correlation of house form and resident social levels: Schema One and Two and the lower and middle classes go together; Schema Three and middle and upper classes do. Nevertheless certain anomalies must be pointed out. The occupants of several Designed houses are no longer of the same class as the original upper-middle-class owners or their descendants, but are lower-class buyers, former servant inheritors, and room renters. Yet the overall consistency of the relationship between Spanish and

130 PUERTO RICAN HOUSES

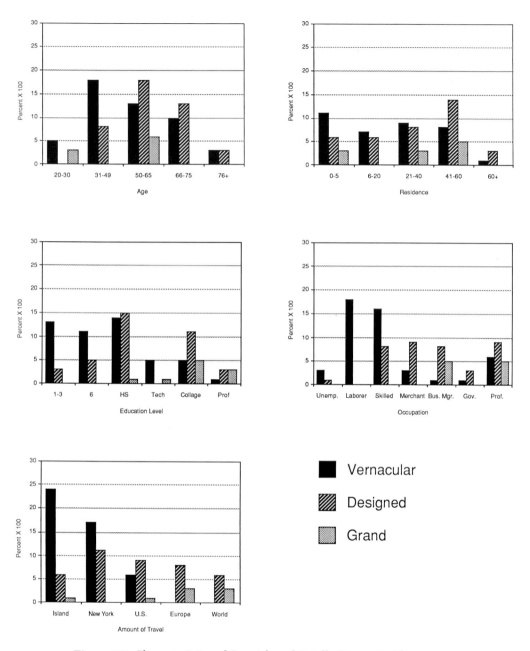

Figure 105. Characteristics of Spanish and Criollo House Residents.

Criollo house type and form, and the social level of residents makes a strong case for the predictability of these associations.

House Types of the Eclectic Period, 1875–1910

Two-Story One-Family Mansion

The advent of large pretentious residences toward the end of the nineteenth century introduced new concepts and formal innovations into the organization of houses. Thus large, complex two-story buildings, often asymmetrically arranged around a central hall, differ from simpler but equally large-scale Hacienda or House and Tienda types.

The Grand houses had two types of plans. The first, associated with Victorian Queen Anne, though organized as a square with rooms at the corners, has an irregular outline with bays and verandas extending outward (figures 106a and 106b). This irregularity and the asymmetrically organized axes allow for variation in room size, with small ones tucked into odd-shaped spaces and large ones expanding out from the center. The exterior, enlivened by turrets, conical roofs, and jutting bays, is equally irregular. The second type, associated with Greek Revival style, though equivalent in scale, has a symmetrical plan which is more self-contained within a square or cube (figures 107a and 107b). It often includes a circular or oval central hall with rooms around it and an imposing stairway leading to the second level.

Though differing in plan, these two types are comparable in scale and formality of design. In contrast to the more open-ended modular designs of Schema Two and Three houses, these are conceived as total entities, with each room fitted into a formal plan. Each unit, delineated and separated by enclosing walls and doors, is also more specialized by size than rooms in Schema Two and Three types. Moreover, although the master *dormitorio* is sometimes situated on the first floor, others are confined to the second floor, separated from living areas. Some of the formality of these Grand houses and certain of their features were incorporated into more modest Designed and Vernacular houses of the same period.

Figure 106a. Grand Queen Anne Two-Story One-Family Mansion. Naguabo.

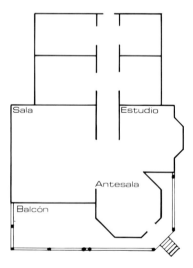

Figure 106b.
Plan of Naguabo House.

Figure 107a. Grand Greek Revival Two-Story One-Family Mansion. San Sebastián.

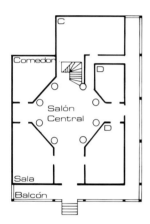

Figure 107b.
Plan of San Sebastián House.

Partial-Second-Story Houses

Different and simpler two-story forms were adopted for Designed and Vernacular wood houses of this period. A number have a partial second story at the back which resembles the Louisiana Camelback. Others have towers or miradors at the front, and some have central belvederes. The second-story room or rooms, used variously as *dormitorios* or as separate sitting areas for enjoying the view and evening breeze, are reached by an interior spiral stairway within the tower or mirador structure, by a stairway within the house proper, or by an outside stair. Though conceptually and formally related, the houses differ in appearance because of the variable shapes of tow-

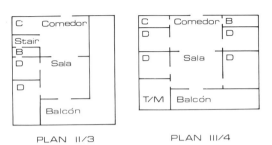

Figure 108.
Plans of Partial-Second-Story Houses.

ers, camelback partial second stories, and belvederes. Their plans, though related to Schema Two and Three, differ from them because the stairways and towers must be accommodated. A common solution, regardless of addition or schema, is to use the *balcón* space forward of the front wall at left front for this purpose. Either a tower occupies this space, or a *dormitorio* or other room is moved forward to allow for an interior stairway in back. The *balcón* then continues across the remaining two-thirds of the house front and sometimes around one side to form an L shape. When the plans fit within Schema Two or Three and manifest such specific patterned modifications, they are termed Plan II/3 and Plan III/4 (figure 108). Plan II/3 consists of the two-division central core with *dormitorios* on one side and *sala/comedor* on the other. Plan III/4 has a three-section central core with *dormitorios* on either side of a *sala/comedor*. When the core plan is unchanged and an addition is added at the back, as is most common, the type is referred to as a "camelback addition." There are also a number of idiosyncratic solutions.

Plan II/1: Camelback Addition, Vernacular

The majority of Vernacular examples of both Camelback and Tower houses are located in the southern part of the island. Their number attests to their popularity.

A Camelback was added recently to a Plan II/1 house in Puerto Real (figures 109a and 109b). To accommodate the inside stair on the left at the back, which now takes up the space of the former *comedor* or a *dormitorio*, the former *balcón* was enclosed to create a large living room across the front, and a new *balcón* was constructed in front of it. The addition of the camelback permitted *dormitorios* to be moved to the second floor and space made available for a larger kitchen and

TYPOLOGY OF HOUSES 135

Figure 109a. Vernacular Camelback. Idiosyncratic plan. Puerto Real.

Figure 109b.
Rear View of Puerto Real
House.

eating area. This idiosyncratic solution resulted in the complete transformation of the house. One now enters into the *comedor* kitchen area at back left; the stairway is on the left and the large living room at right.

Plan III/2: Camelback Addition, Designed

A ninety-four-year-old man lived all his life in a Criollo Camelback house in Mayaguez (figure 110). The camelback with interior stair was incorporated at the back without disturbing the central core. The house is notable for the fine details of craftmanship characteristic of the period, especially an interesting *mediopunto* and tile entrance steps.

Plan II/3: Tower House, Vernacular

A tower occupies the front left corner of this house in Rio Piedras. The tower with its L-shaped *balcón* exemplifies the configuration of this type. In this house (figure 26) a very narrow spiral stair built inside the tower walls leads to a small *dormitorio* above.

Figure 110. Designed Camelback Addition (Plan III/2). Four-opening facade. Mayaguez.

Figure 111. Designed Tower House (Plan II/3). Four-opening facade. Aguadilla.

Plan II/3: Tower House, Designed

A mirador house in Aguadilla (figure 111) has a similar plan except for its three-quarter *balcón*. Stairs enclosed within the mirador structure are no longer safe for use. According to its owner, an old man who inherited the house, this mirador always was used for its designed purpose.

Plan III/4: Belvedere House, Designed

The Queen Anne belvedere was the inspiration for a third type of partial-second-story house. A house in the center of Juana Díaz (figures 112a and 112b) has a *comedor* extending out at left front and an L-shaped *balcón*. In back on the left, the interior stairway leads to the belvedere, clearly designed for viewing the town plaza which it overlooks. The house has not been greatly altered, but rooms are no longer used for the purposes intended. However, it is still possible to see the original Schema Three spatial order.

Figure 112a. Designed Belvedere House (Plan III/4). Three-opening facade. Juana Díaz.

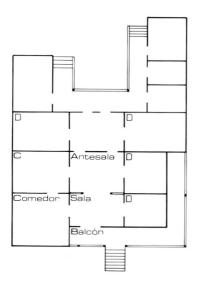

Figure 112b.
Plan of Juana Díaz House.

Plan III/4: Belvedere House, Grand

Such accommodations are not observable in the exterior configuration of large Designed or Grand houses. As in Queen Anne and Greek Revival houses, stairways or other specialized features are designed into the plan. A large belvedere now used as library study by the lawyer owners enhances a Grand house in San Germán (figures 113a and 113b). This interesting, lavishly ornamented house has an idiosyncratic design created by an architect. It nevertheless incorporates some Schema Three configuration. The main part of the dwelling is on the second level above the first-floor work areas, stores and storage. The entrance from the *balcón* at right leads to a foyer; then there is an *antesala* and a *sala,* rather small considering the size of the house. These three rooms occupy the front of the house. A very large *comedor* takes up the center, with *dormitorios* on the right and kitchen areas on the left. At the right of the *comedor* a stairway leads to the belvedere.

Discussion

The above structural innovations are linked with the styles characteristic of late-nineteenth-century economic prosperity and the ensuing conspicuous consumption, but changes in family relationship and overall social structure also must be reflected. Few Grand houses of the scale illustrated were built, so the degree of their architectural presence should not be exaggerated. But their effect on style and certain structural features and on concept was disproportionate to their number. Complex and formal plans, with rooms separated by fixed walls and areas of the house divided by level—*dormitorios* above and living areas below—occur more frequently after the houses of this period. Such formality signals not only ostentation, but also a diminution of family unity.

Designed and Vernacular Camelback, Tower, and Belvedere houses were influenced by but did not imitate the Queen Anne, Italianate, and Greek Revival styles of the Grand mansions. Nevertheless, the formality exhibited in Tower and Belvedere structures must reflect similar social needs. Novelty was also an important aspect of these houses, which, like the Grand mansions, were intended to impress.

Figure 113a. Grand Belvedere House. Idiosyncratic plan. San Germán.

Figure 113b. *Comedor* of Grand San Germán House.

Residence Pattern

There are only thirteen Eclectic houses in the survey, two of them Vernacular. About the same proportion of Eclectic to Criollo houses is represented in the survey as in the island as a whole, although the representation of Vernacular houses is disproportionately small, the data (figure 114) reveal that the majority of residents are fifty to sixty-five years old, have resided in their houses twenty years or more, are skilled workers and merchants with high school or better education, and have traveled extensively. On the basis of these data, one could predict that Eclectic houses, ostensibly no longer built, are the homes of relatively affluent older people and are generally either unsuitable for or inaccessible to the younger and less affluent.

U.S. INFLUENCE HOUSES, 1920–1940

The American styles that were introduced brought further formal changes to the plans and configuration of Puerto Rican houses such as the American two-story house. These styles also added entirely new features including hallways, Bungaloid roofs and *balcones*. The innovations are primarily represented in Designed houses; Vernacular houses generally incorporate only such particular features as the Bungaloid roof, while retaining a basic Schema Two organization.

North American Architectural Features

Hallways

Hallways have the dual functions of facilitating and limiting access; they lead to rooms but also separate them from each other, thereby increasing privacy. Hallways can also inhibit cross-ventilation—a detriment in the tropics.

Except in Grand Eclectic Houses, interior hallways (beyond short passageways) apparently did not exist in houses built before the United States occupation of Puerto Rico. However, they do occur in association with such post-1900 styles as a Ponce architect-designed Beaux Arts house (figures 115a and 115b) and were also introduced into a few Criollo houses. A corner entrance modifies the Schema Two plan of one house (figures 116a an d116b), as does its dividing

142 PUERTO RICAN HOUSES

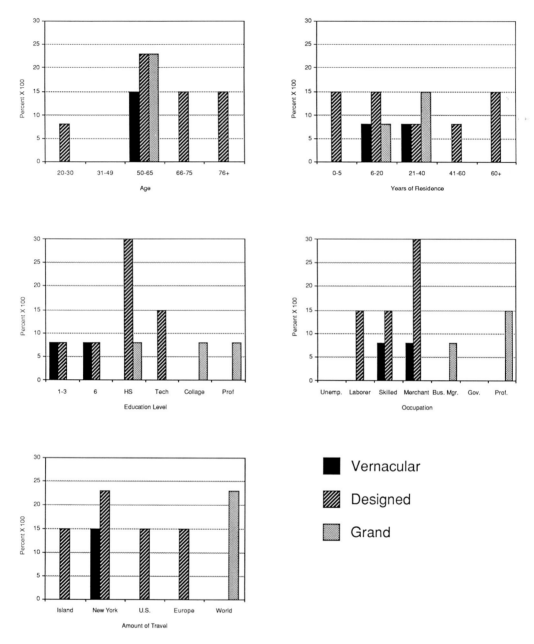

Figure 114. Characteristics of Eclectic House Residents.

TYPOLOGY OF HOUSES 143

Figure 115a. Grand Beaux Arts House. Ponce.

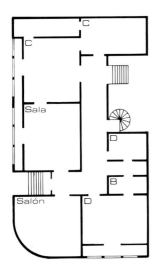

Figure 115b.
Plan of Ponce House.

Figure 116a. Designed Criollo Corner-Entrance House. Schema Two plan, modified by hallway. Aguadilla.

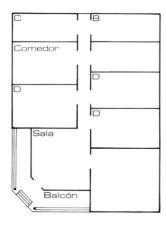

Figure 116b.
Plan of Aguadilla House.

hall, but the two sections are still visible. Owned by a music teacher, the large room at right front is used for lessons.

The Schema Two plan of a house in Humacao is also changed by a dividing hall (figures 117a, 117b, and 117c). The front room, formerly a *sala*, now serves as a formal *antesala* or reception room. A large *comedor*/sitting room, situated near the back *galería*, has been transformed into a porch. The bungaloid roof and porch-like character of the *balcón* in front are further evidence of North American influence.

Bungaloid Roofs and Front-Porch–like *Balcón*

Bungaloid, probably the most influential American style, brought changes in roof structure and the transformation of the *balcón* into a front porch. The bungaloid roof was merged with a wide range of house types, including even a Plan III/3 O, illustrated by an Aguadilla example (figure 118) as well as such modern buildings as a reinforced concrete house in Cayey (figure 119).

Prairie

Prairie, found only in Designed examples, changed the configuration of urban houses by horizontal amplification. The hip roof spread out over a broad front porch, which often was extended around one or more sides of the house and sometimes covered a porte-cochere or carport as well. Room sizes were also enlarged.

Art Deco and Spanish Colonial Revival Styles

As noted previously, these two styles were primarily influential through their decorative elements; Art Deco stepped frets and diamonds and Spanish Colonial Revival roof tiles, arches, and wood balustrades were widely adopted. However, the flat roof of Art Deco and the reinforced concrete construction of both styles were major structural contributions to Vernacular, in particular. Both styles are also associated with an American-type Two-Story One-Family House with a typical American plan consisting of a square or rectangle, with rooms in each corner on both the first and second story and a central hall with stairway.

Figure 117a. Designed Criollo Neoclassic House. Schema Two plan, modified by hallway. Humacao.

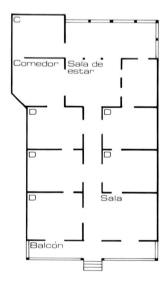

Figure 117b.
Plan of Humacao House.

Figure 117c.
Hallway of
Humacao House.

TYPOLOGY OF HOUSES 147

Figure 118. Designed Bungaloid Influenced (Plan III/3 O). Three-opening facade. Aguadilla.

Figure 119. Designed Bungaloid Influenced Reinforced Concrete House. Cayey.

In their formal organization U.S. Influence houses divide into two main categories: Schema Two or Three houses modified by Americanisms; and American-Type houses. Each of these two categories is subdivided into one- and two-story buildings and into Vernacular, Designed and Grand types. Vernacular houses generally fall into the first category, while Designed houses may be modified by Americanisms or may be American type. Country houses of the period are described separately.

Schema Two and Schema Three Houses Modified by Americanisms

One-Story Houses

Plan II/2 O: Bungaloid, Vernacular

Spanish Colonial Revival roof tile and Art Deco fret designs used as decorative elements are the most common evidence of U.S. influ-

Figure 120. Vernacular Bungalow. (Plan II/2 O). Two-opening facade. Fajardo.

Figure 121. Vernacular Bungalow (Plan II/2 W). Ciales.

ence on Vernacular houses, but Bungaloid roof structure, which allowed for the expansion of the *balcón,* was widely adopted. For example, a Fajardo Bungaloid front *balcón* seems to have been attached to a Plan II/2 O house (figure 120).

Plan II/2 W: Bungaloid, Vernacular

The *balcón* included within the structure of a Ciales house, Plan II/2 W (figure 121), which was built as a bungalow with sheltering hip roof, assumes more of a front-porch character and is used as an outside living area.

Plan II/2 W: Art Deco, Vernacular

Art Deco has great appeal for Vernacular house owners, who frequently incorporate some of its structural features as well as decorative elements when remodeling their Schema Two houses. A flat roof

Figure 122a. Vernacular Art Deco. (Plan II/2 W). Two-opening facade. San Juan.

Figure 122b. Entry, Art Deco House.

and bold facade, masking a former Plan II wood house, are the most common forms. A small Plan II/2 W house (figures 122a and 122b), remodeled by its owner into a concrete structure, illustrates the type. This house is painted white with red band trim. Art Deco frets and diamonds are added as decoration to the facade.

Plan II/2: Bungaloid, Designed

Except for its slender posts, the bungaloid *balcón*/porch of a Barranquitas house (figures 123a and 123b) is American in appearance. Glass window panes give further evidence of U.S. influence, but, like the two previous examples the house retains a traditional plan.

Plan II/3: Bungaloid, Designed

Bungaloid features are occasionally incorporated into Designed houses. One notable example in San Juan (figure 124), designed by an architect, has a bungaloid roof structure in front, a mirador/camelback at the back and a Plan II/3 with "L" shaped *balcón*. The large, handsomely appointed house successfully combines nineteenth- and twentieth-century features.

Two-Story Houses

Plan III/3 W: Two-Story, One-Family House, Vernacular

Certain two-story houses also give evidence of U.S. influence. The hip roof and dormers of an Arroyo house (figure 125) with a Plan III/3 W resembles houses in the South of the U.S. Another United States architectural element is its side porch.

Two-Story One-Family House, Designed

A Hatillo house built of brick (figure 126) eclectically combines a bungaloid front porch with such Queen Anne features as decorative balustrades and complex roof structures. The plan is asymmetrical like Queen Anne.

Figure 123a. Designed Bungaloid (Plan III/2). Three-opening facade. Barranquitas.

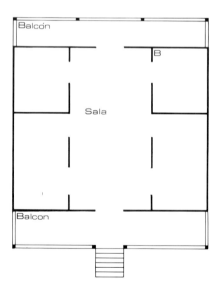

Figure 123b.
Plan of Barranquitas House.

Figure 124. Designed Bungaloid with Partial-Second-Story Camelback (Plan II/3). San Juan.

Figure 125. Vernacular U.S. Influence Two-Story One-Family House. Arroyo.

Figure 126. Designed U.S. Influence Two-Story One-Family House. Hatillo.

American-Type Houses

One-Story Houses

Prairie-Style Houses, Designed

The formal organization of Prairie style houses departs from Schema Two and Three to a greater extent than that of Bungaloid houses. Not suited to urban Vernacular, Prairie occurs most frequently in average-sized Designed houses similar to a Nechodoma example (figures 127a and 127b). This house has such Nechodoma hallmarks as a tile hip roof and projecting front portico included as part of the design. Although Schema Three still underlies its present plan, it now contains some more recent North American features. Somewhat oriented to the back, the *comedor* opens onto a porch that overlooks the

TYPOLOGY OF HOUSES 155

Figure 127a. Designed Nechodoma/Prairie (Modified Plan). Coamo.

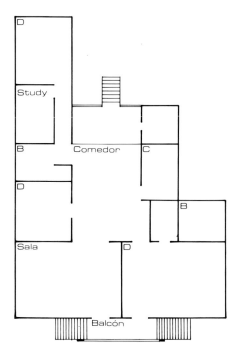

Figure 127b.
Plan of Coamo House.

garden. A counter wall divides *comedor* and modern kitchen. One bedroom has been converted into a study, and a second bathroom has been added next to the parent's bedroom; the other is used by the sons. In contrast to conventional Schema Three plans, the bedroom sections are organized as units, separate from the living area.

A corner house on the plaza in Naguabo (figure 128) is another example of Prairie in Puerto Rico. Both are built of reinforced concrete.

Art Deco Style Houses, Designed

Reinforced concrete construction is also the material of a fine Art Deco architect-designed house (figure 129). Its idiosyncratic plan includes a hall and formal dining room. A garage is within the house structure.

The original simple Schema Two plan (II/2) of a Guayama house (figures 130a and 130b), was first modified by the addition of an interesting Art Deco facade and more recently changed again. Formerly, the partial octagonally-shaped room at the left of the entrance was the *antesala*, now it is a *dormitorio*. The *sala/comedor* was previously in the center, but without the present separating wall, and

Figure 128. Designed Prairie. Naguabo.

Figure 129. Designed Art Deco (Idiosyncratic Plan). Moca.

the other *dormitorios* were arranged as they are represented. Now further Americanized, the *cocina* is separated by only a counter wall.

Spanish Colonial Revival Style Houses, Designed

Though two-story one-family houses are most typical of the original Spanish Colonial Revival style, one-story examples exist in greater numbers. Built of reinforced concrete with red tile roofs, they include such other familiar elements as Mudejar arches and Spanish tile decoration around doors. Their plans occasionally manifest vestiges of primarily Schema Two order in the situation of *sala/comedor* and *dormitorios* but have more formal room separation. The plan of an architect-designed house (figure 131) is similar to Plan II/1 W. The

Figure 130a. Designed Art Deco (Modified Plan II/2). Guayama.

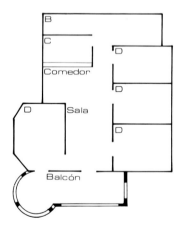

Figure 130b.
Plan of Guayama House.

Figure 131. Designed Spanish Colonial Revival (Modified Plan II/1 W). San Juan.

balcón, screened with *rejas*, is in constant use as an informal sitting area. The room at left of entrance, previously used as a *dormitorio*, was converted into a formal dining room, while the former *sala/comedor* became a large living room. The second example has a plan related to Plan II/2 and its small *balcón* entrance retains more of a traditional *balcón* character (figure 132).

Prairie Style House, Grand

Pretentious mansions, no longer in vogue, were superseded by equally large but less elaborate houses. Prairie was considered to be one of the appropriate styles. A Grand Prairie suburban house (figure 133a and 133b) has large bedrooms, a hip roof spreading over wide porches, and adequate but comparatively less ample living room areas. The *sala* has become a seldom-used formal front parlor, supplanted as family gathering place by the *comedor* and back *galería/balcón*. Like other Prairie examples, the house was built of reinforced concrete.

Figure 132. Designed Spanish Colonial Revival (Modified Plan II/2). San Juan.

Two-Story One-Family Houses

Two-story American houses, which are either Art Deco or Spanish Colonial Revival in style, brought new plans and new conceptions of spatial organization. Modest in comparison to Grand Eclectic two-story houses, their designs are directed more toward practicality than display. They are quite rare in Puerto Rico and while apparently adopted to some extent in the 1920s and 1930s never became popular. The majority of examples are located in Humacao, Cayey, and the newer areas of San Juan. Only Designed examples were seen.

Art Deco Style House, Designed

A Humacao house (figures 134a and 134b) is a handsome example of an American-type two-story one-family house in Art Deco style. The plan, as described above, has four rooms, one in each corner on both upper and lower levels and a central stair hall. The terrace in back projects out beyond the upper story, and a two-car garage lies below it. The interior is very American, with wall-to-wall carpet, sep-

TYPOLOGY OF HOUSES 161

Figure 133a. Grand Prairie House (Idiosyncratic Plan). Humacao.

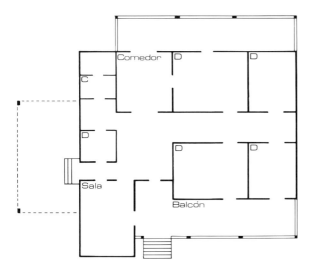

Figure 133b.
Plan of Humacao House.

Figure 134a. Designed Art Deco Two-Story One-Family House. Humacao.

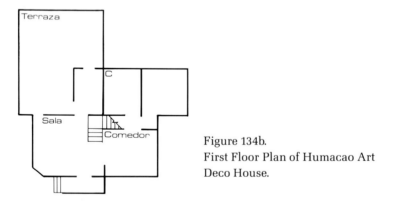

Figure 134b.
First Floor Plan of Humacao Art Deco House.

arate bathrooms for parents and children, a living room apart from the dining room, and a large enclosed porch at the back.

Spanish Colonial Revival Style House, Designed

As designed, a Spanish Colonial Revival San Juan house had a Schema Two *sala/comedor* arrangement, but through modification the house is now more like the Humacao house. At present one enters into a foyer. To the right is the *sala* and beyond it a *balcón* expanded into a terrace porch. At left a wall encloses a library, formerly a *comedor* connected with the *sala*. The dining room is now in back of the library. A stairway to the second floor is behind it.

Spanish Colonial Revival Style House, Grand

The well-known large two-story "Castillo" above Ponce (figure 39), which bears reference to California Mission architecture, is one of

Figure 135. Designed Spanish Colonial Revival Two-Story One-Family House. San Juan.

Figure 136. Vernacular Finca House (Plan III/2 W). Three-opening facade. La Parguera.

the earliest Spanish Colonial Revival examples of the two-story form. There are several others in the Condado section of San Juan.

Country Houses

Country houses of the 1920–40 period differ from their city counterparts primarily in their *zocos*, which vary from two to eight feet in height, and in their simplicity and lack of adornment. Their main impact depends on their three-dimensionality, overall shape, or mere bulk. Prominent gable or hip roofs amplify these impressions.

Plan III/2 W: Three Opening Facade, Vernacular

A fairly common country house (figure 136), raised abut three feet above the ground, usually has a *balcón* surrounding three sides. The hip roof with central ridge that spreads over all is the outstanding feature. Found on *fincas* (farms), such houses are now used either as tenant farmer residences or weekend retreats.

Plan II/2 W: Two Opening Facade, Vernacular

The plan of an administrator's house on a sugar plantation (figure 137) is like Plan II/2 with half-*balcón*, except that here the *balcón* is also extended out to cross the full width of the front. It is a very plain wood house except for its prominent concrete front stair entrance.

Plan III/2 W: Grand

A very large house (figure 138) with a structure somewhat like the finca house in figure 136 is situated outside of Mayaguez near the coast. The height of the house and the belvedere rising from the hip roof are designed to take advantage of the broad sea vista.

At the turn of the century and later, when the sugar industry was

Figure 137. Vernacular (Plan II/2 W). Two-opening facade. Patillas area.

Figure 138. Grand Belvedere House (Plan III/2 W). Outside Mayaguez.

consolidated, houses were built on *factoría central* property for engineers, chemists, and other professionals working for the industry. These buildings are typical of Caribbean architecture, with high pitched roofs and verandas. Their most striking characteristics are their size, simplicity of design, and occasionally refinement of carpentered detail. They resemble industrial buildings of the period. The hip roof with central ridge of one (figure 139) covers the entire house, including the open porch. The second (figure 140) has a gable roof that is extended to cover the screened veranda at the sides. An additional connecting section of roof covers the front part. This building has more finished detailing and a prominent stairway entrance.

TYPOLOGY OF HOUSES 167

Figure 139. Designed Engineer's House Sugar *central*. Patillas area.

Figure 140. Designed Engineer's House, Sugar *central*. Patillas area.

Discussion

Unlike Criollo ones, U.S. Influence houses are not a unified family of styles and types. Their variety points toward an increasingly diversified, pluralistic society. Moreover, the variable adoption of Americanisms implies that people of different social levels with diverse interests adapted differentially to American influence. Though pervasive in the 1920s, when the majority of these houses were built, American influence was narrow. Puerto Ricans for the most part appropriated structural components that could be incorporated into conventional Puerto Rican houses and styles compatible with their aesthetic needs.

American influence introduced a degree of informality to the exterior of Puerto Rican houses but greater formality to the interior of Designed houses, in particular. In contrast to earlier styles, facades became less pretentious, and greater emphasis was placed on the entire house as a unit. Such changes suggest a shift away from a family-centered society to one focused more on the community and the individual.

Residence Pattern

According to the data (figure 141), residents of U.S. Influence houses are relatively younger than residents of earlier house types, and the time of residence is shorter. A high proportion consist of professionals, government officials, and business managers; has a college or professional education; and has traveled extensively in the United States, Europe, and other parts of the world. U.S. Influence houses apparently suit educated people in upper social levels. Presumably, families living in them have adapted to a North American middle- to upper-class family lifestyle with a certain degree of independence among members.

Urbanización Houses, 1950–1980

Urbanización houses depart markedly from other Puerto Rican domestic architecture, since they are based on a foreign model that is unrelated to Puerto Rican design and that uses manufacturing methods rather than artisanry. Although some formal variation exists among Urbanización houses, their appearance belies it. In most de-

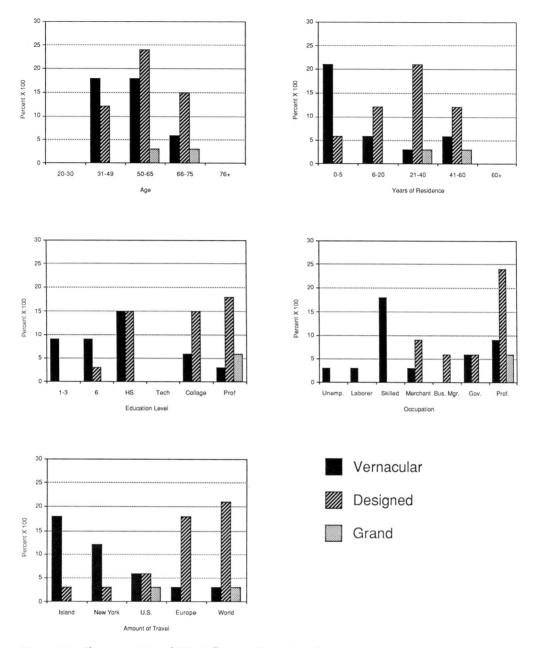

Figure 141. Characteristics of U.S. Influence House Residents.

velopments, whether publicly or privately funded, potential residents can choose among three or four facades, but plans are alike except for minor differences in room orientation: the entrance on the left or right side of the *sala*. General configuration and, above all, uniformity of reinforced concrete material account for the similarity of appearance. Standardized component modules—wall height, door and window sizes—which are used in all grades of developments and adapted by architects to their buildings, further contribute to the general sameness of appearance. Yet, although reinforced concrete construction promotes standarization, its flexibility and versatility enable architects to create original, sometimes even fanciful, designs.

The distinction between Vernacular and Designed Urbanización houses is chiefly a matter of quality and size. Vernacular houses in government-funded housing developments, built to meet low-cost minimal standards, are smaller and less finely finished than Designed houses in private developments. Individually built International Style designs created by architects especially for clients (classified here as Grand) have a quality that cannot exist in mass-produced houses. The majority of all these reinforced concrete dwellings, are one-story, with flat roofs, diverse front roof lines, and varying amounts of plate glass and louvered windows. Despite similarity, the eventual addition of individually selected ornamentation enlivens and differentiates even the most uniform.

Vernacular[9]

The simplest type of Urbanización house is a rectangle, nearly always with a carport at the side. It is usually set back from the street, with a walkway leading to the front visitor entrance; the family uses the kitchen door, entered through the carport. The generally small rooms consist of a *sala/comedor* without *mediopunto*, a kitchen, and three bedrooms and a bath reached by a narrow hallway. To increase living space, many families remodel the carport into a family room. Others convert it into a *tienda,* and a few use it to garage their car.

The illustrated house (figures 142a and 142b), with typical louvered "Florida" windows, has been remodeled by its owner, who converted the original carport adjoining the kitchen at entrance left into a family room and built a new carport at entrance right. He also created a retaining wall decorated with diamond patterns to support a front

TYPOLOGY OF HOUSES 171

Figure 142a. Vernacular Urbanización House. Carport modification and second carport added. A second story has been added to house at right. Carolina.

Figure 142b. Retaining Wall and Front Garden of Carolina House.

garden, which effectively takes the place of a *balcón*, although he plans to build one eventually.

Designed

Such modifications are rare in more affluent neighborhoods, where elements of specific styles, particularly Spanish Colonial Revival, are integral to houses. Red tile roofs, arched windows, Mudejar arches, and tiled floors may be part of the original design. Yet whatever their style, houses are fundamentally similar. The example (figure 143) is more spacious and occupies a larger lot than the Vernacular house. The house is oriented to the side, where there is a small entrance patio, but family interests are directed to the large garden in back.

Another Designed house in the same area (figure 144) has a more open plan. One large living room, rather than *sala/comedor*, occupies the center of the house, with bedrooms on the left, kitchen on the right. A broad terrace overlooks a back garden.

Figure 143. Designed Urbanización House. Río Piedras.

TYPOLOGY OF HOUSES 173

Figure 144. Designed Urbanización House. Río Piedras.

Architect-Designed House

A relatively modest house designed by the architect Henry Klumb serves as an example of an International Style house. Klumb, a follower of Wright, in this instance used a LeCorbusier vocabulary modified to fit Puerto Rican climate and family needs. This two-story structure is designed, in apparent reference to Puerto Rican architecture of the past, with living quarters above (figure 145a) a garage and small *tienda* below (figure 145b).

Country Houses

Urbanización reinforced concrete and modular units are also used in the construction of contemporary houses in rural areas.

174 PUERTO RICAN HOUSES

Figure 145a. International Style House Designed by Henry Klumb. Upper level. San Germán.

Figure 145b. Tienda on Lower Level of Klumb House.

Vernacular

A reinforced concrete farm house (figure 146) follows general country house 25 conventions, with *zocos* raising it about eight feet above the ground to provide sheltered space for equipment, vehicles, laundry, and various outside tasks. The eight-foot height is itself a standard, since forms for pouring concrete or preconstructed posts are available in this dimension (figure 147). Moreover, modular units of this size are favored because they can be handled without special machinery. This particular house has no decoration of any kind, but others, such as a comparable fisherman's house (figure 148), are ornamented with balustrades, Spanish roof tile, or Art Deco motifs.

Many Urbanización houses in rural areas must be categorized as suburban. Some, strung along country roads, face forward as if on a city street; others are more rural in their adaptation to particular settings or orientation to scenic vistas.

The manufacturing method of construction puts the Urbanización house into a category similar to an automobile or refrigerator and thus lessens its potential for manifesting individual expression in comparison to other house types. The relative amount of investment in embellishment reflects a resident's need to express identity and status. The fundamental sameness of Urbanización houses is overridden by differentiation which, sometimes forcefully, asserts individuality.

Residence Pattern

Although inconclusive because of the small sample, the evidence on Urbanización house residents is supported by general observations and other data gathered (figure 149). On average, residents of Urbanización houses were young to middle-aged, and, as a consequence of the newness of the houses, the time of their residence was relatively short. Those in Vernacular dwellings tended to be either skilled workers with a high-school education or, in a few cases, government officials with college degrees. Some typical jobs held by residents of one government-subsidized Urbanización included plumber, *público* (transportation) driver, and factory worker.

Residents of Designed houses in privately funded developments were more often professionals with graduate school degrees, but with a larger sample one would find a wider range of occupations and probably a higher percentage of businessmen, bankers, lawyers,

Figure 146. Vernacular Farm House. Built of reinforced concrete. Luquillo area.

and, above all, government employees, since this latter group represents the highest proportion of employed workers in Puerto Rico (Sanchez Vilella 1984). Residents of Urbanización houses showed a proportionally high amount of travel. As a group, they have adapted to these contemporary houses. Designed house residents have tended to adjust to Urbanización houses as built, while owners of Vernacular Urbanización houses tend to modify their dwellings to suit their preferences.

Second Houses

Numerous city dwellers retreat each weekend to country houses, which range from old Hacienda houses to small beach cabins. A second house is not a new phenomenon for the affluent, who in the past lived on their haciendas and owned a house in town or vice versa.

TYPOLOGY OF HOUSES 177

Figure 147. Reinforced-Concrete Vernacular Country House. In process of construction. Luquillo area.

Figure 148. Vernacular Fisherman's House. Built of reinforced concrete. Puerto Real.

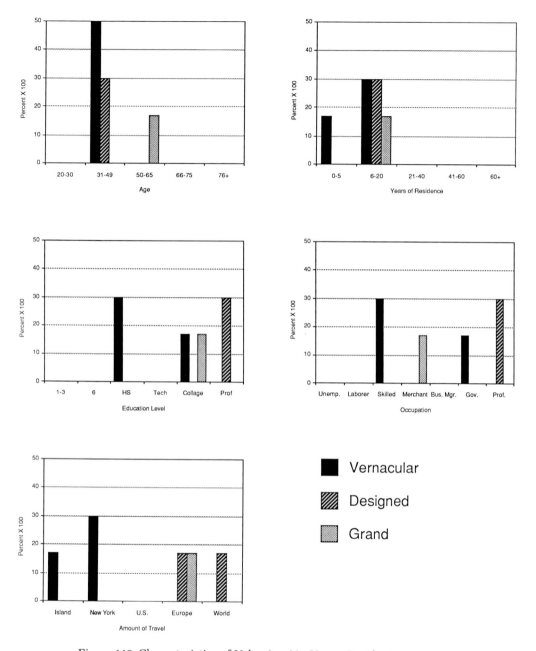

Figure 149. Characteristics of Urbanización House Residents.

Today, second houses are more common among the middle class and are apt to be principally vacation or weekend retreats.

For example, a type built on the water at La Parguera,[10] where houses range from simple fishermen's shacks to more elaborate specially-built structures, allows the city dweller to indulge fantasies of living with nature. A good example of this romantic attitude is a former shack (figure 150) which has been made part of the environment through the removal of walls and close proximity to the water level. It is approached through the mangroves by a board walk.

Parcela, Jíbaro, and Arrabal Houses

With few exceptions, the foregoing house types represent the mainstream of Puerto Rican domestic architecture. In each period, Vernacular and Designed houses have differed in certain fundamentals

Figure 150. Second House: Water House. La Parguera.

and are generally easily distinguished. But having evolved together, they are also interrelated. The Vernacular houses discussed below are at times similar to Criollo and Urbanización Vernacular houses, but in many aspects follow different rules.

Parcelas

Few poor Puerto Ricans are able to live in *urbanizaciones* because they lack such qualifications as full employment and specified income level. Those without such resources resort to a variety of options, including subsidized apartments in multistory housing projects, building or acquiring a house in an *arrabal,* and rentals in rundown older houses. Occasionally, a town or individual builds a one-room house for an indigent old person. *Parcelas,* the favored choice for those who meet the employment requirement, were devised during the 1940s through cooperative efforts of the United States and Puerto Rican governments to offer poor *arrabal* inhabitants the opportunity and means to build and own their own homes. Still in effect, the program provides for qualified individuals, who are able and willing to build a house and occupy it, to acquire by contract with the government a *parcela* (lot, or piece of government land) equal to a *cuerda* (a measure of land in Puerto Rico). At set times, parcels of land are chosen by lot and then distributed. This system now is often criticized on the grounds that parcels frequently go to relatives of government officials, who sell them at a profit. Nevertheless, as a result of the program, a number of people manage to acquire previously unobtainable property, and land has been more equitably apportioned.

Through contractual agreement, the owner can acquire government plans for his house as well. He carries out the actual construction with the help of his *parcela* neighbors and his relatives, sometimes under the guidance of government technical experts (for the specific details of *parcela* acquisition and house construction, see Vásquez Calcerrada 1960). About 187 families were living at one of the visited *parcela* sites, but some of the houses, still unfinished, were for sale.

Parcela houses are built of wood, as in two examples (figures 151, 152a, and 152b), and also of reinforced concrete, as in a third (figure 153). The first is a Pueblerino, Plan II/1, structure, while the other two show Urbanización influence. Because they are quite varied at any given site, Parcela houses bear some resemblance to Arrabal

Figure 151. Parcela Wood House (Plan II/1 O). Two-opening facade. Luquillo.

houses, but they are constructed of better materials and are more widely separated on larger lots.

Jíbaro Houses

Arrabal and Jíbaro houses are alike in their mode of accrual and assemblage construction, but serve somewhat different needs. Originally the Jíbaro house was the home of independent country people who lived apart from cities and other populated areas, subsisting as families on produce they raised. As described above, the property included not only the house but also outbuildings for animals, supplies, and equipment. The increasingly rare Jíbaro house is represented here by three examples.

One in the coastal lowlands, raised on *zocos*, is surrounded by

182   PUERTO RICAN HOUSES

Figure 152a. Parcela Wood House. Urbanización-related plan. Naguabo.

Figure 152b. Sideview of Naguabo Parcela House. Note waterfront situation.

Figure 153. Parcela Reinforced-Concrete House (Modified Plan II/2). La Parguera.

coops for fighting cocks and other animal pens (figure 154). Characteristically, the house began with one or two rooms and later was enlarged by additions to accommodate a growing family.

A roughhewn hundred-year-old house in the mountains, some of its supporting *zocos* still bark-covered, has a different shape (figure 155). Its plan approximates a square, with a large all-purpose *sala* occupying most of the space, two small *dormitorios* divided off at the right, and a lean-to *cocina* in back. Large by Jíbaro house standards, this house was altered—the entrance, which formerly faced the *dormitorios*, was moved to its present location—but rooms were not added until recently. Among the nearby outbuildings are a *tormentera* (storm shelter) and another building which still has *yagua* roofing and some siding (figure 156).

A third example (figures 157a, 157b, and 157c), located near Luquillo, is quite typical of many houses seen in mountain areas. It consists of one room with an alcove-like sleeping area divided off at one

Figure 154. Jíbaro House. Some sections of the house are unpainted, others are painted different colors. Piñones.

end. Water is piped to this house, but it is sparsely furnished and otherwise bare of amenities. Paradoxically, a sister of the owner lives closeby in a substantial concrete house.

Jíbaro houses are consistently devised to fit the basic needs of individual families. Built of wood and scraps of other materials, zinc in particular, and resting on crudely fashioned *zocos*, they have an improvised, extemporaneous character. The plans of a few bear casual resemblance to Schema One, but generally, disregarding plan, rooms are added and improvements made as necessary.

Arrabal Houses

Arrabal houses (the word *arrabal* means outskirts, but in Puerto Rico signifies squatter settlements) are built close together in marginal

TYPOLOGY OF HOUSES 185

Figure 155. Jíbaro House. More than a hundred years old. Later addition at right. San Germán area.

Figure 156. Jíbaro Building. Note roof of yagua. On same property as San Germán area house in figure 155.

186 PUERTO RICAN HOUSES

Figure 157a.
Jíbaro House with *Balcón*.
Near Luquillo.

Figure 157b.
Back of Luquillo House.

Figure 157c.
Interior of Luquillo House.

areas. Unlike independent *jíbaros,* who own their property or have sharecropper rights, the commonly unemployed or underemployed Arrabal house builder seeks to survive by joining his fellows on unclaimed, presumably valueless lands. At the time of their construction, Arrabal houses are similar in form, partly of necessity: builders have sufficient resources for only one room and only six hours to construct the house. Moreover, as a result of lack of differentiation attention may not be drawn to their presence. As previously noted, Arrabal houses, especially around San Juan, are often built over water or swampy areas,[11] raised on posts just above flood level. Wherever located, they are constructed of whatever materials are available, such as packing cases and scraps of wood and metal (figure 158).

The process of building Arrabal houses is almost never-ending. In

Figure 158. View of "El Fanguito," 1946 (Archivo General de Puerto Rico, No. 5472).

arrabales, owners paint, decorate, and individualize their houses to a greater extent than either *jíbaros* or Puerto Ricans in other kinds of neighborhoods. The Arrabal house is constantly added to and modified, with the goal of a final transformation into concrete.

A wide variety of structures can be seen in present-day *arrabales*, but the majority of the types are Schema Two, Plans II/1 and II/2, raised on *zocos* and two-story House and Tiendas (figure 159). Though improvised like Jíbaro houses, Arrabal houses are also linked to both Urbanización and Criollo Vernacular houses. Indeed, because of their accrual mode, the improvements made to the Vernacular Urbanización house discussed above (figure 142a) may be indicative of the owner's *arrabal* background.

Residence Pattern

The people who live in Parcela, Arrabal, and Jíbaro houses differed from each other as well as from the residents previously discussed,

Figure 159. Arrabal House and Tienda, Under Construction. The construction worker who is owner-builder of this house has access to better materials than the average *arrabal* inhabitant. Carolina.

TYPOLOGY OF HOUSES 189

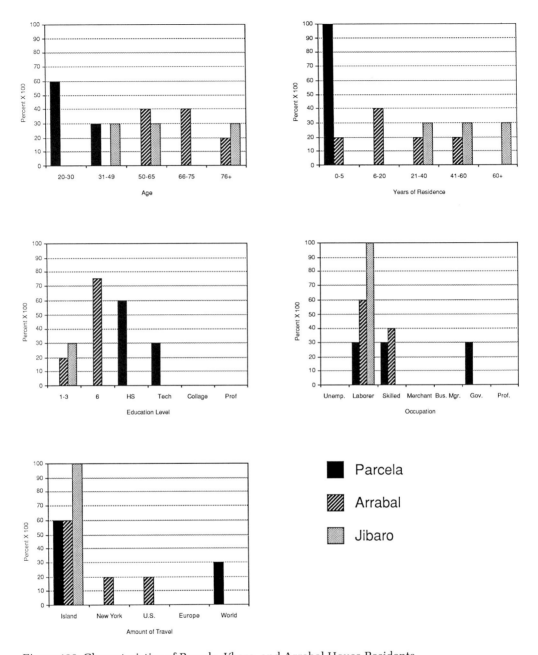

Figure 160. Characteristics of Parcela, Jíbaro, and Arrabal House Residents.

although Parcela and Vernacular Urbanización residents were somewhat alike. The limited data reveal that those who lived in *parcelas* had attended technical and high schools, worked at skilled and government jobs, were relatively young, and had lived in their houses a short time (figure 160). Their travel was apt to have been related to their occupations, especially military assignment.

Jíbaro houses residents tended to be middle-aged or older people who had resided in their houses since birth. They generally had very little education; some had never attended school, and their exposure to other parts of the world depended on television, when accessible, rather than on travel.

Arrabal residents displayed a wide age range. Many had lived in their houses for more than twenty years. Most had not attended school beyond the sixth grade and, when employed, tended to work at unskilled occupations. They traveled to New York to visit relatives; indeed, many returned migrants reside in *arrabales*.

Summary of Residence Patterns

A comparison of residence patterns across all house types shows consistent relationships between age of resident and age of house; older house types tend to be the dwellings of elderly people who may have lived in their houses since birth, while more recent house types tend to be the habitations of younger people (figure 161). There is also a clear relationship between social level and type of house. People with less education and lower-paid occupations reside in Vernacular, Parcela, Jíbaro, and Arrabal houses; those who are better educated and with higher paid occupations live in Designed houses. Though not unexpected, these fairly clear-cut results are valuable not only because they confirm general assumptions, but also and more significantly, they demonstrate the existence of a patterned relationship between residents and houses types.

A less obvious connection between U.S. Influence house types and professionals and managers is also revealed. The large number of Urbanización houses and the character of their inhabitants is visible evidence of their popularity among younger people of lower and middle social levels. Urbanización houses are popular not only for the practical reasons of hurricane and insect resistance, but also because owning a reinforced concrete house is a mark of status for peo-

TYPOLOGY OF HOUSES 191

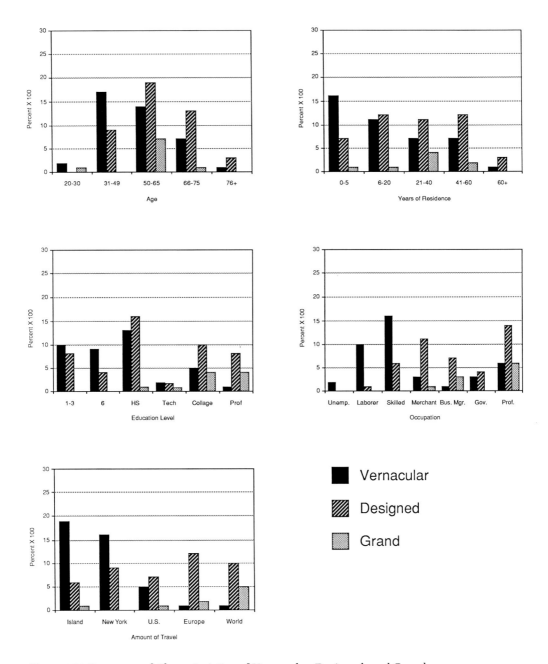

Figure 161. Summary of Characteristics of Vernacular, Designed, and Grand House Residents.

ple at lower social levels (Pérez-Chanis 1975:99). There may also be an underlying reference to historical differences between the stone houses of the Spanish, and the wood and cane houses of workers and slaves. In any event, judging by the proliferation of these houses as well as of owner-built Vernacular and Arrabal imitations, for a large proportion of the population the most desirable residence is an Urbanización house.

These findings on residence pattern provide useful demographic information related to the various types of Puerto Rican houses. However, the connection between a house and its residents involves meaning as well as economic and social factors. Although the issue of meaning is addressed more specifically in Chapter 3, at this juncture it is useful to review some implications that have emerged from the examination of house form.

Social Implications of House Form

Importance of Single-Family Houses

The most noticeable and consistent characteristic of all Puerto Rican houses, regardless of style and structure, is that the majority are built for single families. Although residents ordinarily make room for aged parents or other close relatives, planned provision for a second family is rare. Many Puerto Ricans live in multiple dwelling units, but they are not the choice of the majority, and public housing apartments are largely regarded as a last resort for poor people. Nor are townhouses or single houses with adjoining walls favored. When for economic reasons families must share a building, the norm is the Two-House Two-Story type. The arrangement of houses stacked one above the other with separate entrances minimizes visual as well as actual contact. Because most Puerto Ricans desire to have their own house standing apart from their neighbors, one has to assume that possession of one's own house has great meaning.

Change and Continuity

The variation in rate of formal change to house, according to time period and house type, is also striking. Although the distance of time and lack of evidence influence this conclusion, it is probable that in the early years, continuity rather than change was the mode. So it has continued to be in Vernacular houses. After 1850, change in Designed houses took place rapidly, even abruptly, and such changes were often definitive. The implications are that the conventional form of Vernacular houses serves the needs of its conservative residents, who preserve a traditional family structure. This contrasts with the more innovative Designed house form, which suits independent-minded individuals with ties to the world outside Puerto Rico. The differences are more complex, however, and reflect disparate modes of maintaining continuity and incorporating change. Through renovation and incorporation of innovations, Vernacular houses cling to their basic form but are gradually transformed. When new Designed types are adopted, old ones are not replaced but continue to endure. These contrasts persist in the kinds of alterations made. Remodeling of Designed houses is usually confined to the interior; the integrity of the exterior is maintained or enhanced. Vernacular and Arrabal houses are conventionally altered on the exterior, usually by the addition of a *balcón* and transformation into concrete, but retain a Schema One or Two organization and sometimes the original wood walls.

Complexity and Differentiation

Throughout Puerto Rican history, as the society grew in complexity, houses became more differentiated. Variable house types allow individuals to select preferred or suitable habitations within obvious socioeconomic constraints; or, from a system or societal point of view, variable house types are a means of sorting the society. Homogeneity is the present trend, but social diveristy and personal preference continue to be expressed in the retention of the old along with the new, and in the individualization of every house.

CHAPTER 3

Messages and Meanings

Theoretical Considerations

Certain questions are raised by this research. Why do all these house types and styles still exist in Puerto Rico? Why are houses built in other eras still functional in the contemporary built environment? And more precisely, what is the "social fit" of Puerto Rican houses? Most Puerto Ricans openly express great pride in their houses and are pleased to display them, but only a few have considered such questions or could respond to them. Therefore, the principal sources of the contextual data supporting the analysis of house forms and their messages were, first, observations of the behavior of Puerto Rican residents in relation to their habitations and, second, their responses to the informal interviews conducted during the survey. Arising out of a dialectical process, the information was constantly changing (Geertz 1977: 480–92). Moreover, it came not only from the residents, who themselves represent a wide spectrum of social and educational levels and backgrounds, but also from professionals, the author's friends and acquaintances, and the "man in the street." The range of sources and the mode of data-gathering make it difficult to draw an exact line between Puerto Rican beliefs and my own observations. However, direct expressions of opinion by Puerto Ricans are identified.

Further, since houses embody sentiments and social values of which Puerto Ricans themselves may not be aware, penetrating the meanings of houses requires interpretation of their forms. This line of inquiry is pursued with emphasis on the messages emanating from the particularly salient elements of spatial organization and ornament.

A fundamental assumption is that the form or physical reality of houses can be and often is separate or disassociated from meaning, which is culturally derived and attaches to form (Bonta 1979:1–25; see also Rapoport 1982:15–27). Furthermore, meaning depends on how well the code is known, not on the object's shape or technical qualities alone (Jencks 1980:72). Yet, since it is contended that the built environment not only reflects cultural norms, but also shapes and reinforces social behavior, there must be specific connections between the physical reality and meaning. Following Eco's analysis: a house, or form of habitation, can be conceived as denoting particular functions; that is, a primary function of the form itself is not only to make its function possible but also to denote it. The secondary function, or connotation, or meaning, rests on the primary. In Eco's example, a seat is the primary function denoted by a throne, dignity its connotation or meaning or symbolic function. Expressiveness, or meaning, arises from a dialectic between the primary function, or relatively stable significative forms, and the constantly changing codes of interpretation (Eco 1980:11–30). Thus, one way of detecting meanings is to identify specific elements or forms that are the sources or "emitters" of information,[1] as well as the messages they convey. Assuming that redundancy is as common in this communication process as elsewhere, the messages conveyed by Puerto Rican houses are doubtless less diverse than the emitters. Other communication systems, both animal and human, have been shown to have a few basic messages, including identity, position or status, territoriality, and ideas of attracting or repelling, which are differentially presented (W.J. Smith, 1977:85; see also M.O. Jones, 1980:338). It is likely that each houses states and restates these messages and a few others by indexes and signals. Here the purpose is to examine the diverse emitters and identify their messages. Such analysis is directed toward exact interpretation of the meanings of Puerto Rican houses and ultimately their social fit, but for reasons stated previously, the validity of the analysis must rest on concurrence with the sociocultural codes.

The discussion is cast within a communications model, but, owing to the limitations of the survey method used, the data are insufficient to permit precise semiotic analysis. The following definitions, devised by Bonta (1979:26–30), are used, however, to specify elements in the communication process in which Puerto Rican houses are involved. An *indicator* is a directly perceivable event by means of which it is possible to learn something about other events which are not perceivable. *Signals* are a class of indicators that are (1) deliberately produced for the purpose of communicating, and (2) recognized by the interpreter as such. Signals communicate, indicators indicate. Signals communicate states of mind rather than matters of fact.

Indicators which are not purposeful are *indexes*. They are supposed to originate directly from reality, as opposed to being produced by an emitter.[2] It is not always possible to determine intention with certainty, and in such cases the term *indicator* is used. In more clearcut instances the terms *signal* and *index* are used. For example, bright paint on a house is assumed to be an intentional form of communication and is therefore termed a signal; the siting of the average house is an index. Most Puerto Ricans would give aesthetic reasons for the first, and practical or circumstantial explanations for the second.

A further, not unrelated, idea is that it is essential to discriminate between signals and contextual information (W.J. Smith, 1982), which here refers to the spatial and temporal setting of a house. Understanding contextual information, which could be considered an index according to Bonta's scheme, is indispensable for the interpretation of meaning.

Contextual Information

Beyond sociohistorical background, among the chief contributors of material contextual information are the relation of a house to its environment, and its locale (geographical location). The first source is more significant with regard to houses in rural areas, the second to those in urban areas.

The role of the environment is primarily culturally determined (Kniffen 1976), but the sea, prevailing winds, and sun were the principal constant elements that Puerto Ricans considered when siting and constructing their houses in the past. Puerto Rican houses are of several kinds: wood or *mampostería* structures adapted to the tropical climate; those that overcome environmental conditions by use of air-conditioning or other twentieth-century technological solutions; and compromises between these approaches. Adapting to the environment is currently again the acceptable position, so Klumb and other more contemporary architects design with that in mind. But in constructing *urbanizaciones,* developers seldom concern themselves with preserving or taking advantage of environmental features. In one development at Luquillo, air-conditioned houses are built at right angles to the sea view so it cannot be appreciated, and every tree was bulldozed to simplify construction. The economic decisions that govern this kind of house construction are out of the hands of residents, who must adjust to preestablished built environments rather than adapting their dwellings to the natural setting. Whether houses incorporate adaptive or technological solutions supplies valuable background information for understanding resident response and thus contributes to the interpretation of meaning.

Location near or away from the sea provides more direct messages. Puerto Ricans have traditionally turned their backs to the sea, for multiple reasons: dislike of the sea is believed to be a Spanish characteristic; to protect against pirate invaders, early cities were built inland or as fortresses; periodic hurricanes with high seas promoted preference for inland sites; and elevated sites away from malaria-endemic coasts were chosen for health reasons. In the early history of Puerto Rico, coastal areas were first inhabited by Taíno Indians and later by people of African descent, usually freed slaves, either by preference or because these lands were not valued by the Spaniards. As a result of such environmental and cultural influences, major residential areas in coastal towns and cities are situated inland from the waterfront, which is the locale for port and fishing activities and for habitations of poor or low-income people. In Old San Juan, the principal residential area is located in the center of its narrow boundaries, while the *arrabal* of La Perla clings to a narrow shelf between sea and fortress wall (figure 49). But proximity to or distance from the sea, although once useful as identifying marks of class for Spanish and Criollo houses, now provides conflicting messages, since some younger and more affluent people currently prefer seaside locations.

The situation of houses in rural areas probably reflects deliberate choice based on environmental considerations, without the con-

Figure 162. Hotel Francés, Vieques.

straints imposed in towns. The majority of such houses surveyed were built to take advantage of the breeze and view, and most are shaded by tall trees. A large Vieques house is an example (figure 162).

Geographical Location

Geographical location, or place in region or town, contributes contextual information that pertains more to sentiment and experience than to practical considerations. Sense of place—relationship to a particular area—is an important identity marker for Puerto Ricans. Well-known, usually Spanish, family names are connected with particular towns and regions. This characteristic, brought from Spain where regional identity is also significant, still links Puerto Ricans of Spanish descent with particular locales in Spain as well. Such association incorporates gradations of significance that include both class and history. To some extent Spanish ancestry continues to distinguish the upper class, so many Puerto Rican descendants of nineteenth-century immigrants refer frequently to their Catalan, Mallorcan, or Galician heritage.

More common is the continuing tie most Puerto Ricans have with their natal town or city. Migrants to San Juan or New York frequently return for annual *fiestas patronales* (celebrations in honor of a town's patron saint) and special family gatherings, and eventually they retire to the place of their birth. All Puerto Ricans have bonds to region, town, and family, which are not only social and familial but also conceptual—connections to an image or schema of a particular town or hacienda that enhance self-esteem, even if only in memory (Rapaport 1976:124).

But attitudes differ, in confirmation of diverse experience. Older people and regionally prominent families claim affiliation with their place of origin; family connection to the Grand house on a town plaza is still a source of pride. Poor and younger people relate more closely to their present situation, especially when it is an improvement over the past. Many older Puerto Ricans express national pride in terms of personal geographical ties, but for better educated professionals or younger people, with a greater sense of the unity of the country, national pride is linked with recognition of the diversity of the island and the individuality of each town. Members of the latter group do not lose sight of their ancestral town or region, but their ties become more tenuous.

Such ideas of identity through attachment to place are expressed in the distinctive architecture of many towns, each of which has its own unique flavor that arises from its history and situation. Ponce, for example, is noted for its remaining High Neoclassic buildings; Manatí, for interesting Criollo dwellings. The affinity displayed by houses in the central streets near the plaza, not replicating each other but sharing formal conventions of style and type, proclaims pride in that particular town.

Location of houses in town and region is a primary identifying statement for Colonial Spanish and Criollo houses and their residents. In contrast, residents of contemporary suburban development houses are allocated to areas according to income level, a system that is believed to have emerged in response to modern social complexity. Clustering of people according to perceived homogeneity probably reduces stress (Rapoport 1977:334–35), as it is easier to relate to people who are "the same" (see also Sommer 1969). Thus identity with geographical location has shifted, from a sociohistorical connection to a particular town or region, to an address in a suburban neighborhood which is associated with a population group of approximately the same socioeconomic level. Residents of *arrabales* also identify with geographical location, usually sardonically named places where they are supported by social networks of family and friends. Some places provide "thicker" experience than others (Tuan 1984:4), but despite their diversity they all signify to the residents "the place where I belong."[3]

Siting

The term "siting" refers to the specific situation of a house in its urban or rural setting.

A nineteenth-century town plan is a guide to the town's social order (Markham 1977). The houses of the most prominent citizens were situated on the town square, with the largest and grandest house, usually the home of a wealthy sugar or coffee plantation owner, standing on a corner, and less pretentious residences distributed in descending order outward from the center (figure 163). Lots and houses dwindle in size as they move farther away from the plaza, with mere shanties located at the edge of town. There, on unclaimed property, are the *arrabales*, further distinguished from the central grid by their apparently haphazard disposition.

In each neighborhood setting, further contextual information is available. Distance from the town center indicates social level, but on a given street, houses are differentiated by gradations in property size and situation. The siting of Colonial Spanish, Criollo, and Eclectic houses was a means of ordering the society by social level and thus indicated social status.

The present wide distribution of people into *urbanizaciones* has fragmented what were formerly town neighborhoods into separate developments. Relationship to the center is no longer of consequence, since improved transportation enables the affluent as well as the middle-class to locate where they choose, which often is as far from the center as the dwellings of the poor. However, certain residential areas quite obviously consist of expensive houses, while others are sites for people of low-income. Moreover, there are gradations of property value which convey status within a development; corner lots are larger and more advantageously situated, for example. Though

Figure 163. Town Plan of Añasco, 1978. (Taken from Mapa de Zonificación de Añasco, Hoja #5.)

the siting of twentieth-century houses differs from that of nineteenth-century ones, it still indicates socioeconomic level (see also Sternlieb and Hughes 1980). The context differs, but messages are similar, though the resonance with history evident in Criollo towns is clearly not characteristic of *urbanizaciones*.

Contextual information supplements that communicated by the exterior and interior spatial order of the house and by the ornamental elements which embellish or complete the house (plants, boundary walls, fences, and decorative ornaments on the outside, and the spatial arrangement, furnishings, and decoration on the inside).

Spatial Organization

The exterior spatial features of a house and its site include the site; its size, shape, and boundaries; their relationships to the house; and the exterior organization of the house—size, general morphology, and enclosure features. In varying degrees, all these elements convey messages of territoriality, relative dominance, attraction or exclusion, and status. The equally informative interior, which consists of public and private zones and their organization, enclosures, and means of circulation, similarly is an index of family relationships and behavior. The articulation of exterior and interior is also an important source of information (Doll 1981:173–98) for interpreting the desired form of interaction between residents and nonresidents (the latter will be referred to here as "the public" or "outsiders").

Exterior Spatial Organization

Space surrounding a house is shaped by the house's dimensions; contours; and relationship to such neighboring objects as buildings, streets, and vegetation—its field of forces (Arnheim 1988:15–31). Space in front is public and relates the house to the outside world; at the sides, space creates a separation from or barrier between adjacent houses; and in back, space is private and in some cases integral to the house. Each house, within its three-dimensional bubble (Hall 1966; Sommer 1969), manifests its relationship to the surrounding natural and built environment by such dimensions as height above the ground, distance between houses, and distance from street or road to facade. Though transmission of information involves multiple formal components and their composition, at the simplest level the site and its boundaries are explicit signals of territoriality. Size and sometimes height above the ground are indicators of relative status. Formality—that is, the clear delineation of form—emits messages of attraction or exclusion. Such components and their spatial arrangements not only convey messages about the kind of interaction expected by residents, but also facilitate behavior. Thus, the front of an urban house and its mode of relating to the street and to neighboring houses communicate messages of invitation or exclusion, and at the same time the spatial order guides or supports behavioral interaction (see also Rapoport 1982:191).

Exterior Ornamentation

Exterior ornamentation, which supplements and usually concurs with information provided by spatial organization, is also a mode of expressing identity—somewhat analogous to clothing, which defines individual personality. Degree and type of ornamentation thus send messages variably signifying respectability, ostentation, modesty, conformity, or individuality, among other qualities. There appear to be different norms for each social level as well as for each time period, so the amount and kind of ornamentation vary along both axes—Vernacular, Designed, and Grand houses; and Colonial Spanish, Criollo, Eclectic, U.S. Influence, and Urbanización styles. Ornamentation on Designed houses is usually conventional and integral to specific style. Grand houses display greater complexity, manifested in amount and elaboration of ornamentation as well as in perfection of detail. A Grand house is designed to be preeminent and often also ostentatious, but the mode of achieving these goals varies according to style. Vernacular houses, in contrast, rely primarily on paint and on individually selected ornament for decoration.

Color

The color of paint or construction material is frequently the most immediately discernible characteristic of a house. Inspired in part by the varicolored tropical environment, color is a fundamental component of the Puerto Rican aesthetic (Martorell 1976), although at times it is countermanded by other cultural influences. Lime white, for example, was used by the Spaniards.

Color became important during the nineteenth century as a means of displaying status and respectability. According to a student at the University of Puerto Rico School of Architecture, "Yo no soy peón" ("I am not a peon") was the explanation given for painting Vernacular houses. First balustrades were painted to protect them from oxidation, and later came the house exterior. With the introduction of North American paints after 1898, painting of houses became more common. A custom still followed by many Puerto Ricans is to paint the house at Christmas, apparently a retical expression of renewal (Fernández 1977).

Currently, a palette of Caribbean or Mediterranean color is widely followed. Many colors appear constantly, most notably aqua and light green—sometimes almost indistinguishable—and cream, white, blue, salmon, and pastel shades of olive, pink, blue, green, yellow, and gray. The most common colors for the body of the house are aqua, blue, green, and yellow, and for trim, red, white, and brown. Frequently-seen color combinations are aqua with salmon trim, blue with red, and pale green with white.

Use of color varies according to stylistic period. Colonial Spanish houses were white, and Spanish Colonial Revival houses continue this tradition. Art Deco and Prairie houses are generally white or cream, though Vernacular Art Deco examples have brightly colored motifs. Criollo and Bungaloid wood houses and High Neoclassic, Beaux Arts, and some Eclectic Queen Anne houses are distinguished by livelier color.

Designed Criollo houses are painted pastel colors—green, blue, pink, and yellow—often only on their facades, with the form of balustrades, columns or capitals, and window and door openings accentuated by white. Two well-known Grand houses are painted all white. Brighter colors, including many of the combinations noted above, are used on Vernacular houses. *Arrabales* display the most vivid colors, presenting lively backdrops from their hillside settings. *Arrabal* residents, like tropical fish, resort to color as the principal means of differentiating their homes and indicating territoriality.[4]

Regional diversity is evident in the use of certain colors (Anonymous N.D.:No. 145). In areas where people of African descent are concentrated, deep blue is prevalent.[5]

Color is a contemporary signal which expresses the aspirations of current residents, who conform either to past tradition or present norms. Thus, because a bright aqua color reduces the formality of a Designed High Neoclassic house, it not only conveys a more welcoming message than was the intention of the style, but also links the residents with the present (figure 80). The use of bright paint has a damaging or enlivening effect, depending on the point of view. The grace of some early buildings has been diminished by individualistic application of strong colors which dissolve or overwhelm simple proportions (figures 164, and 165). On the other hand, colors are considered by many to be in keeping with the island's tropical setting.

Quality of Appearance

Before discussing the messages signaled by the ornamentation of specific house types, the question of overall quality of appearance must be addressed. A rundown house clearly conveys neglect due to poverty or absentee ownership. Conversely, a freshly-painted and well-maintained house signals pride in ownership. Such evidence sends messages that may override those intended when the house was constructed. Indeed, a Grand house in bad repair may be a rooming house. Moreover, several examples of fine architecture have been transformed for commercial use into offices, funeral homes, or country inns. Sometimes the transformation has been carried out with respect, but often the building has been desecrated by inappropriate painting (figures 162 and 166). Disjunctive signals are quickly noticed, as are other irregularities—a lavishly decorated house among plain ones, an unpainted house in a carefully tended neighborhood.

Figure 164. Sports Store, Ponce. This is a fine example of Puerto Rican Criollo architecture.

Figure 165. Commercial Building, Adjuntas. Patches of bright red or blue-green paint occur randomly around doorways.

But idiosyncratic aberrations are included here only when they contribute to general patterns.

The Analysis

The following analysis of house messages and meanings relies primarily on a communications model, but supplements it with symbolic anthropology in the discussion of certain contextual referents and nonspatial elements. The discussion will concentrate specifically, though not exclusively, on the messages of territoriality, identity, status, and exclusion or welcome conveyed by the spatial order and ornamentation of Puerto Rican house types. Through such a focused comparison not only should meanings emerge, but disparities among meanings, according to house type and social level, also should be disclosed. To point up similarities and differences, the discussion separates Designed houses from Vernacular and Jíbaro/Arrabal houses.

However, Designed and Vernacular Urbanización houses are discussed together.

Designed Houses

Colonial Spanish and Criollo

Exterior Spatial Organization

Territoriality is clearly indicated by the facades of Colonial Spanish and Criollo houses and by the relationship of each house to its site. Since the space each house occupies almost corresponds with its site, from the front Colonial Spanish and Criollo houses appear to fill the entire property. The common or abutting walls or joined fa-

Figure 166. Funeral Home, Arecibo. Though used for commercial purposes, the facade of this building has been treated with respect.

cades of Colonial Spanish houses, which as a group form a continuous flat surface with no interrupting spaces, present a protective wall along the street, an explicit indicator of territoriality as well as a barrier, a signal of exclusion (figure 50). At the time of construction, interaction with the public took place in the street or from a second-story *balcón* (when one existed).

At times there is more space between the street and a Criollo house facade, and boundaries of fences or walls define the territory. The Criollo *balcón*, while tentatively inviting, also increases distance and is thus a signal of exclusion as well, though a less formidable one than a wall-like facade. The *balcón* provides for and thus facilitates public interaction within the domain of the house. Similarly, the *zaguán* of the Colonial Spanish House and Tienda, in effect a continuation of the street, permits public entrance into house domain. In both cases, however, interaction takes place in controlled space. Criollo houses are not only distanced from the street but also raised above ground level, further discouraging or controlling entrance. Height, which elevates residents above other citizens, is also an indicator of status.

Size, or the occupation of comparatively larger amounts of space, also signals relative status or social rank, especially when other differentiating features are minimal or lacking. Thus size is more obviously distinguishing among relatively homogeneous Colonial Spanish houses than in Criollo houses.

The messages emitted by the regularity of space on a street of Colonial Spanish facades (figure 167) contrasts with those of the advancing and receding spaces created by the morphological variety of Criollo facades (figure 168). Colonial Spanish signals exclusion; the receding spaces of Criollo, such as the recessed *balcón* type, are more inviting, yet their formality imposes limits.

With their two-dimensional facades and forward axis, Colonial Spanish and Criollo houses are more directly and formally related to the street than to juxtaposed neighbors. The space between Criollo houses, divided by walls or fences and seldom of consequence, is ignored or taken up by driveways or entrances to the back. These spatial arrangements send less forceful messages of exclusion than the aligned front walls of Colonial Spanish, but they clearly convey restrictive signals to outsiders.

Walled patio gardens in back of houses, a Spanish heritage, are small spaces with informal assemblages of fruit trees and flowers.

Figure 167. Street of Colonial Spanish Houses, San Juan.

They contrast with similarly located, fairly rare, formal gardens which were apparently introduced through nineteenth-century European or U.S. influence (figures 169 and 170). Both types, conceived as private spaces inside the territory of the house, are often accessible only from within. In varying degrees of cultivation and care, they are found in the majority of houses built before 1920. By bringing the natural environment into the private domain of the house for the personal enjoyment of residents, away from public view, the house is extended to incorporate property remaining unbuilt upon. The house itself is thus the territorial unit defined by its side walls, or fenced boundary, the back wall of the garden, and the street in front unless there is an intervening wall or fence. Space beyond these boundaries is "outside" the domain. All these indicators of territory, exclusion, and control in Colonial Spanish and Criollo houses point to meanings of the house as family center and haven.

Exterior Ornamentation

Exterior embellishment of Colonial Spanish houses is limited to architectural features, including *balcones*, balustrades, and window grilles, although a few houses are now painted in pastel colors. However, there may have been precedents for these colors, since in South America and therefore probably Puerto Rico, some Colonial Spanish houses were tinted rose or yellow depending on whether oxblood or cow fat had been added to the white lime mixture. Decorative elements on Criollo Designed and Grand houses are also almost entirely determined by architectural convention. Yet, because of the variants inherent in Criollo styles, the facades of Criollo houses display greater diversity than those of Colonial Spanish houses. In both types, individual expression arises from the colors chosen, validity of design, and perfection of detail—in other words, from the quality of performance in meeting a standard. Apparently each homeowner aiming to achieve recognition for superior performance extended the limits by selection of ornament, color, and special materials such as stained glass windows.

Such messages of identity sometimes conflict, but more often coincide with those of territoriality, exclusion, and status. In general, both Colonial Spanish and Criollo present formally coherent, clearly defined statements—unequivocal messages of identity, status, and territoriality. Less differentiated Spanish exteriors are an index of

Figure 168. Street of Criollo Houses, Arecibo.

community solidarity, while the more individualized Criollo exteriors are indicators of family confidence and pride.

Interior Spatial Organization

"Perceptually and practically, the worlds of outside and inside are mutually exclusive" (Arnheim 1977:92). The exterior of the house is presented to the public; the interior is an enclosing family shelter. The spatial order of rooms and the circulation among them convey information about the family, the relative importance of its members, and their relationships.

Colonial Spanish and Criollo Schema Two and Three houses are strictly organized according to public and private zones, which indicate the preferred locations of interaction and withdrawal. House plans provide a system of spaces that order interaction between the family and the public, and among family members. With the Criollo house as a model, and moving from front to back, as one enters onto the *balcón*, proceeds into the *sala*, through to the *comedor*, and beyond to the *cocina*, one passes from formal public areas to less for-

MESSAGES AND MEANINGS 213

Figure 169. Patio Garden of Designed Criollo Neoclassic House, Humacao. (House also shown in figures 117a–c.)

Figure 170. Patio Garden of Criollo Neoclassic House and Tienda, Añasco. (House also shown in figures 95a–c.)

mal private ones (see also Tuan 1974:27). The central axis facilitates flow through the house from front to back, and also sets out a clear sequence of room order.[6]

The *sala*, the public space within the house where the family meets, presents itself to outsiders, and entertains them, conveys signals of status and family identity. It provides a formal arena like the town plaza, which also orders and simplifies such interchanges. In certain Grand houses, an *antesala* precedes the *sala* and serves as a more formal reception room. The *sala* is the domain of the father, in the traditional Hispanic family usually an autocratic paterfamilias. His personality and values are those projected by the facade. As the family's leader and guardian, he has the responsibility of interacting with the public. The mother's domain is private, the area of withdrawal in the center of the house, where, in fulfillment of her nurturing role, she provides the family's food (Buitrago-Ortiz 1973). The *comedor*, with dining table and encircling chairs, is an index of the family's unity. In some Designed houses a room designated *antesala*, located between *sala* and *comedor*, is used as a less formal family sitting-TV room. The *cocina*, once a separate building, is now incorporated into the house plan though still relegated to the back. The master bedroom of the parents, the best furnished *dormitorio* and often the repository of treasured mementos and valuables, is sometimes on display off the *sala*, the public space within the house, as the town's prominent citizen was strategically located on the plaza (Rykwert 1976:25). Moving from front to back, other *dormitorios*, diminishing in quality of furnishings, are assigned to other family members according to their importance; smaller servants' rooms are located at the end of the *galería* or behind the house. Situated at the back near the *cocina* is the *baño*, which is sometimes only a storage area with a tub or basin for bathing.[7] The house order is an index of family order—of the relative status of its members, the values ascribed to men and women, and the roles of father and mother within the family (see also Rapoport 1977:291).

From within, Colonial Spanish and Criollo houses seem contained. The Criollo *balcón* provides a formal, sheltered passage to public space, and the Colonial Spanish open *galería* in back is protected with patio walls or fences. Such control of boundaries implies a certain segregation and, when combined with the interior plan and its room-to-room circulation, is an index of family self-reliance as well as family unity. Family homogeneity is indicated by room size, which, except for a larger *sala* and master bedroom, varies little. The separate *comedors* and more diversified room sizes of Grand houses are indicators of additional messages of status and identity.

Interior Ornamentation

In most houses ornamentation is concentrated in the *sala*, the setting for the aesthetic display of the family's history, religious beliefs, and values. The *sala* is intended to provide a pleasing ambiance which confirms status and identity at family gatherings and when entertaining outsiders. It includes the architectural features of the room—doors, windows, floors, ceiling, walls—and the furnishings and their arrangement.

Colonial Spanish house interiors rely for interest on materials of construction, simple lines, wood beams and doors, and tile floors, many of these features dating from the Colonial period. Their high

Figure 171. Interior of Colonial Spanish House. (Historic American Buildings Survey [HABS] photo.)

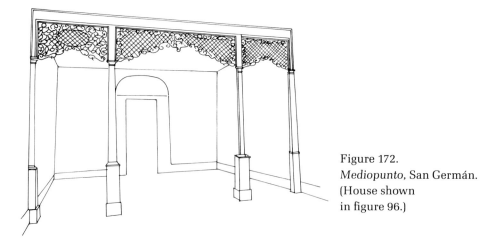

Figure 172.
Mediopunto, San Germán.
(House shown in figure 96.)

beamed ceilings impart spaciousness to even small rooms. Furniture varies, but Spanish antiques—chests, tables and, more rarely, chairs—are interspersed with contemporary upholstered sofas and chairs (figure 171). Nineteenth-century Puerto Rican furniture made of native wood often is found in Colonial Spanish as well as Criollo houses.[8]

The most noteworthy feature of the Criollo interior is the *mediopunto* or divider between *sala* and *comedor*. As the *mediopunto* was a means of display, distinctive and frequently elaborate examples can be seen in almost every house (Canino 1976). Some of the most attractive are graceful filigree scrollwork arches supported on thin columns (figure 172). On one, the white curvilinear design is highlighted by silver, shading its carved edges. Another in a hundred-year-old house resembles a triptych, with two window-like openings on either side of a central arch (figure 173). *Mediopuntos*, like proscenium arches, indicate the stage on which public interaction takes place. They also serve as gateway barriers—signals of exclusion from private areas.

The *mediopunto* is commonly complemented by other stylistically related architectural details such as scrollwork or geometric carpentry filling the spaces in transoms or fanlights over windows (figure 174). Doorways entering into bedrooms are curtained or have louvered or solid doors variously painted either to match walls or with contrasting colors to emphasize carving or paneling (figure 175).

Ceilings are usually plain wood or pressed metal, but a few are treated especially to fit the design, such as one created of thin pieces of wood to resemble pleating. Floors are typically of wood but sometimes are of cement with Spanish or imitation Spanish tiles. The contrast between the refined details of *salas* and the plain unadorned *dormitorios* in many houses is quite striking. It is an index of the importance of the public presentation of family identity and status.

Many Criollo houses are furnished with native Puerto Rican furniture made of hardwood with cane seats and backs. A standard set apparently includes a settee, rocker, two or three armchairs, and one or more tables conventionally arranged in a circle below a central chandelier (figure 176). Other pieces commonly found are: a cabinet holding the family's best dishes, placed against the back wall of the *comedor*; desks and chests located against *sala* walls; and variously, special pieces such as secretaries, pianos, and grandfather clocks. The spacious but specific arrangement of furnishings in most Designed houses is an index of public and private areas as well as status.

An array of decorative objects displays the interests, social status, and aesthetics of the family. At every social level certain sets of objects are apparently essential for personal esteem, status, and enjoy-

Figure 173. *Mediopunto*, Mayaguez. (House shown in figure 110.)

Figure 174.
Doorway, Añasco. (House shown in figure 81.)

ment. Some, such as family photographs, are generally present, while others are specific to certain social levels. The objects provide contextual information. Their grouping and patterned placement reinforce their messages of status, identity, and territoriality. The items fall into several categories, including religious, family mementos, and aesthetic.

Certain possessions are important in themselves, and their patterned arrangement and location are indexes of additional meanings. Religious paintings and shrines, mainly of a few types, are usually located near the center of the house, on the wall of the *comedor* or on the wall at the side of a *dormitorio* entrance. In this situation the objects apparently signal territoriality or protection of the private zone of the house. Prints or paintings of the Sacred Heart, which has particular connotations of family solidarity (Firth 1973:233), are seen most frequently (figure 177). Portrayals of the Last Supper are also fairly common and similarly express group unity. Other similar representations, usually commercial reproductions selected for conventional reasons, are talismans rather than devotional objects. They occur in all types of houses but differ qualitatively.

MESSAGES AND MEANINGS 219

Figure 175.
Doorway Paneling, Arroyo.
(House shown in figures 92a–c.)

Figure 176. Puerto Rican Nineteenth-Century Furniture. Made of native hardwoods and cane.

Figure 177.
Interior, with Painting of Sacred Heart, in Grand High Neoclassic House, Guayama. (House shown figures 80a–c.)

Collections of family heirlooms and framed photographs of weddings, family groups, young men in uniform, and small children repeat or amplify the messages of identity and family heritage conveyed by geographical location. Family pictures, often grouped with albums on a table, and other family memorabilia such as diplomas, certificates, or clippings hanging on a wall are signals of family solidarity and status. Their clustering for display emphasizes the messages.

Designed house residents choose many objects for their particular interest or aesthetic value and others as signals of status. Possession and display of a requisite set or complex of things that conform to externally imposed conventions or are inspired by home-decorating magazines is apparently an essential mark of identity and self-esteem. Sets are variable in Designed houses, but frequently include Criollo-style *sala* furniture, a few conventional pictures, and small rugs as floor coverings. The interiors of Grand houses sometimes are ostentatiously furnished but more often contain antiques, special collections, and less standardized furniture (figure 178).

Discussion

The formality—that is, the clear delineation of house structure and spatial organization, and adherence to style—common to both Colonial Spanish and Criollo Designed houses emits purposive signals which define territory and exclude more than welcome. These signals restrict and control social interaction outside the family. The barrier facades of Colonial Spanish houses show less individuality than those of Criollo houses and seem to be indexes to meanings of greater conformity to community norms and an overriding need to express Spanish solidarity.

The spatial organization of both types clearly orders and reinforces a pattern of closely-integrated family behavior, but Criollo houses are less formal in the interior, because of their incomplete walls and room-to-room circulation. The self-contained segregation of Criollo

Figure 178.
Interior of Designed Criollo Neoclassic House, Humacao. Note antique furniture and oil paintings. (House shown in figures 117a–c and 182.)

houses implies greater reliance on family than on community, but above all, indicates the salience of the house itself. At once a family-centered haven and a vehicle for establishing family reputation, the Criollo house is also an incisive signal of status and *dignidad*. Moreover, Criollo, like Colonial Spanish, was an index of ethnicity, in this case, identifying nineteenth-century Catalans, Mallorcans, and migrants of other origins.

Depending on the context of site and geographic locale, with simple modernizing, and few alterations, many present-day residents still find Colonial Spanish and Criollo houses suitable habitations. Some such houses retain echoes of their original meanings.

Eclectic and U.S. Influence Houses

Exterior Spatial Organization

The spatial order of most Eclectic and U.S. Influence houses differs markedly from that of Colonial Spanish and Criollo ones. Eclectic Queen Anne and Greek Revival houses introduced new conceptions of house siting as well as structural and stylistic innovations. Large surrounding pieces of land, extending rather than encompassed by house boundaries, indicate the territorial limits. The territorial unit consists of house plus property, rather than of a house occupying the total property on which it rests. Moreover, the surrounding space, usually defined by walls, fences, or planting, distances these houses on all sides. As a result, the sides and often the back of the house are exposed instead of the facade alone, so the house is treated three-dimensionally. The openness to public view emits less excluding messages than the confrontational forward-axis facades of Colonial Spanish and Criollo houses. However, the size and ostentation of the Eclectic houses almost negate this message. Few of them could be considered welcoming.

Eclectic houses were designed not only to signal the owner's status by their size and two-story height, but also to dominate the surrounding town or landscape. As the walls of Queen Anne houses pushed outward, their gardens and other land also expanded away from the house. A large garden adjacent to the entrance of the Naguabo house (figure 106) spreads out in unconcealed public display. A Queen Anne house in San Germán is centered on a large corner lot near the church (figure 28). Such presentations thrust these houses into the community but clearly signal domination and power more than participation.

Most U.S. Influence houses are also designed three-dimensionally. The majority are oriented on a forward axis, with a walkway leading from the front boundary of sidewalk or street to the entrance. Lawns and shrubbery intervene to distance houses from the street and also to separate them from adjacent houses, with a greater proportion of land in the back—essentially an American suburban arrangement. Although the territorial unit is actually the property on which the house stands, since the land often appears vacant or unused, the definition of territory shifts ambiguously between house and property. The frontal axis is less confrontational than that of the showy Criollo facade and is further weakened by the space between adjacent houses. Despite separating hedges and fences, boundaries are generally not clearly defined, and many houses are visibly accessible on all sides. The relatively informal presentation of the majority of U.S. Influence houses—their morphologically simple geometrical shapes, ground-level situation, reduced frontality, base planting of shrubbery that conceals and softens the formal stucture, and indefinite boundaries—are indexes of invitation rather than exclusion. Aside from a closed front door, there are few architectural means of controlling or restricting interactive behavior, leaving choice and mode to circumstances (figure 179). Such informality indicates not only welcome but also inclination to participate and interact with outsiders. The informal exterior thus seems to provide material evidence of the democratizing effect associated with United States influence.

Variations in size among U.S. Influence houses have the same implications of status difference as in other house types. Grand Spanish Colonial Revival houses, typically separated by a height barrier and set off behind high walls or iron fences, constitute exceptions to the general informality. The territorial and other messages emitted by Eclectic and U.S. Influence houses are indexes of outward communication with society—on the one hand, a commanding presence; on the other, open participation.

Exterior Ornamentation

The exterior ornamentation of Eclectic and U.S. Influence houses, like that of Colonial Spanish and Criollo houses, is generally integral

224 PUERTO RICAN HOUSES

Figure 179. Doorway of Grand Spanish Colonial Revival House, San Juan. (House shown in figure 135.)

to the architectural style. The setback situation of the former two styles fosters surrounding lawns, decorative walls, statuary, shrubbery, and front gardens as exterior embellishment. Shrubbery around U.S. Influence houses provides variable visual barriers for privacy as well as boundary indicators, but many gardens invite or permit ingress and are open to view. Yet *rejas*[9] (grilles) on *balcones* (figures 180 and 181), introduced to protect against uninvited entrance, signal exclusion. They imply a certain reluctance to adopt the openness of U.S Influence styles. Most U.S. Influence houses are modestly painted in neutral colors, indicators of a participatory or conforming and less individualistic or dominating attitude. Eclectic houses, in keeping with their ostentatious style, are often painted less discreetly in rosy pinks and yellow, though some are white and gray.

Interior Spatial Organization

The introduction of increased separation through formal barriers within private as well as public zones in the interiors of both Eclectic and U.S. Influence houses provided for greater public access to specialized areas within the house. The interior spatial organization is thus consistent with the messages of outward communication signaled by the exterior. Furthermore, the *balcón* on U.S. Influence houses is transformed by screening *rejas* into an outdoor sitting area. Its function as a place to interact with the public is assumed by an interior foyer or vestibule, and a smaller entryway takes its place outside. Though formal interaction with outsiders takes place within the house, the confined space still provides control. Grand Eclectic and many U.S. Influence houses incorporate such spatial innovations, but others, reflecting their transitional character, retain the public-private axis, general configuration, and freer circulation of Criollo houses. Nevertheless, as previously noted, alterations—addition of a *comedor*/sitting area on the back *galería* near a modern kitchen, and the introduction of hallways—are made to many of these (figure 182).

Interior Ornamentation

The changes in ornamentation introduced to the interiors by Eclectic and U.S. Influence were more broadly acceptable. *Mediopuntos* disappeared from *salas,* and furnishings called "Maria Teresa" became the standard set (figure 183). Derivative of French Louis XV

Figure 180. *Rejas* on Designed Spanish Colonial Revival House, San Juan. (House shown in figure 131.)

rococo style, this set consists mainly of small elegant chairs and sofas, mirrors, and carpets or rugs. Probably widely adopted earlier, it still occurs but generally has been replaced by contemporary upholstered living room furniture.

Consistent with the status display of the exterior, the walls and ceilings of Eclectic, High Neoclassic, and Beaux Arts houses are often embellished with elaborate plaster moldings (figure 184). Small mural landscape paintings or fruit and floral still lifes, created by itinerant European artists of the late nineteenth century, also decorate the walls.

The *salas* of U.S. Influence houses are plainer and usually painted in neutral colors. They lack architectural ornamentation, except for the ubiquitous Spanish tiles and arches in Spanish Colonial Revival

Figure 181. *Rejas* on Designed Spanish Colonial Revival House, San Juan. (House shown in figure 132.)

houses. The centering chandelier is often moved to the *comedor*. In the *salas* of many Designed houses, contemporary upholstered and some antique furniture is dispersed away from the center into one or more groups, depending on room size, replacing the circular arrangement of Criollo furniture. Such changes in type and arrangement of furniture reflect fashion, but also arise from personal and cultural aesthetics (Patterson 1968:358). Though modestly, furnishings signal status and identity. As compared with Criollo furniture arrangement, the more open later arrangement is an index of greater informality and less family control.

The same categories of objects—religious, family memorabilia, and aesthetic—exist in Eclectic and U.S. Influence houses as in the houses examined earlier. Fewer religious objects and family photographs appear in the *sala*; they may be situated in private areas. Some decorative objects, acquired for their aesthetic appeal or as me-

Figure 182. Informal *Comedor*. Sitting area on back *galería* of Criollo Neoclassic house in Humacao. (House shown in figures 117a–c and 178.)

mentos, are common in all houses. Floral prints and landscape paintings are typical wall decorations in older houses; prints by recognized artists, contemporary paintings, ceramics, and other kinds of ornaments are seen in Urbanización and U.S. Influence houses. Other objects specifically signal status. For example, certain porcelain figurines, often grouped on a coffee table, are apparently considered "correct" possessions to own (figure 185).

Discussion

The spatial formality and ostentation of Eclectic houses were compatible to relatively few Puerto Ricans even at the time of their introduction. Now these houses are rarely valued and preserved (figures 112a and 112b). Some are maintained for personal reasons connected with pride in family heritage; a Naguabo house (figures 106a and 106b) is very well kept. But its twin on an adjacent site is a ruin.

Figure 183. "María Teresa" Style Furniture. Interior of Designed Art Deco house in Moca. (House shown in figure 129.)

Figure 184. Plaster Moldings, Ponce. (Interior of house shown in figures 115a and 115b.)

Figure 185. Interior of Spanish Colonial Revival house, San Juan. (House shown in figure 132.)

Other houses survive because of the continuity of their contextual meanings. Grand houses situated on the plazas of small towns were originally conceived as the palaces or castles of their owners, wealthy sugar or coffee planters. They are now the homes of furniture merchants, doctors, or pharmacists, persons of consequence in the contemporary town hierarchy and economy but not equivalent to the planters. With the fading of the towns' importance as centers, the meanings of such houses are attenuated to nostalgic references.

The formal interior spatial order of U.S. Influence houses was more popular, though two-story one-family houses were less acceptable. Yet, at the time of introduction and since, the commodious simplicity of U.S. Influence houses seems to have been found a fitting expression by many Puerto Ricans. Symbolizing a break with the past in their use of modern materials, U.S. Influence houses connote ties to science, technology, and modernity. Bungaloid and Art Deco styles were more often taken up as Vernacular expressions, and only a few Prairie houses remain but Spanish Colonial Revival has continued to be popular. It provides for a relatively neutral and thus adaptable habitation. This style is also a unifying materialization for Puerto Ricans. The combination of references to both Spanish heritage and U.S. contemporary form and construction typifies present-day Puerto Ricanness for many professionals, in particular.

Country Houses

In certain aspects Designed Country houses are similar in exterior spatial organization to urban Designed ones of the same period. For example, Criollo Hacienda houses resemble town houses of the same period in their *balcones* and stairways for controlling access. But in rural areas territoriality is indicated variably and idiosyncratically, by size of property and specific boundary markers of fences and walls, which are also the principal signals of welcome or exclusion. Distance from entrance or road, size of house, and its height above the ground are the other major indicators of these messages. Modern farmhouses are closer to the road and appear more accessible.

Country houses are commonly situated to take advantage of features in the natural setting, which are often indexes of territoriality. Lack of order in the surrounding natural landscape—forests, marshland, and even disarray around house grounds—is tolerated in rural areas, a probable consequence of the space available and resulting privacy. At times the spatial arrangement of country houses also imposes order on the landscape. The spatial order of buildings on haciendas sometimes echoes the order of the town plaza. Farms are less formally laid out.

With few exceptions, country houses of every style are simpler on both exterior and interior than those in the city. On the exterior, their simplicity indicates welcome, but their boundaries, usually clearly and unambiguously marked, define the limits of ingress and interaction. The relatively informal interiors of country houses are also welcoming. Yet, considering also the territorial boundaries on the exterior, these houses seem designed to receive primarily family and close friends. The idiosyncracy of spatial control and boundary delineation of each farm and hacienda are indicators of independence and self-reliance, characteristics essential for survival in rural areas.

Discussion

Differences among Puerto Rican Designed houses can be elucidated in terms of gradations of formality in both relative complexity and definition.[10] Formal structures, in combination with defined spaces, emit clear signals of territoriality and control as exemplified by Colonial Spanish, Criollo, and to some extent Eclectic houses. The less clearly defined or informal order of U.S. Influence houses combines with ambiguous boundaries to send imprecise signals of territoriality. In the absence of barriers or countervailing information, messages of openness or welcome are assumed (Ruesch and Kees 1972: 89–95). The variable emphases of size, height, spatial distance, and irregular morphology related to each type further reinforce such differences. The disparities between early and later types seem to indicate changing attitudes toward social control, from a society tightly ordered by convention to one in which decisions were more often left to individuals. The increased variety of later house types gives further evidence of the opportunity for individual choice. The variety also seems to be an index of demographic diversity.

Gradations of formality also occur in the interiors of houses. There formality is manifested chiefly by degree of room separation, seen in incomplete or complete walls, presence or absence of doors, and the number of levels. Interiors and exteriors do not always coincide in degree of formality. Criollo houses are formal on the exterior and informal on the interior. Outwardly informal U.S. Influence houses are formally organized on the interior. The increased separation of rooms in the more formal interiors of U.S. Influence houses seems to indicate greater independence of family members after 1920. The greater formality also seems to imply that the house was open to a wider range of visitors and guests.

The principal characteristic of all Designed Houses is their reliance on external standards or models. Their aesthetic and their original designs arise from the tension between demands that they conform to standards, on the one hand, and that they adapt or transform them to fit Puerto Rican imperatives, on the other. The specialized knowledge required to construct Designed houses according to proper styles and modes demonstrates superiority, the characteristic of an elite. "An elite partakes in the culture of the wider society, but develops boundaries through style of life—accent . . . style of dress, patterns of . . . etiquette, manners" (Cohen 1976:15). Houses meeting architectural standards are one such means of distinction. Designed houses, though introduced through historical circumstances, were selected for their practical and aesthetic suitability. They were also chosen because their prototypes were models to be emulated (Kubler 1980:235). They express a desire to belong to a special, at times exclusive segment of society. Thus, a fundamental meaning of all Designed houses of whatever period is to distinguish an elite: the Spanish from Taino Indians and African slaves, Spanish and Caribbean planters from *jíbaros,* educated professionals and bureaucrats from workers, and from *peones* and *agregados* in *arrabales.* Each Designed house displays its individual distinctiveness within the canons of a style and type—more or less ostentatious, restrained, or original. Designed houses, built as complete entities and then periodically outmoded, are superseded by newer external models. Older types continue to stand alongside newer ones. Each new type sets off another elite group—Criollo from Spanish, very wealthy from less affluent, educated professionals from the less knowledgeable.

Distinctive messages emanate from the different types of Puerto Rican houses, but the context of setting is often critical to the interpretation of meaning, especially of older houses. The survival of Colonial Spanish, Criollo, Eclectic, Prairie, and Art Deco houses is dependent primarily on (1) the continuity of their use as family heritage, (2) their transformation into Vernacular habitations or commercial buildings, and (3) their preservation and recycling. The examples discussed generally fall into the first category, and brief reference to the second has been made. Now we must touch on the present role of preservation and its relationship to the meaning of elite.

Colonial Spanish houses, for example, have disappeared or been transformed into commercial buildings throughout most of the island, except in Old San Juan. This area formerly was becoming rundown, but it has been renovated in recent years, partly because of the current regard for historic preservation. A historic site, Old San Juan provides a stimulating environment for the dense population of government officials, professionals, shopkeepers, workers, and tourists who occupy government, commercial, and residential buildings. Today, as in the past, the form of Colonial Spanish houses is in harmony with the setting. Though many have been remodeled, their commercial residential functions are similar to those of the past, and the formal facades appropriately still signal messages to restrain public ingress. Old San Juan itself, defined in part by Colonial Spanish architecture, condenses multiple meanings. It refers to Puerto Rican history; it denies United States dominance by the current use of Spanish buildings, with their references to the colonial period; but it also alludes to independence from Spain by its American lifestyle. Its shops, restaurants, museums, and government buildings bring it into the present. These characteristics and other circumstances have made it attractive to an elite population. Residence in a Colonial Spanish house in Old San Juan signals status and identity. Yet the current meanings attached to Colonial Spanish houses are of the present (Tuan 1984:4) even though "enriched by [the] accretion" (Eco 1979:31) of the layers of meanings that existed historically. Furthermore, these meanings are integral to the particular setting but lacking apart from it. Similar buildings elsewhere, in Mayaguez, for example (figure 73a), though restored and appreciated, for want of equivalent context are not imbued with equal meaning.

Criollo houses undergoing restoration in San Germán, a contrasting quiet, uncrowded environment, similarly have ties to history and to the "correct" and knowledgeable behavior of architectural preservation that confirms elite status. Locale as well as the historical or architectural significance of a building being restored affects meaning. Symbolically, Criollo styles stand for opposition to Spain, especially in western towns which were the centers of independence movements (Lewis 1983:265–77). Even without specific sociohistorical significance, modernized old Criollo houses are regarded as charming, comfortable dwellings with pleasing aesthetic qualities and symbolic references to Caribbean history. These meanings are contextual, however, and attach more often to houses which belonged to well-known families in towns such as San Germán, Manatí, and Guayama. Many Criollo houses, especially Hacienda houses, are considered outmoded, beyond restoration, or impractical and are falling in ruins for want of care.

The meaning of elite still clings to many old Designed houses, while others lose their elite significance and take on the characteristics of Vernacular houses. The messages emanating from some still hold, but others are overridden by the present context. The easily readable codes of nineteenth-century geographical location and siting have been replaced by new dispersed patterns of residence.

Vernacular Houses

Vernacular wood houses, although similar in certain aspects to Designed houses of the same periods, follow a separate course of development. In contrast to the episodically introduced changes of Designed houses, Vernacular habitations conserve tradition, evolving over time through slow adaptation (Hubka 1980:70). Built by homeowners or their friends and neighbors, Vernacular wood houses vary more in quality of construction than professionally constructed Designed houses. The types common today evolved from thatched-roof *bohíos* with wood, cane, or *yagua* siding, which were still prevalent as late as the 1940s. The process of transformation from *bohío* to concrete Schema II/2 half-*balcón* or Bungaloid types, which takes place in most Vernacular neighborhoods, is exemplified by a row of houses in Camuy (figure 186). Within living memory, *yagua* siding was gradually replaced, first with wood and currently with concrete. A few of these houses reveal their original *bohío* shape, but others have acquired *balcones* and Schema Two–like interiors.

Vernacular houses resemble Criollo and Bungaloid Designed more than they do other types, but they are generally smaller. Measure-

Figure 186. Street of Criollo Vernacular Houses, Camuy.

ments show their average size to range from 15 by 15 feet to 20 by 27 feet, as compared to Designed houses, which range from 30 by 30 feet to 40 by 45 feet and larger (Roberts and Stefani 1949:49).

Criollo Vernacular

Exterior Spatial Organization

The spatial order of Vernacular houses varies little from one style-period to another. Criollo Vernacular houses, usually situated fairly close to the street, with an occasional front boundary wall or fence, like Criollo Designed houses, themselves define territoriality (figure 186). Schema Two houses, scarcely accommodated by narrow lots, are sometimes so closely packed that only inches of space separate them. No matter how meager, the space defines the territorial line between adjacent houses. Moreover, though actually an unordered no man's land, and disadvantageous because of noise transmission, the space serves the useful purpose of ventilation by creating a flue that channels air to the windows (Marvel 1978, personal communication). Because of the quality and varying size of this dividing space, the general simplicity of facade morphology, the variable height of *balcones*, and the diverse use of fencing or other restrictive barriers, the messages of territoriality and exclusion or welcome emitted by Vernacular houses are less consistent than those conveyed by formally defined Criollo Designed houses. The implication of the diverse but specifically direct messages is that restrictions on interaction with outsiders are imposed more often by individuals than by architectural and social convention.

Exterior Ornamentation

Ornamentation is applied variously to Vernacular houses, often without regard for stylistic period, so the houses generally appear idiosyncratic. For a combination of reasons—lack of knowledge, economic means, incentive, and different aesthetic preferences—Vernacular houses do not replicate Criollo or other Designed styles, but use only selected elements of certain stylistic repertoires for their design and their perceived meanings. They exhibit originality more by novel combinations of architectural features and decorative forms than by the creation of innovative ornament. Reliance is placed on color and occasionally on original decorative creations to signal identity and status, and on fencing or other barriers to indicate territoriality and exclusion or welcome. Selections are patterned, however, and thus presumably are limited by unstated Vernacular rules.

In many Vernacular neighborhoods, embellishment consists primarily of manufactured ornaments. Balustrades of *balcones* are made of commercial ornamental concrete blocks, painted or plain, which present a rich surface pattern reminiscent of Criollo carpentry details, albeit in different material and design (figures 187). Cast-concrete spindles are used in place of wood balusters on *balcones* as well. These materials are not costly, considering their overall effect and structural utility. In 1979, the prices for blocks were $1.25, $1.50, and $1.75. Balusters cost $1.50 each.

a.

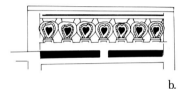
b.

c.

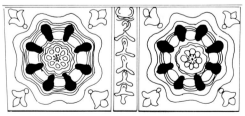
d.

Figures 187a–d. Four Patterns of Decorative Concrete Block Used on *Balcones*.

To assess the diversity of Vernacular houses, a count was made of the variable components represented on one short block of twenty-three such houses.

The following results were found:

Stories	22 one-story; 1 two-story
Material	8 wood; 15 concrete (conversions)
Roofs	10 flat or extended gable; 11 gable; 2 hip
Balcones	8 half; 14 full width; 1 lacking
Concrete blocks	19 patterns
Rejas	15 patterns (painted black or white)
Colors of houses	*Colors of trim*
White	Red, green, aqua, mustard, gray, brown, pink, salmon
Cream	Ochre, olive, red, aqua, green
Blue	Brown
Green	White, brown, cream
Aqua	White
Gray	White
Yellow	Green

No two houses were alike, although they appeared so at first glance. Such concern for individual distinction within overall similarity underscores the importance of expressing not only territoriality and status, but also personal and neighborhood identity.

Interior Spatial Organization and Ornamentation

Throughout all periods most Vernacular houses of every type are simple and quite informal in the interior. They are usually organized according to Schema Two. The *sala* is larger and more carefully painted and furnished than other rooms. Possessions to display status and identity are present, but the *sala* remains a relatively intimate place (sometimes a work space) for family and close friends. *Mediopuntos*, when they exist, are elementary arches or brackets. Curtains often take the place of doors, and furnishings tend to be contemporary and sometimes crowded together. The required set usually consists of a plastic upholstered sofa and two chairs. Other items apparently considered essential include: in the *sala*, a chandelier, television set, stereo, wall clock, and sometimes a fish tank; and in the *comedor*, a china cabinet and refrigerator (figure 70c). In most Vernacular houses, furniture is deployed against the walls, and only rarely in a center circle. Walls are sometimes painted in bright colors, especially aqua, or in white or cream. Floors are of wood covered with linoleum, or tile on concrete.

The same categories of ornaments—religious, family memorabilia, and aesthetic—exist in Vernacular houses, sometimes in proportionately greater numbers than in Designed houses, but their quality is not equivalent. The location and arrangement of items are similar to Criollo Designed, although pictures of John Kennedy, religious pictures, and family photos are grouped together near the *comedor* or, in some Vernacular houses, on one of its walls. These arrangements, as well as the choice of objects, appear individualized and spontaneous, but the recurrence of some in many houses implies selection on the basis of convention. For residents of Vernacular houses, objects are both possessions which signal status, and also treasured mementos and religious talismans; all reinforce self-esteem and *dignidad*.

Partial-Second-Story and U.S. Influence Houses

Exterior Spatial Organization

Partial Second Story

Vernacular Camelback and Tower houses, like Eclectic houses, are surrounded by more land than Criollo Vernacular ones. Some have gardens at the front or side. But the height of the second story is their principal spatial difference from Criollo houses. This height, plus the purposely novel and arresting shapes of the towers command attention. Bright colors often further emphasize their eccentricity. The camelback and especially the towers are preeminent signals of status and identity.

Bungaloid. Vernacular Bungalows differ similarly from Criollo houses in their more spacious settings, with gardens at front or side. Their broad and open front porches, often used as sitting areas, signal welcome (figure 188). A small shrine in a front garden adjacent to the low *balcón* of a Fajardo house is an original decorative form

Figure 188. Vernacular Bungaloid House, Camuy.

(figure 120). Its idiosyncracy and placement clearly invite interaction by passersby. It is also a territorial signal and a mark of status and *dignidad*. Indeed, the owners take great pride in explaining it.

Art Deco. In contrast, an Art Deco false-front facade, with elements of Spanish Colonial Revival, signals exclusion. The exterior walls of an old Criollo house, which otherwise retains Plan II/1 spatial order, have been replaced with concrete. A front addition of arches decorated with Art Deco frets blocks in the *balcón* and presents a wall-like barrier (figure 189). The residents of this house also discuss this change with pride. It is a signal of their up-to-date status. Art Deco seems to be an explicit message of modernity.

Figure 189. Vernacular Art Deco Renovation, Rio Piedras.

Interior Spatial Organization

As previously discussed, a partial-second-story addition is an economical means of providing more space for either a *dormitorio* or a separate sitting area. Otherwise the interiors of Partial-Second-Story and U.S. Influence Vernacular houses show few differences from Criollo Vernacular in public-private zoning, types of furnishings, or ornamentation (figure 190).

Recent modifications have changed fundamentally the order of some interiors, however, The clear delineation of the *sala* as a separate public zone has been weakened by the introduction of a bar-counter into the traditional *sala/comedor/cocina* organization. The modernized kitchen is united with the *sala/comedor* and brought into the public area (figure 191). A radical change from the lean-to *cocina* at the back, it seems to imply for the housewife a more public

Figure 190. Interior of Vernacular Bungaloid House, Camuy. (House shown in figure 188.)

role and possibly one with greater equality. "The remodeled home symbolizes the new self, or will channel behavior to make it consistent with the image generated by the remodeled house" (Jones 1980: 338).

Discussion

At present many owners of Vernacular wood houses speak directly of their preference for reinforced concrete homes. Some move to an *urbanización*. Others are preoccupied with transforming their wood houses into concrete buildings. Spanish Colonial Revival, Art Deco, and Urbanización houses all serve as exemplars, but only particular elements are appropriated and incorporated. A concrete camelback addition was being added to a Fajardo Bungalow (figure 120) when the house was visited in 1979.

Generally, Vernacular houses follow the spatial organizational rules of Schema Two Designed Criollo houses but differ from them in aesthetic conventions. "Designed houses are apt to be symmetrical, vernacular asymmetrical . . . or uncouth" (Rudofsky 1977:229). Their structural morphology is simple, their surface treatment complex. Criollo Vernacular houses are small simple structures which make use of ornament primarily related to Designed Criollo and Art Deco. They are painted in strong, often bright colors and have a high proprotion of decorative pattern in balustrades, *rejas,* and sometimes doorway ornament. Indeed, on the exterior, Vernacular houses of all types reveal the existence of a normative level of decorative intensity which is attained by color, ornament, or both in combination, depending on aesthetic preference and economic circumstance. Although there is a specific range of conventional Vernacular pattern and decorative devices, houses are extremely varied. They appear not only to have been created through individual selection but also to be intentionally competitive in aesthetic display. The manifestation of diversity signals status differentiation; its intensity implies that proclaiming personal and family identity and *dignidad* is a fundamental requisite. The basic intention is to demonstrate respectabil-

Figure 191. Interior, Ground Floor of Vernacular Two-Story Two-Family House, Ponce (House shown in figures 93a and 93b.)

ity through a significant house form (see also Hubka 1980:68). The conventions or rules of Vernacular, rather than demanding the observance of external standards, encourage the creation and use of clearly recognizable visual elements that indicate a resident's worthiness within a neighborhood. The general similarity of materials and ornaments indicates that Vernacular homeowners desire not only to stand out among neighbors, but also to belong to the neighborhood. The paramount meaning of a Vernacular house is the worth of the family within its locale.

Adherence to Vernacular rules defines each house and resident and at the same time reinforces community standards. Not to conform—to have an unpainted house without *balcón*—is to be "impure" (Douglas 1966). The Vernacular rules themselves provide for both conformity and individual expression. Moreover, through the employment of elements similar to the Designed vocabulary, Vernacular is fitted into the overall socioarchitectural pattern. But Arrabal and especially Jíbaro houses present some exceptions to this characterization of Vernacular houses.

Jíbaro Houses

Jíbaro houses differ markedly from all other Vernacular houses, even Arrabal houses, in their total lack of conformity to general architectural norms.

Exterior Organization

Because of the variability of Jíbaro houses, patterns of spatial order are difficult to discern. On the exterior, they are organized in relation to the surrounding natural and built environment (if any) in the immediate area. Unlike the geometrical or clearly circumscribed order imposed on the landscape by other rural buildings, Jíbaro houses are surrounded by no more than a cleared space, still called a *batey*. Territoriality is defined by natural barriers and boundary fences.

The rough wood and zinc construction of Jíbaro houses and the absence of embellishment, even paint, give these dwellings a rustic, improvised appearance. Public and private zones are generally not clearly demarcated; indeed, it is sometimes difficult to locate the front of a house. The unclear order makes the habitations incomprehensible and thus excluding to outsiders but not to their inhabitants.

In one instance, a small front-yard garden, clumped together and fenced against foraging barnyard animals, signalled messages of status and *dignidad*.

Interior Spatial Organization

The interior of the Jíbaro house consists of one principal room, the *sala,* which is used also as a work and sleeping area (Buitrago-Ortiz 1973). Small partitioned-off spaces and tacked-on additions qualify as private zones. In one house, images resembling "hex" signs are painted above doors leading to tiny box-like *dormitorios,* one for the parents, the other for the children. They are explicit signals of territory.

Furnishings are very sparse in most Jíbaro houses, limited to a bare minimum of tables, chairs, and beds. Wall decoration, almost nonexistent except for calendars, pictures of John Kennedy, newspaper cuttings, and one or two religious representations, appears idiosyncratic and spontaneous, as if dependent on the fluctuations of fortune rather than having been planned. A chandelier hazardously suspended in the center of one very low-ceilinged *sala* was obviously an object of pride. The resident of a house nearly devoid of possessions without solicitation displayed her treasured family photograph album. These belongings stand out in their very simple surroundings, signaling messages of identity and status far more directly than finer objects in Designed houses. Further, they imply that the display of *dignidad* is a basic need.

Jíbaro houses, considered in the context of their rural situation, differ from other country houses principally in their incomplete order both outside and inside. Hacienda and other country Designed houses conform to external rules; Jíbaro houses, evolved from the early *bohío,* develop out of the needs of specific inhabitants. Shelter is their overriding meaning. The house is a protector within and tied to the natural world (Delgado 1978). The idiosyncratic designs, with little relation to other Puerto Rican houses, reveal that the dwellings belong to people apart from the main social fabric, which is how *jíbaros* have always defined themselves and been defined by others. The scarcity of Jíbaro houses corroborates the fading of this way of life.

Arrabal Houses

Exterior Spatial Organization

When constructed, Arrabal houses are somewhat similar to Jíbaro ones and therefore, unlike Criollo and other styles of Vernacular houses. However, through modification, they eventually become more similar to Criollo, Art Deco, and Urbanización houses.

On the exterior, Arrabal house size and its relationship to adjacent structures are determined by the material available at the time of construction and also by the amount and kind of terrain. Arrabal houses are built on hilly or flat land, over water, or in densely crowded areas. The settlement pattern of an *arrabal* (figure 192) is the result of a compromise between the *jíbaro* and the town, rather than a recreation of the village in the city (Kubler 1980:242).

No matter how crowded the site, each house stands independently. Territoriality is clearly but variably expressed by space, fenced boundaries, surrounding water, color of paint, and sometimes plants. Arrabal houses display greater idiosyncracy than, but use some of the vocabulary of, other Vernacular dwellings. Eventually, through remodeling, they take on a Vernacular schema. Long-established *arrabales* are nearly indistinguishable from Vernacular neighborhoods, except for the irregularity of streets and more vivid colors.

Exterior Ornamentation

Color of paint is the most pronounced means of signaling territoriality, identity, and status in *arrabales*. Color is the means of imposing order in the unordered density of an *arrabal* (Maxwell 1978:76). Choice of a commonly used color may signal conformity or family relationship, according to one resident. A strikingly different one may indicate dominance. The brilliant yellow, with green trim, that decorates one two-story House and Tienda building signals status and probably pride in superiority. Bright colors also enable residents to display *dignidad* and thereby negate the low estimation of *arrabales* and their own reputation as "outsiders" living in "impure" places. In a study of Puerto Rican habitations in Boston housing developments (Jopling 1974), residents were found to paint the entrance doors of their apartments in bright colors even under threat of fine for breach of Boston Housing Authority regulations. Inhabitants evi-

Figure 192.
Arrabal Settlement Pattern,
Hato Rey, San Juan.

dently feel compelled to signal territoriality as well as *dignidad*.

Exterior ornament on Arrabal houses is similar to that on Vernacular ones, although pots of flowers, small novelty figures attached near entrance doors, and other decorative items are more common than *rejas* and ornamental concrete blocks.

Interior Spatial Organization and Ornamentation

Interior walls are as colorful as exterior, and ornamental objects on display are frequently brightly colored and shiny. Some items seem spontaneously chosen as mementos of an excursion to an amusement park or similar outing, others intentionally collected for their social or talismanic significance. Ceramic figurines, especially elephants and tigers with possible *santería* connotations; imitation African sculptures; and souvenir dolls from the United States are common. The objects emit signals of identity, self-esteem, status, pride in property for its own sake, and aesthetic enjoyment. The range of similar objects in many houses suggests another "set" (figures 193 and 194).

The incompletely ordered or even wholly unordered disposition of furnishings in *salas* of Arrabal houses contrasts with conventional arrangements in Designed and, indeed, Vernacular houses. Even in very sparsely furnished and tidy *salas*, the confusion of different patterns, colors, and objects, and the irregular placement of furniture within a small space gives the rooms a chaotic appearance. The disordered effect is the result of "discord between partial orders, by the lack of orderly relations between them ... or a clash of uncoordinate order" (Arnheim 1977:170; see also Ruesch and Kees 1972:89–95). Each object is valued for itself, and relationships among objects and among the colors and designs of objects are either not comprehended or not perceived as significant.

Discussion

Taken together, Arrabal houses, though at times similar to other Vernacular ones, are more diverse in degree of completion, amount of space occupied, size, use, and, especially, quality of material and ornament. Most are actually simple structures that appear complex because of their seemingly unordered organization within crowded areas, combined with the intensity of their colors and patterns. This complexity may stem from a psychological need to displace actual deprivation through investment in intense aesthetic expression. Ar-

Figure 193. Interior, Arrabal House, Camuy.

Figure 194. *Sala* of Arrabal House, Arecibo.

rabal houses vie in status display within the *arrabal*, announcing the end of peonage with paint and the addition of a *balcón*. Each owner imposes his own order but draws upon conventions held in common. Such conventions not only unite the *arrabal* but function to socialize the community, mediating toward its eventual incorporation into the social mainstream. Through an indeterminate process of general consensus, some *arrabales* eventually become similar to other Vernacular neighborhoods and are incorporated into town plans. Then their colors gradually become more subdued as they shift to general Vernacular rules.

All Vernacular houses including Arrabal, and Jíbaro dwellings develop out of the social and aesthetic needs of residents, taking into account economic constraints which at times impose severe limitations. While all are less formal than Designed houses, they are not necessarily accessible. Ordering, which from the social point of view protects against disorder or chaos, is inherent in the conventions of Designed houses and in nineteenth-century town plans. Lack of formal definition, characteristic of many Vernacular structures for economic and technological reasons, is often overcome by the individual addition of controls—such pronounced and clearly marked signals of territoriality and status as intensity of decoration, bright colors, and even strong barriers. Thus, an inverse relationship exists between the degree of individually-imposed control and the level of community or social definition. Arrabal houses explicitly exemplify one extreme.

The fundamental disparity between the broad categories of Designed and Vernacular houses can be explained in terms of the different foci of householders' aspirations as well as the strategies employed to achieve them. Designed habitations conform in order to connote for the residents' elite status, that they belong to a superior segment of the total society. Vernacular houses are individualized within inchoate limits, to express a family's *dignidad* and establish its status in a particular local neighborhood. Though Designed houses do not conform totally and do express individual distinctions, clearly greater latitude for idiosyncracy is demanded of Vernacular houses. The latter appear to be misinterpretations or simplifications of Designed houses and are so construed (Kubler 1980). But this characteristic does not arise from a desire to meet and failure to copy elite standards correctly, but rather from the metonymical use of elements of the Designed vocabulary as specifically meaningful labels to indicate worthiness within the Vernacular neighborhood. The fact that Vernacular houses are assemblages of stylistic forms and features, rather than stylistically complete entities is an index of the self-definition of Vernacular house inhabitants. Disparity in aesthetic preference cannot be dismissed as another underlying factor. Still, the difference in final composition of houses can be interpreted as index of social level but not as measure of asethetic sensibility. Each group of householders has its own aesthetic standards and must be judged accordingly (see also Rapoport 1982:29–30).

Messages of territoriality, status, welcome and exclusion are differentially signaled by each house type, but the message emitters of Vernacular houses are far more idiosyncratic than those of Designed houses. Each group of houses is defined by its own standards of order, yet overall there seem to be pressures toward general norms. Moreover, Designed and Vernacular, though very different at the extremes, tend to come together when Designed houses are simple and Vernacular composed. As noted, older Designed houses sometimes turn into Vernacular, and their meaning of elite dies away as they become lower-class dwellings or rooming houses. More rarely, Vernacular is transformed through rehabilitation into Designed. The persistence and changing use of old types alongside current ones through such malleable accommodation is probably a modern phenomenon; in the past, the separation of classes was clearly delineated by stone, wood, and cane houses. The mediating relationships between Arrabal and Vernacular, Vernacular and Designed, further attest to social blending. The blending of social levels, as well as the disparities between Designed and Vernacular houses, are brought into sharper focus by an examination of Urbanización houses.

Urbanización Houses

Designed

Exterior Spatial Organization

In their exterior organization, Urbanización houses are similar to U.S. Influence houses, though less diverse than the latter in their suburban order of surrounding lawns and shrubbery. The territorial unit is a lot, standardized by size and, in long-established developments, usually marked by boundary fences, walls, trees, and hedges, which frequently also signal status messages. In newer developments, except for the rhythm of evenly spaced, uniformly sized houses, boundaries between houses are often undefined; indeed, distinctions between front, side, and back spaces are unclear, as each flows into the next. Houses are set back from the street, and their forward axes are not only weakened by the space between adjacent houses, but made ambiguous by entries through both an informal carport and a formal front door (figure 195). Moreover, many houses are oriented by usage to recreational or garden areas in back, a message of nonparticipatory separation or withdrawal, despite the public accessibility of the houses and their territories. Such an ill-defined spatial order must be taken as an index of neutrality with respect to interaction with outsiders. The neutrality is intrinsic to the design, leaving to each owner the decision to add indicators of territoriality, identity, and other modifications. Without them the neutrality of the Urbanización house conveys messages of disaffection and impermanence.

Figure 195. Front of Urbanización House, Luquillo.

Exterior Ornamentation

As a repertoire of finely carpentered ornaments—capitals, pilasters, scrollwork—was integral to each Criollo style, a contemporary one now exists for Urbanización houses, consisting of manufactured panels of imitation stone, tile, and brick; novelty ornaments; house numbers; door knockers; lights; and especially *rejas*. The stock, while generally consistent throughout the island, varies in design specifics according to development. Each has its own thematic quality, linked to supplier and contractor choices, no doubt, but also to resident preference. In a count of ornament and color on one street, each house was unlike any other, albeit within a very narrow range. Cream, white, gray, and olive, with varying shades of brown or black trim, comprised the colors. Facades contained broad expanses of contrasting materials: glass, painted concrete walls, and panels of imitation stone or tile.

Interior Spatial Organization

The standardized plans of Urbanización houses define private space, consisting of *dormitorios* and *baño*, by a separating hallway. Public space is imprecisely delineated, but interactions with visitors take place at front and side entrances, in the *sala*, and occasionally on the back patio or terrace. Urbanización houses generally lack *balcones* but incorporate large front picture windows, permitting residents to view the outside from within their domain and in turn be viewed. Actual interaction is thus distanced, in comparison with that afforded by Bungaloid style houses, for example. The *sala* may be an informal living room in some homes or, in others, a place where formal visits take place, the location for family gatherings having shifted to the back terrace.

Interior Ornamentation

Urbanización interiors are painted in neutral colors like those in U.S. Influence houses. Proportionately fewer but more varied objects are chosen for personal enjoyment, to reflect the interests or hobbies of residents, and as stereotypical "correct" possessions. In the *salas* of professionals, who often reside in Urbanización houses, there are books and musical instruments and also special collections such as pre-Columbian ceramics, antique china, shells, or other natural objects.

Vernacular

Exterior Spatial Organization

When constructed, Vernacular Urbanizacón houses differ from Designed ones mainly in size and quality. More regimented in design and spatial arrangement and lacking stylistically differentiating ornamental features, the Vernacular buildings are generally even more neutral. Homeowners immediately introduce walls, gates, and plantings into the surrounding vacant property, to signal territoriality and identity (figures 196a–c). The raised garden in front of the house in figure 142b is an explicit message of territoriality as well as identity.

a.

b.

c.

Figures 196a–c. Facade Variation of Three Urbanización Houses with the Same Plan, Luquillo.

Messages of pride in house ownership, in personal creativity, and in economic status are also signaled—characterstics appropriate to a man deserving of *respeto*.

Exterior Ornamentation

Horror vacui seems to characterize the many residents of government-supported developments who are impelled to fill an empty front yard with arrangements of purchased statuary (costing $15 to $50 or more each), painted rocks, and pools (figure 197), and to define boundaries with elaborate walls and gate entrances (figures 198a–c). It is possible that the neutrality of Vernacular Urbanización houses is intolerable to Puerto Rican residents. But exterior ornament also asserts ownership. In conversation, Urbanización house owners remarked that nothing was more important than owning a house: "Those plain houses over there, they're just rented; the government owns them. Those houses with gardens, trees, walls, and so forth, belong to the people who live in them." In a Vernacular neighborhood, external ornament signals the key message of house ownership. The property owner has the right to modify and decorate his own home. His selections reveal his status and, above all, differentiate his house from his neighbor's.

Interior Spatial Organization

Vernacular Urbanización house interiors generally follow the plan of the house as built, with modification confined to carport remodeling. The renovation usually transforms the carport space into a family room/*comedor* adjacent to the kitchen, and leaves the *sala* as a more formal living room. In *salas* one finds the same sets of plastic upholstered furniture, in contemporary North American arrangements or pushed against the walls, as noted above.

Interior Ornamentation

As in other Vernacular houses, emphasis is placed on the novelty or aesthetic attractivenes of all religious, family, and ornamental items.

Figure 197. Front Yard, Urbanización House, Luquillo.

Discussion

Although the introduction of Urbanización style has brought about a convergence of Designed and Vernacular houses, disparities between the two catagories continue. Originally intended to replace *arrabal* habitations, Urbanización houses are an externally imposed form of popular architecture which is essentially neutral in content or has superficial or stereotypical meaning, like a greeting card (Kaplan 1972). Based on technology rather than cultural norms, they are fundamentally neither Designed nor Vernacular architecture but prepackaged neutral designs constructed in artificial settings. Yet the neutrality is taken to be an asset by a wide variety of people of the middle- and upper-middle social level with diverse aspirations, who either accept Urbanización houses at the simplest level as built or take advantage of the practicality and create their own preferred ambiance. Since so many Puerto Ricans reside in the same type of house, status must depend on address in locale or neighborhood, and identity on discriminating exterior ornamentation. Urbaniza-

MESSAGES AND MEANINGS 257

Figure 198a. *Rejas*, Privately-Constructed Urbanización House, Boquerón.

Figure 198b. Modifications to Urbanización House, Luquillo. Note *Balcón* addition and wall built of decorative concrete blocks.

Figure 198c. Front Extension on Urbanización House, Luquillo. Note *rejas* enclosures on all openings, including the garage.

ción houses are modified to meet the myths and aspirations of inhabitants (Hubka 1980:70).

Despite their sameness, Designed and Vernacular Urbanización houses differ in appearance and therefore ostensibly in meaning, as do other Designed and Vernacular house types.

At the outset Designed Urbanización houses are chosen for the appeal of their facades, which are differentiated by color and stylistically related ornament—Spanish Colonial Revival or International Style. Certain connotations of elite attach to Designed houses so only relatively discreet modifications are made. Such houses generally conform to established standards, which follow Latin American more than United States mainland architectural designs. The meaning of modernity, with ramifications arising from the technology, appearance, and United States origin of Urbanización style, is attached to these houses. The importance given to this meaning is probably an overriding reason for the acceptance of Urbanización houses.

Vernacular Urbanización houses also signify modernity. But *dignidad* and the respectability acquired through ownership are more fundamental meanings. Thus such houses are ostentatiously distinguished from each other with diverse exterior embellishment. Vernacular Urbanización house messages of status and identity are directed to the local neighborhood. The degree of investment reveals them to be prime conveyors of status messages.

The general architectural equivalence of Urbanización houses implies a democratic merging of social levels; the essentially vacuous decoration, orientation of the populace toward the present (see also Sánchez 1980); and the variation, the value placed on individuality. The following observation is partially true of Puerto Rican Urbanización houses: "The old preoccupation with meanings and messages, with emotional signs and signals ... is giving way. What matters now is appearance for its own sake" (Frazier 1982:116).

Urbanización houses are fundamentally unifying, colloquial expressions of Puerto Rican as well as personal identity. They state in Puerto Rican terms the significance of the house to each family and also proclaim the family's status and identity within Puerto Rican society. Their general affinity with Latin American and divergence from United States development styles specifically underline their role in confirming Puerto Ricanness (see also Acevedo 1983:26).

Conclusions

Reading the messages of Puerto Rican houses has brought out a cumulation of meanings. Differences in meanings, according to social level, have proved to be more a matter of degree than kind, far less disparate than the modes of expression. The totality of meanings associated with each house type had not been penetrated, but the range and variation of social meanings have emerged.

Despite differences, for the majority of houses, home seems to be the primary meaning. Home signifies a locus, the place where one feels at home, where one belongs, and, for Puerto Ricans especially, where family is (see also Tuan 1984). In Spanish the word for home is *hogar* (literally, hearth), connoting the primal significance of haven. However, *casa* (house), also signifies home, as in the phrase, *Estás en tu casa* ("Make yourself at home," or literally, "You are in your house"), connoting shelter and also possession. Jíbaro and some Arrabal dwellings may contain few meanings beyond the fundamental ones conveyed by *casa* and *hogar*, but most houses are endowed with these and many more. The majority of Puerto Rican houses were intentionally built not only for shelter, but also to display, through possession of property, the owners' worth, family status, *dignidad*, and identity. Furthermore, simultaneously houses condense for the householder myriad family and community meanings which confirm self-identity. The striking individuality of every Puerto Rican house testifies to the importance of its dual function. The number of single-family houses further underscores the point that owning one's own house and distinguishing it from every other are paramount aspirations for the majority of Puerto Ricans. The old proverb, *Mi casa y mi hogar cien dobles val* ("My house and my home are worth a hundredfold"), denotes the value set on possession of one's own house. Yet the individuality that expresses this meaning also conveys by its schema cultural attachment to Puerto Rico. This attachment is typically manifested by varied colors, as well as by the decorative patterns of Colonial Spanish, Caribbean Criollo, Early Gothic gingerbread, contemporary *rejas*, concrete block designs, and Urbanización ornament.

Examination and analysis of Puerto Rican houses and their meanings have led to a few answers to the questions posed at the outset of the study and at the beginning of this chapter. Finally, the existence of different types of Puerto Rican houses, whether introduced or indigenous, and their social fit, have always depended on their selection as suitable habitations by particular individuals, according to cultural and personal preferences. Leaving aside the many Puerto Ricans living by choice or necessity in multifamily structures who have been excluded from this study, currently the requirements of some Puerto Ricans are best met by older houses as originally built or rehabilitated; of others, by contemporary houses. The resulting differentiation of each house, by type and individualization, presumes relationships among them and thereby reinforces the social order (see also Rapoport 1982:191). The dispersal of the Puerto Rican people into many different house types, a kind of template of the society, thus confirms the social order and displays its history, which is reinterpreted anew by each generation (Jencks 1980:86) and also continues to shape the future.

Notes

Introduction

1. Regrettably, because of foreign residence I was unaware of Rapoport's 1982 publication, *The Meaning of the Built Environment*, before completing this book. I was pleased to discover that, although the terminology differs, the approach of this analysis is in general agreement with his views.

Chapter 1

1. From Henri Focillon, *The Life of Forms in Art* (New York, Wittenborn Schultz, 1948).

2. Unless otherwise noted, the historical information in this chapter is based primarily on Salvador Brau, *Historia de Puerto Rico* (Río Piedras, Editorial Edil, 1973); and Eugenio Fernández Méndez, *Historia Cultural de Puerto Rico, 1493–1968* (San Juan, Ediciones El Cemi, 1971), pp. 119–178 and 323–42 in particular.

3. Bo-jio was appropriated to signify "territory of the master" in the northern part of Santo Domingo. It was also the term for the hut where the Indian and his family sheltered. The radical "bo" = large was opposed to the radical "bi" = small in Indo-Antillano language (Cayetano Coll y Toste, *Colón en Puerto Rico* [1893], p. 134).

4. Some of the works that discuss the controversies surrounding source material on Columbus's second voyage include by Guillermo Estévez Volkers, *Tarjeto-Historico* (Madrid, Gráficas R. Manzanares, 1960) and its Apéndice (1964), and José González Ginorio, *Suplemento Bibliográfico* ("El Discubrimiento de Puerto Rico") (San Juan, 1938). Discussion of the reliability of Fernando Colón can be found in Manuel Serrano y Sanz's introduction to Fernando Colón, *Historia del Almirante de Las Indias Don Cristóbal Colón* (Buenos Aires, Ed. Bajel, 1944, pp. 7–15). The reliability of both Fernando Colón and Bartolomé de Las Casas is discussed in Samuel Eliot Morison, *The European Discovery of America: The Southern Voyages* (New York, Oxford University Press, 1974, p. 19–20). Descriptions of Puerto Rico by Las Casas and Fernando Colón follow:

Salieron en tierra algunos cristianos y fueron a unas casas por muy bien artificio hechas todas, empero, de paja y madera, que tenían una plaza con camino, desde ella hasta el mar, muy limpio y seguido, hecho como una calle, y las paredes de canas cruzadas o tejidas, y por lo alto también con sus verduras graciosas, como si fueran parras, o verjeles de naranjos o cidras, como los hay en Valencia o en Barcelona; y junto al mar estaba un miradero alto, donde podían caber diez o doce personas, en la misma manera bien labrado; debía ser casa de placer del señor de aquella isla, o de aquella parte della (Las Casas, taken from Pérez Chanis 1976:7).

... despues aporto a la isla que llamo San Juan Bautista, que los indios llamaban Boriquen, y surgio con la armada en una canal de ella a Occidente, donde pescaron muchos peces, algunos como los nuestros, y vieron halcones y parras silvestres; y mas hacia Levante fueron unos cristianos a ciertas casas de indios que segun su costumbre estaban bien fabricadas, las cuales tenian la plaza y la salida hasta el mar y la calle muy larga, con torres de cana a ambas partes, y lo alta estaba tejido con bellisimas labores de plantas y yerbas como estan en Valencia los jardines, y lo ultimo hacia el mar era un tablado en que cabian diez o doce personas, alto y bien labrado (F. Colon 1944:128).

5. Captain Gonzalo Fernández Fernandez de Oviedo y Valdes described *caney* construction in *Historia* Natural de las Indias. Asunción, Paraguay, Editorial Guaranía, [1946]. Tomo I, Libro 5, Capitulo 12 pp. 293–94:

Hincaban muchos postes á la redonda de buena madera, y de la groseza (cada uno) conviniente, y en circuyto á quatro ó çinco passos el un poste del otro, ó en el espaçio que querian que oviesse de poste á poste: é sobre ellos, despues de hincados en tierra por ençima de las cabeças, en lo alto pónenles sus soleras, é sobre aquellas ponen en torno la varaçon (que es la templadura para la cubierta), las cabezas ó grueso de las varas sobre las soleras que es dicho, é lo delgado para arriba, donde todas las puntas de las varas se juntan é resumen en punta, á manera de pabellón. E sobre las varas ponen de través cañas, ó latas de palmo á palmo (ó menos), de dos en dos (ó sencillas), é sobre aquesto cubren de paja delgada é luenga: otros cubren con hojas de *bihaos*: otros con cogollos de cañas; otros con hojas de palmas y tambien con otras cosas. En lo baxo, en lugar de paredes desde la solera á tierra, de poste á poste, ponen cañas hincadas en tierra, someras é tan juntas, como los dedos de la mano juntos; é una á par de otra haçen pared, é atanlos muy bien con *bexucos*, que son unas venas ó correas redondas que se crían revueltas á los arboles (y tambien colgando dellos) como la corehuela: los quales bexucos son muy buena atadur, porque son flexibles é taxables, é no se pudren, é sirven de clavaçon é ligaçon en lugar de cuerdas y de clavos para atar un madero con otro, é para atar las cañas assi mismo. El buhio ó casa de tal manera fecho, llamasse *caney*.

6. Buildings of the first city founded by Columbus in 1493 were excavated in 1983 in Isabela del Castillo, Dominican Republic. The archeologists found that the early Spanish residents lived in conditions similar to those of the Taino (Estrella de Panama, 13 Oct. 1983:B–16).

7. The first colonists came mostly from Andalusia and Estremadura. The lower-class Iberian house, familiar to most of Puerto Rico's early population, consisted of a one-story two- or three-room dwelling, built of adobe in the south of Spain, and of stone in the north with either a thatched or tile roof depending on the owner's resources. Later migrants probably brought knowledge of the Renaissance house, a larger structure which followed the Roman plan of four sections around a central patio (A. H. de Oliveira Marqués, *Daily Life in Portugal in the Late Middle Ages* [Madison Univ. of Wisconsin Press, 1971], pp.

8. The term *jíbaro* currently signifies primarily a folkloric personage who represents an idealization or symbol of Puerto Rican characteristics. *Jíbaro* dances, music, and poetry have become part of Puerto Rico's folkloric presentations (see also Ramon Luis Acevedo in *The Hispanic American Aesthetic*, 1983). The term *jíbaro* also still refers to rustics from mountain areas, although there is little recognition of their continued existence.

9. A drawing by R.P. Breton of houses of escaped slaves on Guadeloupe (*Relations de l'Ile de la Guadeloupe* [Basse-Terre, Societé d'Histoire de la Guadeloupe, 1978]) shows them built on the ground of wood, cane, and thatch, and grouped together in two rows on either side of an open space in front of a larger two-story wood, cane and thatch building (*Kaz Antiye Jan Moun Ka Rete, Caribbean Popular Dwelling*, ed. J. Berthelot and M. Gaume [Guadeloupe, Ed. Perspectives Creoles, 1983], p. 12).

10. Thomas Jefferys' compilation of various memoirs probably dating from the seventeenth or early eighteenth centuries (*A Description of the Spanish Islands and Settlements on the Coast of the West Indies* [London, 1762] pp. 95–97) has the following description of Puerto Rico and its people:

Called by its antient inhabitants Boriquen, was discovered by Columbus in the year 1493, but it cost the Spaniards a great deal of trouble to reduce it, the inhabitants being a brave gallant people, and extremely fond of liberty. They however succeeded at last, and not only conquered, but extirpated the natives. . . . The rains which generally render the season unhealthful fall in June, July, and August, when the weather would otherwise be extremely hot. The soil, which is beautifully diversified, is extremely fertile, abounding with fine meadows, well stocked with wild cattle, which were brought originally from Spain. . . . The sides of the hills are covered with trees of various kinds, proper for building ships and other useful purposes: but its principal commodities for commerce are sugar, ginger, hides, cotton, thread, cassia, mastic, &. Great quantities of salt are also made on the island. . . . The number of inhabitants who are chiefly Mulatos at present on the island amount to about 10,000.

The genius of the people, and the convenient situation of this island would render it the most flourishing of all the Spanish colonies, if some great inconveniences did not keep the people under. There are principally three; great droughts . . . hurricanes . . . and the descent of privateers.

The capital of the island [San Juan] . . . is the see of a bishop; large, and well built; though the beauty of the city is greatly diminished by the canvas, or wooden lattice that they use instead of glass windows; they have no water, except rain, which they preserve in cisterns.

This place is better inhabited than most Spanish cities, being the center of the contraband trade carried on by the English and French with the subjects of Spain, notwithstanding the severity of the laws.

11. A *jornalero* was defined by Governor López de Baños as any person free or freed, who had neither property, profession, nor position by which to live. A *jornalero* was obliged to work as a hired hand for some employer. Among the issues leading to the passing of laws compelling all landless unemployed to work on local plantations were the scarcity of slaves, the abundance of free land available to the landless, and the "high" cost of labor. Workers had to carry workbooks recording their services, to be maintained by plantation owners. Forced labor laws ended in 1873. This discussion draws on Sidney W. Mintz, *Caribbean Transformations* (Chicago, Aldine, 1974), pp. 88–101 in particular.

12. José Gómez Brioso, "La Casa del Pobre," in *Conferencias Dominicales dadas en la Biblioteca Insular de Puerto Rico*, vol. 2 (San Juan, 12 Oct. 1913–19 Apr. 1914), pp. 254–77, records not only the overcrowded and unhealthful conditions of the poor at the time, but also the exact dimensions and number of inhabitants of many slum buildings. The space of 331 habitations encompassed less than 32 cubic meters; 875, less than 64 cubic meters; and 751, approximately 64 cubic meters. Most of these dwellings were occupied by large families. Here are examples of specific relationships between inhabitants and dwellings called *ranchones*:

Dimensions	No. of Apartments	No. of Inhabitants
1. 72 x 26 ft.	12	56
2. 86 x 37 ft.	16	64
3. 57 x 128 ft.	51	212

13. The term "Urbanización" is capitalized and not italicized when it refers to the style of houses that are mass-manufactured at development sites and others resembling them, including owner-built structures of cement block or wooden ones transformed by cement. The word is italicized when used to signify a housing development.

Chapter 2

1. The Puerto Rican house is characterized as comprised of a varying number of modular spaces (rooms) in J. Berthelot and M. Gaume, eds. *Kaj. Antiye Jan Moun Ka Rete: Caribbean Popular Dwelling* (Guadeloupe, Ed. Perspectives Creoles 1982) pp. 13–24.

2. Plans are not scale drawings but are based on informal sketches made at the time of a visit. Because it was not always possible to view an entire house, some rooms are not identified.

3. "Spanish-Criollo" is a stylistic designation which includes houses built both during this period and subsequently.

4. "Grand" is the term used to identify more elaborate, more refined, or very large Designed houses.

5. Judging by examples seen in Central and South American countries as well as Puerto Rico, the plans of Spanish houses differed somewhat in size and number of rooms, but were alike in the arrangement of rooms around or along the side of one or more interior patios.

6. The kitchen was set apart to keep smoke, heat, the smell of cooking, and the danger of fire away from the main house.

7. *Zaguán*, a word of Arab derivation, signifies portico, doorway, lobby, carriage entrance. As applied to Puerto Rican architecture, it means the arcade entry leading to a shop or shops on the ground level of a House and Tienda.

8. The term "needs" is used broadly here to signify not only the basic requirements of shelter, but also aspects of personal preference and satisfaction. Psychosocial needs for human development include security, equity, participation, and individuation (Michael Maccoby, "Human Development in Villages," in *Village Viability in Contemporary Society*, ed. Priscilla Copeland Reining and Barbara Lenkerd [Boulder, Colo., Westview, 1980], pp. 315–32). Houses can fulfill specific needs for shelter and security in a hostile environment, and may express degrees of equity and participation experi-

enced by inhabitants. The house also is an instrument for expressing individuation or creative work.

9. The term "Vernacular Urbanización," seems to combine conflicting terms, but it refers to the individualized modification to Urbanización houses that is characteristic of *urbanizaciones* occupied by middle-class people who formerly lived in Vernacular or Arrabal houses.

10. There are approximately 1500 inhabitants and 500 dwellings in all of La Parguera. The buildings on the water have no rights to the land (Jorge Menéndez Pérez, "La Parguera" [student paper, School of Architecture, University of Puerto Rico, Rio Piedras, n.d.]). The pollution resulting from the discharge of sewage directly into the bay destroys fish and other marine organisms, so further building has been prohibited, and all water house property will eventually revert to the government.

11. According to P.B. Vásquez Calcerrada (personal communication), the advantages of locating *arrabales* near or on bodies of water include access to water supply, resources such as fish and other aquatic animals, and sewage disposal.

Chapter 3

1. Information is an abstract property of things and events. Each kind of information that a referent (thing or event) provides is a message. The study of messages is concerned only with the kinds of information that are shared among users or participants of referents. Nonbehavioral displays (presentations of information) provide information about the identity of the communicator, the kinds of groups of which it is a member, and its location. Providing information includes the idea of prediction, in the sense that in the course of analysis a pattern emerges that enables the prediction of behavior (W. John Smith, *The Behavior of Communicating: An Ethological Approach* [Cambridge, Mass., Harvard Univ. Press, 1977], pp. 69–73).

2. Bonta lists several other terms which fall outside the scope of this investigation. *Intentional indexes* are indicators which are deliberately used to communicate, but are not recognized as such by an interpreter; *pseudo-signals* are indicators which are believed by the interpreter to have been deliberately produced by an emitter to communicate, but which were not.

3. A family that had resided for more than ten years in an *arrabal* near Martín Peña canal was forced to move because the *arrabal* was being destroyed. Although the adjacent house had been moved away, and time was running out, the family members were unable to act. They could not bring themselves to face a future in a different house, without familiar neighbors and community networks. They had the choice of selling their house to

the government for approximately $50, or dismantling it and moving it to another location. If they chose to sell, they could move to a government-supported multistoried housing development or rent a rundown house. Even though the daughter had saved enough money from her work in New York for the down payment on a government-supported Urbanización house, the family lacked the employment qualifications.

4. Konrad Lorenz observed in "The Function of Colour in Coral Reef Fishes," *Proceedings of the Royal Institute of Great Britain* 39: 282–96, that the diverse and brilliant color of coral reef fishes was a means of signaling territoriality. The color of *arrabal* houses apparently has a similar function.

5. Robert F. Thompson (personal communication) has noted the importance of blue among Yoruba in both Africa and the Western hemisphere. In many Caribbean countries, blue is believed to ward off evil spirits.

6. In Colonial Spanish houses, there was an entrance area or front courtyard where uninvited visitors were received and which blocked off the private areas beyond.

7. Modern bathrooms, with tub or shower, washbasin, and toilet, became a part of upper-class houses around 1890–1900. Latrines in back of the houses were common until after 1940. Many Country and Arrabal houses have running water but not sewerage.

8. In early Colonial Spanish houses, following Andalusian custom which derived from Moorish tradition, a dais of brick or adobe, covered with rugs and furnished with low tables and stools, was located at one end of the *sala* for the women of the house. If these furnishings existed in Puerto Rico, they were not seen, but larger antique chairs used by men occur in a few houses.

9. *Rejas*—the metal grillwork used to screen and enclose *balcones*, carports, and windows—are made in multiple geometric and curvilinear patterns and are painted black or white. They are purchased in sections, so mixed or matched patterns can be installed according to homeowner preference. Used for protection against intrusion, they are also considered essential for the display of status and *dignidad* in many neighborhoods. Their complex lacy patterns transform many otherwise simple Vernacular houses.

10. In essence, complexity signifies density of information. Too much—that is, too many unpredictable things going on to be immediately processed—causes "overload" or lack of comprehension. Reduction of complexity is achieved either by changing the stimuli through organization or by simplifying through homogeneity (Berlyne 1966: Rapoport 1977). The diverse architectural features of Criollo Neoclassic and Beaux Arts houses are defined formally by hierarchical organization; the homogeneity of the simple geometric forms of Colonial Spanish and U.S. Influence houses defines them. The complexity of Vernacular and Arrabal houses arises from their lack of order.

Bibliography

Acevedo, Ramón Luis
   1983   Toward an Aesthetic of Hispanic-American Literature: A Puerto Rican Point of View. *In* The Hispanic American Aesthetic: Origins, Manifestations, and Significance, 23–26. San Antonio, Tex.: Research Center for the Arts and Humanities.

Alegría, Ricardo E.
   n.d.   El Instituto de Cultura Puertorriqueña 1955–1973. San Juan: Instituto de Cultura Puertorriqueña.
   1975   Los dibujos de Puerto Rico de naturalista Frances Augusto Plee (1821–1823). Revista del Instituto de Cultura Puertorriqueña 18 (68): 20–41.
   1978   Apuntes en Torno a la Mitología de los Indios Taínos de las Antilles Mayores y sus Orígenes Suramericanos. San Juan, Puerto Rico: Centro de Estudios Avanzados de Puerto Rico y El Caribe: Museo del Hombre Dominicano.

Alfonso, Guillermo
   1975   Viaje de Estudios in Puerto Rico. Student Paper No. 60. School of Architecture, University of Puerto Rico, Río Piedras.

Alonso, Manuel A.
   1974   El Jíbaro. Barcelona: Editorial Vogos, S.A. [First published in 1849.]

Anderson, E.N.
   1972   On the Folk Art of Landscaping. Western Folklore 31:179–88.

Anderson, Wayne V.
    1977   Perception and Expression in Art and Environmental Design. "Course notes in authors possession, spring semester. Harvard University.

Anonymous
    n.d.   Color in Architecture: Plan of Investigation. Student Paper No. 145. School of Architecture, University of Puerto Rico, Rio Piedras.

Arias Peña, Etanislao, and Eduvigis Martínez Arroyo
    1981   El Habitat Rural en Panamá. Panama: Panamá Talleres Diálogo.

Arnheim, Rudolf
    1971   Art and Visual Perception. Berkeley: Univ. of California Press.
    1977   The Dynamics of Architectural Form. Berkeley: Univ. of California Press.

Arquitecture Vernacular
    1980   Cuadernos de Arquitectura y Conservacion del Patrimonio Artístico. No. 10. Mexico City.

Ashcraft, Norman, and Albert E. Scheflen
    1976   People Space: The Making and Breaking of Human Boundaries. Garden City, N.Y.: Anchor Books.

Bachelard, Gaston
    1964   The Poetics of Space. Boston: Beacon Press.

Badillo Veiga, Américo
    n.d.   Los Estudios de las Migraciones Internas en Puerto Rico: Apuntes Para Una Crítica. Manuscript. Río Piedras: Universidad de Puerto Rico, Facultad de Ciencias Sociales.

Barth, Frederick, ed.
    1969   Ethnic Groups and Boundaries. Boston: Little, Brown.

Bateson, Gregory
    1972   Steps to an Ecology of Mind. New York: Ballantine.

Becker, Franklin
    1977   Housing Messages. Stroudsburg, Pa.: Dowden, Hutchinson, and Ross.

Bennett, Corwin
    1977   Spaces for People: Human Factors in Design. Englewood Cliffs, N.J.: Prentice-Hall.

Bennett, J.W., ed.
    1975   The New Ethnicity: Perspective from Ethnology (Proceedings of the American Ethnological Society). St. Paul, Minn.: West.

Berlyne, D.E.
    1958   The Influence of Complexity and Novelty in Visual Figures on Orienting Response. Journal of Experimental Psychology 55: 289–96.

    1966   Conflict and Arousal. Scientific American 215:82–87.
Berthelot, J., and M. Gaume, eds.
    1982   Kaz Antiye Jan Moun Ka Rete: Caribbean Popular Dwelling Guadeloupe, Edicions Perspectives Creoles.
Bloomer, Kent C., and Charles W. Moore
    1977   Body, Memory, and Architecture. New Haven: Yale Univ. Press.
Bonta, Juan Pablo
    1979   Architecture and Its Interpretation. New York: Rizzoli.
    1980   Architectural Semiotics: The State of the Art. In Meunier 1980, 8–13.
    1980   Notes for a Theory of Meaning in Design. In Geoffrey Broadbent, Richard Burt, and Charles Jencks 1980, 275–310.
Boorstin, Daniel J.
    1958   The Americans: The Colonial Experience. New York: Vintage.
Boza D., Christián, and Hernán Duval V.
    1982   Inventario de una Arquitectura Anónima. Santiago de Chile: Editorial Lord Cochrane.
Brau, Salvador
    1973   Historia de Puerto Rico. Río Piedras: Editorial Edil.
Braudel, Fernand
    1973   The Mediterranean and the Mediterranean World in the Age of Philip II. 2 vols. New York: Harper and Row.
Brioso, José Gómez
    1914   La Casa del Pobre, 1914. In Conferencias Dominicales dadas en la Biblioteca Insular de Puerto Rico. Vol. 2 (12 Oct. 1913–19 Apr. 1914), pp. 254–77. San Juan.
Broadbent, Geoffrey; Richard Burt; and Charles Jencks, eds.
    1980   Signs, Symbols, and Architecture. New York: Wiley.
Brolin, Brent C., and John Zeisel
    1968   Mass Housing: Social Research and Design. Architectural Forum, 129 (1):66–71.
Brooklyn Institute of Arts and Sciences
    1979   The American Renaissance, 1876–1917. Exhibition catalog.
Brown-Manrique, Gerardo
    1980   Searching for Clues in History: The Primitive Hut and Beyond. In Meunier 1980, 128–37.
Brunskill, R.W.
    1978   Illustrated Handbook of Vernacular Architecture. London: Faber and Faber.
Bryce-Laporte, Roy Simon
    1970   Urban Relocation and Family Adaptation in Puerto Rico: A Case Study in Urban Ethnography. In Peasants in Cities. William Mangin, ed., 85–97. Boston: Houghton Mifflin.

Buisseret, David
    1980   Historic Architecture of the Caribbean. London: Heineman.

Buitrago Ortiz, Carlos
    1972   La Percepción de la Desigualdad en una Comunidad Campesina en Puerto Rico. *In* Rafael L. Ramírez, Barry B. Levine, and Carlos Buitrago Ortiz, 1972, 77–95.
    1973   Esperanza: An Ethnographic Study of a Peasant Community in Puerto Rico. Tucson: Univ. of Arizona Press. Viking Fund Publications in Anthropology No. 56.

Cadilla de Martínez, María
    1937   La Campesina de Puerto Rico. Rptd. *in* Eugenio Fernández Méndez 1975, 653–65.

Canino, Marcelino
    1976   El Folklore en Puerto Rico. *In* La Gran Enciclopedia de Puerto Rico. Vol. 12, pp. 3–18. San Juan: Puerto Rico en La Mano y La Gran Enciclopedia de Puerto Rico. Publicado Madrid, Spain, C. Corridera.

Carroll, Henry K. (Special Commissioner for the United States to Porto Rico)
    1899   Report on the Island of Porto Rico . . . Respectfully Submitted to the Hon. William McKinley, President of the United States. Oct. 6, 1899. Washington, D.C.: U.S. Government Printing Office.

Carver, Norman F., Jr.
    1981   Iberian Villages: Portugal and Spain. Kalamazoo, Mich.: Documan Press.

Centro de Estudios Puertorriqueñas, City University of New York. Conferencia De Historiografía.
    1976   Los Puertorriqueñas y La Cultura: Critica y Debate.

Centrón, Celia F. de, and Barry B. Levine
    1972   Quienes son los Pobres en Puerto Rico? *In* Rafael Ramírez, Barry B. Levine, and Carlos Buitrago Ortiz 1972, 9–28.

Child, Irvin L., and Leon Siroto
    1971   BaKwele and American Aesthetic Evaluations Compared. *In* Art and Aesthetics in Primitive Societies. C.F. Jopling, ed., 271–89. New York: Dutton.

Cohen, Abner
    1976   Two-Dimensional Man: An Essay on the Anthropology of Power and Symbolism in Complex Society. Berkeley: Univ. of California Press.

Coll y Toste, Cayetano
    1893   Colón en Puerto Rico. Puerto Rico: Tipografía al vapor de la correspondencia, 1893.

Colón, Fernando
   1944   Historia del Almirante de Las Indias Don Cristóbal Colón. Buenos Aires: Editorial Bajel.

Cooper, Clare
   1974   The House as Symbol of the Self. *In* Designing for Human Behavior. Jon Lang, et al., eds., 130–46. Stroudsburg, Pa.: Dowden, Hutchinson, and Ross.

Cordasco, Francesco
   1973   The Puerto Ricans, 1493–1973. Dobbs Ferry, N.Y.: Oceana.

Cowgill, George L.
   1977   Review of "Spatial Analysis in Archaeology" by Ian Hodder and Clive Orton. *Science* 196:972–3.

Cripps, L.L.
   1974   Puerto Rico: The Case for Independence. Cambridge, Mass.: Schenkman.

Deetz, James
   1977   In Small Things Forgotten: The Archaeology Early American Life. Garden City, N.Y.: Doubleday.

Delgado, Osiris
   1978   Mi Bohío. San Juan: Ramallo Bros. Printing.

Doll, Larry A.
   1980   Morphologies: A Theory and Case Study in Design Education. *In* Meunier 1980, 173–98.

Douglas, Mary
   1966   Purity and Danger. London: Routledge and Kegan Paul.
   1975   Implicit Meanings. London: Routledge and Kegan Paul.

Downs, Anthony
   1977   The Impact of Housing Policies on Family Life in the United States since World War II. Daedalus, 106 (2): 163–80.

Downs, Roger M., and David Stea
   1973   Image and Environment. Chicago: Aldine.

Doxiadis, C.A.
   1976   How Can We Learn About Man and His Settlements? *In* Amos Rapoport 1976, 77–117.

Eco, Umberto
   1979   A Theory of Semiotics. Bloomington: Univ. of Indiana Press.
   1980   Function and Sign: The Semiotics of Architecture. *In* Geoffrey Broadbent, Richard Burt, and Charles Jencks, 1980, 11–69.

Edwards, Jay
   1980   The Evolution of Vernacular Architecture in the Western Caribbean. *In* Cultural Traditions and Caribbean Identity: The Question of Patrimony. S. Jeffrey K. Wilkerson, ed., 291–339. Gainesville Center for Latin American Studies, University of Florida.

Fernández, James W.
    1976   Fang Architectonics. Philadelphia: ISHI. Working Papers in the Traditional Arts, 1.
    1977   Symbolic Anthropology Evolving. Reviews in Anthropology 4:132–41.

Fernández de Oviedo y Valdés, Gonzalo
    1959   Historia General y Natural de Las Indias. Edición y Estudio Preliminar de Juan Pérez de Tudela Bueso. Madrid, Ediciones Atlas.

Fernández Méndez, Eugenio
    1970   La Identidad y La Cultura: Críticas y Valoraciones en Torno a Puerto Rico. 2d ed. San Juan: Ediciones El Cemi.
    1971   Historia Cultural de Puerto Rico, 1493–1968. San Juan: Ediciones El Cemi.
    1972   (ed.) Portrait of a Society. Río Piedras: Univ. of Puerto Rico Press.
    1975   (ed.) Antología del Pensamiento Puertorriqueño. Rio Piedras: Editorial Universitaria.
    1979   Arte y Mitología de los Indios Taínos de las Antillas Mayores. San Juan: Ediciones El Cemi.

Figueroa, Loida
    1976   Breve Historia de Puerto Rico. Rev. ed. Rio Piedras: Editorial Edil.

Firth, Raymond
    1973   Symbols: Public and Private. Ithaca, N.Y.: Cornell Univ. Press.

Fletcher, Sir Banister
    1975   History of Architecture. London: Athlone.

Flores, Jean
    1978   The Insular Vision: Pedreira's Interpretation of Puerto Rican Culture. New York: Centro de Estudios Puertorriqueños, City University of New York. Centro Working Papers, 1.

Focillon, Henri
    1948   *The Life of Forms in Art*. New York: Wittenborn Schultz.

Foley, Mary Mix
    1980   The American House. New York: Harper and Row, Colophon ed.

Foster, Donald W.
    1972   Housing in Low-Income Barrios in Latin America: Some Cultural Considerations. Paper presented at the 71st Annual Meeting of the American Anthropological Association, Toronto.

Frank-Paganacci, Jaime
  1976   Evocaciones y Semblanzas. Rio Piedras: Ediciones Edil.
Frascari, Marco
  1978   Ut Rhetorica Architectura: A Study of the Relationship Between Rhetorical Modes of Production and Architectural Design Production. Paper presented at the 3rd Annual Meeting of the Semiotic Society of America, Providence, R.I.
Fraser, Kennedy
  1982   Architectural Fashion. Part 1. New Yorker, 8 Nov., pp. 116–21.
Freedman, Jonathan L.
  1975   Crowding and Behavior. New York: Viking.
Fried, Marc, and Peggy Gleicher
  1961   Some Sources of Residential Satisfaction in an Urban Slum. Journal of the American Institute of Planners 27:305–15.
Friedl, Ernestine
  1964   Lagging Emulation. American Anthropologist 66:569–74.
Galíndez Suárez, Jesus de
  1969   Puerto Rico en Nueva York: Sociología de Una Immigración. Buenos Aires: Editorial Tiempo Contemporáneo.
Gamble, Robert S., and José Augusto Puig Ortiz
  1978   Puerto Plata: La Conservación de Una Ciudad; Inventario; Ensayo Histórico-Arquitectónico. Santo Domingo: Editora Alfa y Omega.
Gans, Herbert J.
  1962   The Urban Villagers. New York: Free Press.
Geertz, Clifford
  1966   Religion as a Cultural System. In Anthropological Approaches to the Study of Religion. Michael Banton, ed. London: Tavistock.
  1977   From the "Native's Point of View": On the Nature of Anthropological Understanding. In Symbolic Anthropology. J.L. Dolgin, D. Kemnitzer, and D.M. Schneider, eds., 480–92. New York: Columbia Univ. Press.
Glassie, Henry
  1968   Pattern in the Material Folk Culture of the Eastern United States. Philadelphia: Univ. of Pennsylvania Press.
  1975   Folk Housing in Middle Virginia. Knoxville: Univ. of Tennessee Press.
Gleason, Judith
  1975   Santería Bronx. New York: Atheneum.
Goffman, Erving
  1971   Relations in Public. New York: Harper and Row.

Gombrich, E.H.
    1963   Meditations on a Hobby Horse, or the Roots of Artistic Form. Greenwich, Conn.: New York Graphic Society.

González, Nancie L.
    1975   Patterns of Dominican Ethnicity. In J.W. Bennett 1975, 110–23.

González-Wippler, Migene
    1975   Santería. Garden City, N.Y.: Doubleday/Anchor.

Goodenough, Ward H.
    1970   Description and Comparison in Cultural Anthropology. Chicago: Aldine.

Goodwin, Leonard
    1976   Middle-Class Misperceptions of the High Life Aspirations and Strong Work Ethic Held by the Welfare Poor. In Urban Problems: Psychological Inquiries. Neil C. Kalt and Sheldon S. Zalkind, eds., 110–19. New York: Oxford Univ. Press.

Gosner, Pamela
    1982   Caribbean Georgian: The Great and Small Houses of the West Indies. Washington, D.C.: Three Continents Press.

Gowans, Alan
    1964   Images of American Living. New York: Lippincott.

Gulick, John
    1973   Urban Anthropology. In Handbook of Social and Cultural Anthropology. John J. Honigmann, ed., 979–1029. Chicago: Rand, McNally.

Hall, Edward T.
    1966   The Hidden Dimension. Garden City, N.Y.: Doubleday.

Harrisse, Henry
    1884   Christopher Colomb, son origine, sa vie, ses voyages, sa famille, & ses descendants. 2 vols. Paris: Ernest Leroux.

Hartman, Chester W.
    1976   Social Values and Housing Orientations. In Urban Problems: Psychological Inquiries. Neil C. Kalt and Sheldon S. Zalkind, eds., 155–68. New York: Oxford Univ. Press.

Harwood, Alan
    1977   Spiritist as Needed. New York: Wiley.

Hauberg, Clifford
    1974   Puerto Rico and the Puerto Ricans. New York: Twayne.

Hayward, D. Geoffrey
    1976   Home as an Environmental and Psychological Concept. Landscape 20:1–8.

Hernández, Ivan A.
    n.d.   La Plaza en Camuy. Student paper. School of Architecture, University of Puerto Rico, Rio Piedras.

Herrera, Antonio de
　1740　The General History of the Vast Continent and Islands of America Commonly Called the West Indies from the First Discovery There of . . . Capt. John Stevens, trans. Vol. 1, 2d ed. London: Wood and Woodward.

Hubka, Thomas C.
　1980　The Vernacular as Source: A Vernacular Point of View. *In* Meunier 1980, 67–72.

Ittelson, William, ed.
　1973　Environment and Cognition. New York: Seminar Press.

Jacques, John D.
　1980　Regional Dialects: The Charleston Single House. *In* Meunier 1980, 231–34.

Jefferys, Thomas, comp.
　1762　A Description of the Spanish Islands and Settlements on the Coast of the West Indies. London.

Jencks, Charles
　1980　The Architectural Sign. *In* Geoffrey Broadbent, Richard Burt, and Charles Jencks 1980, 71–118.

Johnson, Roberta Ann
　1980　Puerto Rico: Commonwealth or Colony? New York: Praeger.

Jones, Michael Owen
　1980　L.A. Add-ons and Re-dos: Renovation in Folk Art and Architectural Design. *In* Perspectives on American Folk Art. Ian M.G. Quimby and Scott T. Swank, eds., 325–63. New York: Norton.

Jopling, Carol F.
　1974　Aesthetic Behavior as an Adaptive Strategy. Paper presented at the 41st Congreso Internacional de Americanistas, Mexico City.

Kaplan, Abraham
　1972　The Aesthetics of the Popular Arts. *In* Modern Culture and the Arts. James B. Hall and Barry Ulanov, eds. 2d ed. Pp. 48–62. New York: McGraw-Hill.

Kimber, Clarissa T.
　1973　Spatial Patterning in the Dooryard Gardens of Puerto Rico. Geographical Review 63:6–26.

Kirk, Susan L., et al.
　1977　The Architecture of St. Charles Avenue. Gretna, La.: Pelican Press.

Kniffen, Fred B.
　1965　Folk Housing: Key to Diffusion. Annual of the Association of American Geographers 55:549–77.
　1974　Material Culture in the Geographic Interpretation of the Land-

scape. *In* The Human Mirror. Miles Richardson, ed., 252–67. Baton Rouge: Louisiana State Univ. Press.

Koss, Joan D.
   1975   Therapeutic Aspects of Puerto Rican Cult Practices. Psychiatry 38:160–71.

Kreitler, Hans, and Shulamith Kreitler
   1972   Psychology of the Arts. Durham, N.C.: Duke Univ. Press.

Kroeber, A.L.
   1963   Style and Civilizations. Berkeley: Univ. of California Press.

Kubler, George
   1963   The Shape of Time. New Haven: Yale Univ. Press.
   1980   The Arts: Fine and Plain. *In* Perspectives on American Folk Art. Ian M.G. Quimby and Scott T. Swank, eds., 234–46. New York: Norton.

Kushner, Gilbert
   1970   The Anthropology of Complex Societies. *In* Biennial Review of Anthropology 1969. Bernard J. Siegel, ed., 81–131. Stanford, Calif.: Stanford Univ. Press.

Landy, David
   1965   Tropical Childhood. New York: Harper and Row.

Lange, Yvonne
   1975   Santos: The Household Saints of Puerto Rico. Ph.D. diss. Univ. of Pennsylvania, Graduate School of Arts and Sciences.

Leach, Edmund
   1872   The Influence of Cultural Context on Non-Verbal Communication in Man. *In* Non-Verbal Communication. R.A. Hinde, ed., 315–44. Cambridge, Eng.: Cambridge Univ. Press.

Leavitt, Ruby Rohrlich
   1974   The Puerto Ricans: Culture Change and Language Deviance. Tucson: Univ. of Arizona Press. Viking Fund Publications in Anthropology No. 51.

Leiding, Harriette K.
   1921   Historic Houses of South Carolina. Philadelphia: Lippincott.

Leone, Mark P.
   1973   Archeology as the Science of Technology: Mormon Town Plans and Fences. *In* Research and Theory in Current Archeology. Charles Redman, ed., 125–50. New York: Wiley.

Lévi-Strauss, Claude
   1979   Myth and Meaning. New York: Schocken.

Lewis, Gordon K.
   1983   Main Currents in Caribbean Thought. Baltimore: Johns Hopkins Univ. Press.

Lewis, Oscar
   1965   La Vida. New York: Random House.
   1966   The Culture of Poverty. Scientific American. Oct., pp. 19–25.
   1969   The Possessions of the Poor. Scientific American, Oct. pp. 114–24.

Lockhart, James
   1974   Spanish Peru, 1530–1560. Madison: Univ. of Wisconsin Press.

López, A., ed.
   1980   The Puerto Ricans: Their History, Culture and Society. Cambridge, Mass.: Schenkman.

López de Molina, Diana
   n.d.   La Arqueología como Ciencia Social. Manuscript. Río Piedras: Universidad de Puerto Rico, Facultad de Ciencias Sociales.

Lorenz, Konrad
   1962   The Function of Colour in Coral Reef Fishes. Proceedings of the Royal Institute of Great Britain 39:282–96.

Loven, Sven
   1935   Origins of the Tainan Culture, West Indies. Goteborg, Sweden: Elanders Bokfryckeri Akfiebolag.

Lynch, Kevin
   1960   The Image of the City. Cambridge, Mass.: MIT Press.

Maldonado-Denis, Manuel
   1972   Puerto Rico: A Socio-Historic Interpretation. New York: Random House.

Margolis, Luise
   1979   Introduction: The Process of Social Urbanization in Latin America. Urban Anthropology 8:213–25.

Markham, S.D.
   1977   The Gridiron Plan and the Caste System in Colonial Central America. In Western Expansion and Indigenous Peoples: The Heritage of Las Casas. Elías Sevilla-Casas, ed., 59–78. The Hague: Mouton.
   1984   Architecture and Urbanization in Colonial Chiapas. Philadelphia: American Philosophical Society.

Martorell, Antonio
   1976   La Estética Visual Puertorriqueña. In Los Puertorriqueños y la Cultura. Unit 5:1–19. New York: Centro de Estudios Puertorriqueños, City Univ. of New York.

Mason, J. Alden
   1941   A Large Archaeological Site at Capa, Utuado, with Notes on Other Porto Rican Sites Visited in 1914–15. New York Academy of Sciences, Scientific Survey 18(2): 211–72.

Maxwell, Robert J.
    1978   Looking Into Space. Reviews in Anthropology 5(1): 75–81.

Meléndez Muñoz, Miguel
    1937   La Realidad del Jíbaro. Puerto Rico Illustrado 28. Rpt. *in* Eugenio Fernández Méndez 1975, 647–52. Río Piedras: Editorial Universitaria.

Méndez Santos, Carlos
    1973   Por Tierras de Loiza Aldea. Ponce: Producciones Ceiba.

Menéndez Pérez, Jorge
    n.d.   La Parguera. Student Paper. School of Architecture, University of Puerto Rico, Río Piedras.

Meunier, John, ed.
    1980   Language in Architecture (Proceedings of the 68th Annual Meeting of ACSA). Washington, D.C.: Association of Collegiate Schools of Architecture.

Mintz, Sidney W.
    1974   Caribbean Transformations. Chicago: Aldine.

Mintz, Sidney W., and Richard Price
    1976   An Anthropological Approach to the Afro-American Past: A Caribbean Perspective. Philadelphia: ISHI. ISHI Occasional Papers in Social Change, 2.

Moneo, Rafael
    1978   On Typology. Oppositions. Summer:22–45.

Morales, Elena
    1943   La Vivienda en Puerto Rico. Revista Asociación de Maestros 2:185–90. Rpt. *in* Eugenio Fernández Méndez, 1975, 1027–38. Río Piedras: Editorial Universitaria.

Morales Cabrera, Pablo
    n.d.   Puerto Rico Indígena: Prehistoria y Protohistoria de Puerto Rico. San Juan: Imprenta Venezuela.

Morison, Samuel Eliot
    1939   The Second Voyage of Christopher Columbus from Cadiz to Hispaniola and the Discovery of the Lesser Antilles. Oxford, Eng.: Clarendon Press.
    1942   Admiral of the Ocean Sea. Boston: Little, Brown.
    1974   The European Discovery of America: The Southern Voyages, A.D. 1492–1616. New York: Oxford Univ. Press.

Mumford, Lewis
    1956   From the Ground Up: Observations on Contemporary Architecture, Housing, Highway Building and Civic Design. New York: Harcourt, Brace.

Newman, Oscar
    1975   Design Guidelines for Creating Defensible Space. National In-

stitute of Law Enforcement and Criminal Justice, U.S. Dept. of Justice. Washington, D.C.: Government Printing Office.

1976 Defensible Space: Crime Prevention Through Urban Design. In Urban Problems: Psychological Inquiries. Neil C. Kalt and Sheldon S. Zalkind, eds. New York: Oxford Univ. Press.

Norberg-Schutz, C.
1968 Intentions in Architecture. Cambridge, Mass.: MIT Press.

Oliveira Marqués, A.H. de
1971 Daily Life in Portugal in the Late Middle Ages. Madison: Univ. of Wisconsin Press.

Palm, Erwin Walter
1974 Arquitectura y Arte Colonial en Santo Domingo. Santo Domingo: Editora de la Universidad Autónoma de Santo Domingo. Publicaciones 65. Colección Historia y Sociedad 8.

Patterson, Miles
1968 Spatial Factors in Social Interactions. Human Relations 21: 351–61.

Pérez de la Riva, Francisco
1948 La Habitación Rural en Cuba: El Bohío, la Quinta, el Barracón y la Casa de Vivienda. 3rd Congreso Histórico Municipal Interamericano. Actas y Documentos, 135–219. San Juan.
1952 La Habana. Contribución del Grupo Guama. Antropología 26.

Pérez-Chanis, Efraín E.
1975 Génesis y Ruta de la Arquitectura en Puerto Rico, 1493–1975. Manuscript. School of Architecture, Univ. of Puerto Rico.
1976 Génesis y Ruta de la Arquitectura en Puerto Rico. In La Gran Enciclopedia de Puerto Rico, vol. 9, pp. 1–188. San Juan, Puerto Rico en la Mano y La Gran Enciclopedia de Puerto Rico. Madrid, Spain: C. Corredera.

Perin, Constance
1977 Everything in Its Place: Social Order and Land Use in America. Princeton, N.J.: Princeton Univ. Press.

Pico, Fernando
1983 Los Jornaleros de la Libreta en Puerto Rico a Mediados del Siglo 19: Una comparación entre la montaña (Utuado) y la costa (Camuy). Prepublication version of a paper submitted to Cuadernos de la Facultad de Humanidades. Río Piedras: Univ. of Puerto Rico.

Pinkerton, John
1812 A General Collection of the Best and Most Interesting Voyages and Travels in All Parts of the World, Many of Which are now Translated into English. The History of the Life and Actions of Admiral Christopher Colon, Written by His Own Son, Don Ferd-

inand Colon and of His Discovery of the West Indies, Called the New World. Now in Possession of His Catholic Majesty. Vol. 12:1–155. London: Longman.

Qué Pasa? San Juan, Puerto Rico
   1970   31:1 (and subsequent issues) to 1979.

Quintero Ribera, A.G.
   1972   El Desarrollo de las Clases Sociales y los Conflictos Políticos en Puerto Rico. *In* Rafael Ramirez, Barry B. Levine, and Carlos Buitrago Ortiz, 1972, 31–75.

Rainwater, Lee
   1973   Fear and the House-as-Haven in the Lower Class. *In* Housing Urban America. Jon Pynoos et al., eds., 181–90. Chicago: Aldine.

Ramírez, Rafael L.
   1972   Marginalidad, Dependencia y Participación Política en el Arrabal. *In* Rafael Ramírez, Barry B. Levine, Carlos Buitrago Ortiz 1972, 97–118.
   1976   La Cultura de la Liberación y la Liberación de la Cultura. *In* Los Puertorriqueños y la Cultura. Unit 6:1–20. New York: Centro de Estudios Puertorriqueños, City University of New York.
   1976   National Culture in Puerto Rico. Latin American Perspectives 3(3):109–16.
   1977   El Arrabal y La Política. Río Piedras: Editorial Universitaria.

Ramírez, Rafael L.; Barry B. Levine; and Carlos Buitrago Ortiz, eds.
   1972   Problemas de Desigualdad Social en Puerto Rico. Rio Piedras: Ediciones Librería Internacional.

Rapoport, Amos
   1968   The Personal Element in Housing: An Argument for Open-Ended Design. RIBA Journal, 75(7):300–307.
   1969   House Form and Culture. Englewood Cliffs, N.J.: Prentice-Hall.
   1976   (ed.) The Mutual Interaction of People and Their Built Environment. The Hague: Mouton.
   1977   Human Aspects of Urban Form: Towards a Man-Environment Approach to Urban Form and Design. New York: Pergamon.
   1982   The Meaning of the Built Environment. Berkeley, Calif.: Sage.

Rapoport, Amos, and Robert E. Kantor
   1967   Complexity and Ambiguity in Environmental Design. Journal of American Institute of Planners, V.33(4):210–21.

Reed, Torres, Beauchamp, Marvel
   n.d.   Un Estudio de la Zona Histórica y El Área Central de la Ciudad de Ponce para La Junta de Planificación de Puerto Rico.

Reining, P., and B. Lenkerd, eds.
   1980   Village Viability in Contemporary Society. Boulder, Colo.: Westview. AAAS Selected Seminar Series.

Richardson, Miles
   1984   Place and Culture: A Final Note. Geoscience and Man 24:65–67.
Rifkind, Carole
   1980   A Field Guide to American Architecture. New York: New American Library.
Robbins, Michael C.
   1971   Material Culture and Cognition. *In* Art and Aesthetics in Primitive Societies. C.F. Jopling, ed., 328–34. New York: Dutton.
Robbins, Richard H.
   1973   Identity, Culture and Behavior. *In* Handbook of Social and Cultural Anthropology. John J. Honigmann, ed., 1199–1222. Chicago: Rand, McNally.
Roberts, Lydia J., and Rosa Luisa Stefani
   1949   Patterns of Living in Puerto Rican Families. Río Piedras: University of Puerto Rico.
Rogler, Lloyd H.
   1972   Migrant in the City: The Life of a Puerto Rican Action Group. New York: Basic Books.
Rogler, Lloyd H. and August B. Hollingshead
   1965   Trapped: Families and Schizophrenia. New York: Wiley.
Rosario, José C.
   1934   Nuestra Herencia Social y El Jíbaro de Puerto Rico. Revista Brujala 1(2). Rpt. *in* Eugenio Fernández Méndez 1975, 666–78.
Rouse, Irving
   1941   An Analysis of the Artifacts of the 1914–15 Porto Rican Survey. New York Academy of Sciences. Scientific Survey 18(2):273–303.
   1964   Prehistory of the West Indies. Science 144:499–513.
Rudofsky, Bernard
   1964   Architecture Without Architects. Garden City, N.Y.: Doubleday.
   1977   The Prodigious Builders. New York: Harcourt, Brace, Jovanovich.
Ruesch, Jurgen, and Weldon Kees
   1972   Nonverbal Communication. Berkeley: Univ. of California Press.
Rykwert, Joseph
   1976   The Ideas of a Town. Princeton, N.J.: Princeton Univ. Press.
Safa, Helen I.
   1973   Progress and Poverty: A Study of Relocated Shanty Town Families in Puerto Rico. *In* The Family in the Caribbean: Proceedings of the Second Conference on the Family in the Caribbean, Aruba, Netherlands Antilles, Dec. 1–5, 1969. Stanford N. Gerber, ed., 95–103. Rio Piedras: Univ. of Puerto Rico.
   1974   The Urban Poor of Puerto Rico: A Study in Development and Inequality. New York: Holt, Rinehart and Winston.

Sahlins, Marshall
   1977   Colors and Cultures. *In* Symbolic Anthropology. Janet L. Dolgin, David S. Kemnitzer, and David M. Schneider, eds., 165–80. New York: Columbia Univ. Press.

Salisbury, Richard F., and Mary E. Salisbury
   1972   The Rural Oriented Strategy of Urban Adaptation: Siane Migrants in Port Moresby. *In* The Anthropology of Urban Environments. Thomas Weaver and Douglas White, eds., 59–68. Washington, D.C. *Society for Applied Anthropology* (Monograph No. 11.)

Sánchez, Luis Rafael
   1980   Macho Camacho's Beat. New York: Pantheon.

Sánchez Vilella, Roberto
   1984   Puerto Rico and the US: The Political Economy of Later-Day Bootstrap. Caribbean Review 13(3):4–12.

Sarnoff, Henry
   1974   Measuring Attributes of the Visual Environment. *In* Designing for Human Behavior. Jon Lang et al., eds., 244–60. Stroudsburg, Pa.: Dowden, Hutchinson, and Ross.

Schaedel, Richard P.
   1979   From Homogenization to Heterogenization in Lima, Peru. Urban Anthropology 8:399–420.

Schapiro, Meyer
   1962   Style. *In* Anthropology Today. Sol Tax, ed., 278–303. Chicago: Univ. of Chicago Press.

Scheflen, Albert E.
   1976   Some Territorial Layouts in the United States. *In* Amos Rapoport 1976, 177–221.

Science
   1976   Housing (special issue). June 4.

Scully, Vincent
   1973   American Architecture and Urbanism. New York: Praeger.

Seda Bonilla, Eduardo
   1969   Spiritualism, Psychoanalysis and Psychodrama. American Anthropologist 71:493–97.

Sheehan, Susan
   1976   A Welfare Mother. Boston: Houghton Mifflin.

Silva, Ana Margarita
   1945   La Cultura del Campesino Puertorriqueño. *In* Eugenio Fernández Méndez 1975, 674–704.

Smith, W. John
   1977   The Behavior of Communicating: An Ethological Approach. Cambridge: Harvard Univ. Press.

Sommer, Robert
   1969   Personal Space. Englewood Cliffs, N.J.: Prentice-Hall.
Sperber, Dan
   1974   Rethinking Symbolism. Cambridge, Eng.: Cambridge Univ. Press.
Sternlieb, George, and James W. Hughes
   1980   The Changing Demography of the Central City. Scientific American 243(2):48–53.
Steward, Julian H., et al.
   1956   The People of Puerto Rico. Urbana: Univ. of Illinois Press.
Stiny, George
   1980   Languages of Style. *In* Meunier 1980, 258–262.
Suedfeld, Peter, and James A. Russell, eds.
   1976   The Behavioral Basis of Design. Book I. Stroudsburg, Pa.: Dowden, Hutchinson, and Ross.
Shuttles, Gerald D.
   1968   The Social Order of the Slum. Chicago: Univ. of Chicago Press.
Torres, Beauchamp, Marvel
   1975   Manatí Arquitectura y Conservación. Auspiciado por Fideicomiso de Conservación de Puerto Rico para el Municipio de Manatí . . .
Tringham, R., ed.
   1973   Evidence for the Use and Organization of Space. Andover, Mass.: Warner.
Tuan, Yi-Fu
   1974   Topophilia: A Study of Environmental Perception, Attitudes and Values. Englewood Cliffs, N.J.: Prentice-Hall.
   1984   In Place, Out of Place. Geoscience and Man 24:3–10.
Tumin, Melvin M., with Arnold S. Feldman
   1971   Social Class and Social Change in Puerto Rico. 2d ed. New York: Bobbs-Merrill.
Turner, Daymond, trans. and ed.
   1975   Oviedo y Valdés, Captain Gonzalo Fernández . . . The Conquest and Settlement of the Island of Boriquen or Puerto Rico. Avon, Conn.: Limited Editions.
Turner, John F.C.
   1974   The Fits and Misfits of People's Housing. RIBA Journal, 81(2): 12–21.
   1976   Housing as a Support System. Architectural Design. 46:222–25.
   1977   Housing by People. New York: Pantheon.
Turner, Victor
   1967   The Forest of Symbols: Aspects of Ndembu Ritual. Ithaca: Cornell Univ. Press.

Uzzell, Douglas
   1979   Conceptual Fallacies in the Rural-Urban Dichotomy. Urban Anthropology 8:333–56.

Van den Burghe, Pierre L.
   1973   Pluralism. In Handbook of Social and Cultural Anthropology. John J. Honigmann, ed., 959–77. Chicago: Rand, McNally.

Vásquez Calcerrada, P.B.
   1960   Housing in Puerto Rico under the Mutual Aid and Self-Help Program. International Federation for Housing and Planning, Interamerican Planning Society, Puerto Rico.

Venturi and Rauch
   1976   Signs of Life: Symbols in the American City. Exhibition catalog. Washington, D.C.: Renwick Gallery, Smithsonian Institution.

Vlach, John
   1977   Shotgun Houses. Natural History, Feb:86(4) 51–57.
   1978   The Afro-American Tradition in Decorative Arts. Exhibition catalog. Cleveland, Ohio: Cleveland Museum of Art.

Wampler, Jan
   1977   All Their Own. Cambridge, Mass.: MIT Press.

Watson, O. Michael
   1972   Symbolic and Expressive Uses of Space: An Introduction to Proxemic Behavior. Reading, Mass.: Addison-Wesley. Module 20.

Weaver, Thomas, and Douglas White, eds.
   1972   The Anthropology of Urban Environments. Washington, D.C.: Society for Applied Anthropology, (Monograph No. 11).

Weismann, Elizabeth Wilder
   1976   Americas: The Decorative Arts in Latin America in the Era of the Revolution. Washington, D.C.: Renwick Gallery, Smithsonian Institution.

Welsch, Roger L.
   1979   Front Door, Back Door. Natural History 88(6):76–82.

Whiffen, Marcus
   1969   American Architecture Since 1780: A Guide to the Styles. Cambridge, Mass.: MIT Press.

Wilson, Peter J.
   1969   Reputation and Respectability: A Suggestion for Caribbean Ethnology. Man 4:70–84.

Wilson, Samuel, Jr., and Bernard Lehman
   1974   New Orleans Architecture. Vol. 1: The Lower Garden District. Vol. 4: The Creole Faubourgs. Vol. 5: The Esplanade Ridge. Gretna, La.: Pelican Press.

Wolf, Eric R.
- 1982 Europe and the People Without History. Berkeley: Univ. of California Press.

Wolf, Kathleen L.
- 1972 Growing Up and Its Price in Three Puerto Rican Subcultures. *In* Eugenio Fernández Méndez, 1972, 233–76.

Yancey, William
- 1976 Architecture, Interaction and Social Control: The Case of a Large-Scale Public Housing Project. *In* Urban Problems: Psychological Inquiries. Neil C. Kalt and Sheldon S. Zalkind, eds., 169–79. New York: Oxford Univ. Press.

Zeisel, John
- 1971 Social Research in Architectural Planning. Mimeographed paper.
- 1975 Sociology and Architectural Design. New York: Russell Sage.

Zéndequi, Guillermo de
- 1977 City Planning in the Spanish Colonies. Americas: Feb., supp. 1, 1–12.

Index

adobe, 14, 15, 65
aesthetic, 204, 217, 218, 227, 232, 247, 250; display, 40, 215, 255; investment, 59, 61; needs, 168, 248, 249; preference, 5, 56, 128, 197, 220, 233, 236, 243
Africa, African, 5, 11, 13, 16–23, 198, 233, 247
African-inspired house, 21, 76
agregado, 13, 31, 45, 57, 233; *see also* landless
Aguadilla, 28, 36, 137, 145
Aibonito, 93
alcaría, 20
America, American, 28, 36, 38, 42, 49, 141, 145, 160, 168, 223, 234
American-type, 145, 148, 154–64
Americanism, 148–53, 168
Americanization, 44, 52, 157
Añasco, 40, 99, 115
Andalusia, Andalusian, 13, 29, 92, 263
antesala, 103, 108, 109, 139, 145, 156, 214
Antilles, 1
apartments, 25, 111, 180, 192, 246

Arawak, 5, 7
arches, 23, 34, 46, 48, 49, 93, 145, 157, 172, 216, 226, 238, 240; *see also* Mudejar
architect-designed, 49, 128, 156, 157, 173
Arecibo, 13, 111
arrabal, arrabales, 19, 45, 56, 57–59, 70, 74, 180, 184, 188, 190, 198, 201, 205, 233, 246, 249, 256, 266
arrabal house, 58–59, 64, 115, 179, 180, 181, 184–88, 190, 192, 193, 207, 244, 246–48, 251, 259
Arroyo, 32, 151
Art Deco, 49, 145, 148, 149, 151, 156–57, 160, 175, 205, 230, 233, 240, 243, 246
Art Nouveau, 33
artisan, 12, 15, 20, 28, 40
Asturias, 29
Atlantic, 2
audiencias, 12
ausubo, 15, 66
axis, axes, 31, 204, 209, 214, 222, 223, 251

baile de bomba, 29
balcón, balcones (balconies), 15, 32, 33, 37, 48, 49, 56, 58, 67, 68, 70, 73, 74, 76, 78, 81, 84, 90, 92, 93, 97, 98, 106, 108, 115, 118, 120, 134, 136, 137, 139, 141, 145, 149, 151, 159, 163, 164, 172, 193, 209, 211, 212, 214, 225, 231, 235, 236, 237, 238, 239, 240, 244, 249, 253
balustrades, 29, 34, 37, 70, 75, 81, 84, 90, 97, 145, 151, 175, 204, 205, 211, 237, 243
bamboo, 23, 51, 65
baño (bathroom), 67, 68, 73, 75, 78, 86, 90, 109, 120, 156, 170, 214, 253, 267
Barcelona, 6, 27
barranca (ravine), 52, 58
Barranquitas, 151
barrier, 203, 209, 216, 221, 223, 225, 232, 236, 237, 240, 244, 250
batey, 7, 23, 50, 244
bathroom. See *baño*
beams, 8, 51, 66, 67, 215, 216
Beaux Arts, 46, 141, 205, 226
bedroom. See *dormitoria*
bejucos (vines), 8
belvedere, 37, 39, 133, 134, 165
belvedere house, 137, 139
bihao, 8
blacks, 12, 13, 15, 17, 18, 19, 20, 21, 26
boards, 9, 15, 22, 51, 66, 67
Boca de Cangrejos, 20
bohío, 5–9, 15, 20, 21, 22, 26, 50, 51, 52, 56, 58, 60, 61, 64, 65, 66, 74, 81, 235, 245, 261
Boriquén, 6, 264
boundary, boundaries, 203, 209, 211, 214, 222, 223, 225, 231, 232, 236, 244, 246, 251, 255; see also fences, walls
brackets, 37, 75, 238
brick, 14, 23, 33, 65, 66, 151, 252
bungalow, bungaloid, 47, 49, 50, 69, 141, 148, 149, 151, 154, 205, 230, 235, 242

caballeros, 13
cabildo, 12
Cabo Rojo, 13
cacique, 7, 10, 11
Caguas, 10
California, 39, 47, 48, 163
camelback, 36, 133, 134, 136, 139, 151, 239, 242
caminera, 93
Camuy, 235
Canary Islands, 13, 29, 70
cane, 5, 6, 7, 8, 15, 22, 23, 26, 51, 65, 192, 235, 251
caney, 7, 8, 50
Cangrejos, 28
Caparra, 10
Carib, 11
Caribbean, 2, 21, 29, 38, 61, 93, 205, 233, 234
Caribbean architecture, 70, 91, 166, 259
Carlos III, 27
carpenter, carpentered, 21, 28, 39, 51, 64, 166, 252
carport, 56, 145, 170, 251, 255
casa, 7
Casa Blanca, 14
cast-iron, 34, 36, 100
Castro, Pedro de, 37
Catalans, 28, 32, 108, 200, 222
cathedral, 13
Cayey, 28, 145, 160
Ceiba, 84
ceilings, 14, 215, 216, 226
cement, 56, 217
central hall, 131, 145, 160
chandelier, 217, 227, 238, 245
chapel, 20, 108
church, 11, 15, 20, 43, 44, 223
Ciales, 103, 149
circulation, 73, 74, 127, 203, 212, 214, 221, 225
cisterns, 15, 23
city, cities, 10, 12, 15, 28, 45, 54, 56, 57, 181, 198, 200, 246

class: lower, 9, 13, 26, 45, 54, 59, 129, 250; lower-middle, 49, 54; middle, 26, 34, 41, 45, 49, 52, 54, 59, 129, 168, 179, 201, 256; upper, 13, 14, 21, 23, 26, 40, 41, 45, 49, 52, 54, 59, 129, 168, 200; upper-middle, 49, 52, 129, 256
climate, 1, 2, 38, 45, 47, 173, 198
Coamo, 106
coast, coastal, 10, 12, 27, 28, 29, 52, 181, 198
cocina, 67, 68, 75, 78, 81, 84, 86, 87, 90, 92, 99, 103, 109, 118, 120, 157, 183, 212, 214, 241; *see also* kitchen
coffee, 27, 28, 30, 31, 57, 230
coffee plantation, 30–32, 117, 120, 127, 201
Colonial Spanish architecture, 13–16, 23–26, 61, 64, 65, 66, 67, 72, 78, 91, 92, 198, 200, 201, 204, 205, 208–22, 232, 233, 234, 259, 263, 265, 267
color, colored, 35, 39, 56, 58, 59, 61, 127, 204–5, 211, 216, 225, 226, 237, 238, 239, 243, 246, 247, 248, 249, 250, 252, 253, 258, 259
Columbus, 6, 7, 9, 10, 22, 262, 263
columns, 39, 46, 48, 205, 216
comedor, 67, 68, 74, 75, 78, 84, 91, 93, 99, 103, 108, 109, 118, 120, 134, 136, 137, 139, 145, 154, 156, 159, 163, 212, 214, 215, 217, 218, 255
commerce, commercial, 13, 25, 27, 28, 30, 43, 45, 56, 59, 129, 206, 218, 233, 237, 264
communicate, communication, 4, 127, 196, 197, 202, 204, 207, 223, 225
company, companies, 42
concrete, 56, 58, 66, 70, 78, 81, 84, 90, 151, 165, 175, 184, 188, 193, 235, 239, 240, 242, 252
concrete block, 70, 237, 238, 247, 260
construction, 1, 7, 9, 15, 21, 23, 26, 35, 45, 51, 54, 56, 58, 60, 64, 66, 67, 156, 170, 173, 175, 180, 181, 187, 197, 198, 209, 215, 231, 235, 244, 246

contemporary, 198, 205; furnishings, 216, 226, 227, 228, 238; houses, 64, 66, 173, 176, 200; styles, 252, 255, 260
context, 63, 64, 233, 234, 235
contextual information, 195, 197–203, 207, 218, 230, 234
contraband, 13, 17, 27, 264
control, 211, 227, 232; of interaction, 223; of space, 209, 225, 231, 250
conucos, 11
Convent, 23
converted, 84, 93, 111, 159, 170; *see also* remodeled, transformed
core, 65, 66, 67, 93, 120, 134, 136
core rectangle, 68, 70, 73, 74, 78, 81, 84, 98
corn, 10
corner entrance, 117, 141
cornice, 14, 15, 23, 25
corral, corrales, 12, 15, 52
Corsica, Corsicans, 29, 32
counter, 156, 157, 241
country house, 50, 127, 148, 164–67, 173–76, 231
craft, craftsmanship, 21, 136
Criollo, 29, 32, 34, 40, 44, 59, 69, 84, 87, 93, 97, 103, 106, 109, 111, 115, 120, 127, 129, 131, 136, 141, 168, 180, 188, 198, 200, 201, 202, 204, 205, 223, 225, 227, 231, 232, 233, 234, 235, 236–39, 242, 246, 252
Criollo Neoclassic, 34, 40, 69, 76, 84, 90, 93, 99, 103, 106, 111, 120
Criollo Pueblerino, 32, 34, 69, 78, 81, 111
crop, 13, 27, 28, 30, 50
Cuban vernacular houses, 22
Culebra, 2
cultivable, cultivation, 4, 10, 30
Cumberland, 13

Delfina, 120
Delicias, 120
designed house, 64, 70, 76, 78, 84, 87, 92, 93, 99, 103, 111, 115, 118, 120,

designed house (continued)
127, 128, 129, 131, 137, 139, 141, 145, 148, 151, 154, 160, 163, 170, 175, 176, 179, 190, 193, 204, 207, 208–34, 236, 242, 243, 250, 251–53, 256, 258

developments (residential), 54, 170, 175, 200, 201, 251, 252, 255, 259; see also urbanizaciones

dignidad (dignity), xx, 222, 239, 240, 243, 245, 246, 247, 250, 258, 259

dirt floor, 5, 72, 120

display, 36, 56, 160, 195, 216, 220, 222, 245, 246, 247, 249; aesthetic, 40, 215, 243; status, 226, 238, 249; wealth, 40, 87

dominance, 203, 222, 223, 225, 246

Dominicans, 27

door, 7, 22, 34, 51, 66, 69, 73, 81, 99, 118, 131, 157, 170, 205, 215, 223, 232, 238, 247, 251

doorway, 23, 86, 115, 216, 243

dormer, 47, 93, 115, 151

dormitorio (bedroom), 22, 51, 67, 68, 74, 75, 76, 78, 81, 84, 86, 87, 90, 91, 92, 93, 98, 99, 103, 108, 109, 111, 115, 118, 120, 131, 133, 134, 136, 139, 156, 157, 159, 170, 172, 183, 214, 215, 216, 217, 218, 241, 245, 253

Dos Rios, 120

Drake, Sir Francis, 12

Dutch, 12, 13, 17

Early Gothic, Early Gothic Revival, 36, 37, 93, 259

Eastlake, 39

eclectic, 35, 131–39, 141, 160, 201, 204, 205, 222–30, 232, 233

education, 27, 43, 45, 128, 129, 141, 168, 175, 190

El Fanguito, 19, 57

El Morro, 13

elite, 232, 233, 234, 250, 258

emit, emitters, 196, 197, 203, 209, 221, 222, 223, 232, 236, 247, 250

encomendados, 18

engineer, 90, 166

England, English, 12, 13, 17, 18, 28, 36, 37, 44

entrance, entries, entryways, 9, 47, 49, 52, 69, 70, 75, 78, 90, 98, 106, 111, 115, 117, 120, 136, 165, 166, 170, 172, 183, 192, 203, 209, 218, 222, 223, 231, 246, 247, 251, 253, 255

environment, 47, 61, 72, 179, 195, 196, 197, 198, 204, 211, 234, 244

Esperanza, 30

estancias, 11, 12, 13

Estremadura, 13, 263

ethnic, ethnicity, 5, 19, 40, 222

Europe, Europeans, 4, 5, 6, 20, 27, 29, 35, 36, 40, 49, 61, 129, 168, 211, 226

European Central Hall, 90, 91

European Neoclassic, 25

excluding, exclusion, 203, 204, 207, 211, 216, 221, 222, 223, 225, 231, 236, 237, 240, 244, 250

exterior, 52, 64, 65, 66, 67, 70, 74, 93, 98, 99, 131, 139, 168, 193, 202, 203, 204, 211, 212, 223, 225, 226, 231, 258

exterior ornamentation, 204–7, 211–12, 223–25, 236–38, 246–47, 250, 254, 256

exterior spatial organization, 208–9, 222–23, 231, 236, 239–40, 244–45, 246, 251

facade, 33, 48, 49, 56, 67, 69–70, 71, 72, 76, 81, 84, 98, 99, 115, 120, 127, 151, 156, 168, 170, 205, 208, 209, 214, 221, 222, 223, 233, 236, 240, 252, 253, 258

factoría central, 29, 42, 166

Fajardo, 149, 239, 242

family, families, 7, 30, 40, 99, 111, 127, 139, 168, 170, 172, 173, 180, 181, 183, 184, 192, 193, 199, 200, 201, 203, 211, 212, 214, 215, 217, 218, 220, 221, 222, 227, 228, 231, 232, 233, 234, 238, 239, 243, 244, 245, 246, 250, 253, 255, 258, 259

family room, 84, 99, 170, 255

fanlights, 33, 216
fence, fenced, fencing, 203, 209, 211, 214, 222, 223, 231, 236, 237, 244, 245, 246
FHA, 54
fiesta, 13, 27, 200
finca (farm), 165
five opening, 69, 111, 115, 120
flat roofs, 15, 23, 54, 71, 76, 78, 149, 170, 238
floor, 7, 22, 51, 57, 58, 65, 66, 81, 117, 172, 215, 217, 220, 239
floral, flowers, 50, 99, 209, 226, 228, 247
Florida, 48, 170
fogón (stove), 22
forests, 2, 231
form, xxii, 69, 118, 203, 231; architectural, 29, 52, 56, 61, 151, 250; house, 7, 63, 64, 66, 67, 128, 129, 131, 187, 192–93, 195, 196, 233
formal, 209, 211, 230, 231, 236; design, 74, 90, 99, 131, 139, 148, 157, 214, 249
formal organization, 63, 67–74, 127, 148, 154
formality, 168, 221, 228, 232
fort, fortifications, fortress, 12, 13, 14, 26, 27, 40, 198
four opening, 69, 98–109, 115
France, French, 12, 13, 27, 28, 37, 99, 115, 225
frets, 49, 145, 151, 240
frontal, frontality, 223
fruit, 12, 23, 99, 209, 226
furnishings, furnished, 203, 215, 227, 238, 241, 245, 247, 267
furniture, 2, 22, 39, 216, 217, 220, 221, 226, 227, 239, 247, 255

gable, 8, 36, 37, 47, 71, 72, 75, 78, 86, 98, 103, 109, 120, 164, 166, 238
galería, 72, 78, 84, 91, 92, 99, 103, 108, 109, 115, 118, 120, 145, 159, 214, 225
Galicia, 29, 200

garage, 118, 156, 160, 170, 173
gardens, 7, 23, 84, 90, 93, 99, 156, 172, 209, 211, 222, 225, 239, 244, 251, 255
gente de razón, 26
geographical, geography, 1–4, 61, 197, 199, 200, 201, 220, 222, 234, 264
ginger, 13
gingerbread, 36, 39, 61, 260
glass: stained, 34, 90; windows, 23, 45, 151, 170, 211, 252
gold, gold-mining, 11, 12, 16
government officials, 13, 168, 175, 180, 233
grand house, 84, 90, 99, 120, 127, 128, 129, 131, 139, 141, 148, 159, 160, 163, 170, 200, 204, 205, 206, 211, 215, 220, 223, 225, 230
Greek Revival, 131, 139, 222
grilles. See *rejas*
ground level (height above), 29, 51, 52, 67, 70, 72, 76, 84, 110, 115, 117, 118, 120, 164, 175, 203, 209, 223, 231
Guadianilla, 13
Guanica, 10
Guayama, 13, 32, 60, 84, 93, 99, 103, 156, 234
Guinea Coast, 18

hacendado, 28, 30
hacienda, 19, 27, 28–32, 42, 57, 120, 127, 176, 231
hacienda house, 21, 29–32, 110, 111, 117–27, 131, 176, 231, 234
Haiti, 2, 7, 18
half-*balcón*, 73, 78, 84, 87, 90, 165, 235
hall, hallways, 87, 111, 141, 145, 156, 170, 225, 253
handbooks, 29, 36, 47
Hatillo, 51
hatos, 12, 13
haytinales, 8
herringbone siding, 103, 109
High Neoclassic, 45, 99, 109, 200, 205, 226
High Victorian Gothic, 37

hip roofs, 29, 32, 47, 71, 72, 84, 86, 99, 118, 145, 149, 151, 154, 159, 164, 165, 166, 238
Hispanic, Hispanicism, 30, 44, 214
Hispañola, 2
hogs, pigs, 12, 13
home, 180, 242, 259
homeowner, 53, 59, 61, 211, 235, 244, 253
horcones, 8
Hormigueros, 120
house and tienda, 110, 111, 115–17, 131, 188, 209, 246
housing developments, 45, 54, 170, 180, 192, 246
Humacao, 145, 160, 163
hurricanes, 14, 26, 28, 52, 56, 190, 198, 264

IBEC, 54
identity, 175, 196, 204, 207, 211, 218, 227, 234, 237, 238, 239, 246, 247, 251, 253, 256, 258, 259; family, 127, 214, 215, 217, 220, 243; national, 26; regional, 61, 199–201
immigrants, immigration. See migrants, migration
improvements to houses, 70, 76; see also remodel, transform
independence (political), 28, 234
index, indexes, 196, 197, 203, 211, 214, 217, 221, 222, 223, 227, 231, 250
Indians, 7, 9, 11, 12, 13, 18, 19, 22, 26, 198; see also Taíno
Indias, Indies, 12
indicator, 128, 129, 197, 203, 209, 211, 215, 225, 231, 251, 266
individualism, individualize, 40, 53, 54, 58, 59, 60, 61, 175, 188, 193, 200, 204, 205, 211, 221, 225, 238, 243, 250, 258, 259, 260
industrial, industry, 43, 45, 129, 166
informal, 61, 99, 238; design, 103, 223, 231
informality, 52, 227, 232

inhabitants, 27, 58, 63, 180, 190, 244, 245, 247, 250, 258
innovation, 4, 23, 45, 131, 139, 141, 193, 222, 225, 237
insects, 56, 66, 72, 190
interior, 14, 34, 49, 64, 65, 66, 67, 68, 70, 73, 74, 86, 93, 98, 99, 103, 108, 115, 133, 136, 141, 160, 168, 193, 202, 203, 212, 214, 215, 216, 220, 221, 225, 230, 231, 232, 235
interior ornamentation, 215–21, 225–28, 238–39, 253, 255
interior spatial organization, 212–15, 225, 238–39, 245, 253, 255
International Style, 54, 170, 258
invitation, 70, 204, 209, 223, 225
iron fences, railings, 25, 223
ironwood, 32, 66; see also *ausubo*
Italian, Italianate, 13, 37, 139

jalousies, 33, 34, 74; see also shutters
Jewish, 12
Jíbaro, 21, 30, 59, 187, 188, 233, 245, 246, 263
Jíbaro house, 21, 22, 23, 40, 50, 58, 64, 179, 181–84, 188, 190, 207, 244–45, 259
jornaleros, 28, 30, 57, 264
Juana Díaz, 103, 137

kitchen, 22, 51, 52, 99, 134, 136, 139, 156, 170, 172, 225, 255, 265; see also *cocina*
Klumb, Henry, 173, 198

L-shaped, 20, 134, 136, 137, 151
La Parguera, 179, 266
La Perla, 58, 198
La Vida, 58
labor, 16, 19, 27, 30
laborers, 12, 27, 28, 31
land, 12, 19, 23, 27, 28, 42, 54, 117, 180, 187, 198, 222, 223, 239, 246
landholders, landholdings, landowners, 12, 13, 27, 29

landless, 31, 45, 57, 264; see also agregado
landscape, 222, 228, 231, 244
Lares, 28, 97
Latin America, Latin American, 28, 258
law, 11, 57
Laws of the Indies, 12
Le Corbusier, 173
lean-to, 22, 51, 183, 241
Levitt, Levittown, 54
limpieza de sangre, 12
lintel, 46
loggia, 37
lot, 81, 109, 180, 181, 201, 222, 236, 251
Louisiana, 133
louvered, 23, 170
Luquillo, 2, 78, 183, 198

machine, machinery, 27, 31, 32, 72, 110, 118, 120, 175
mahogany, 66, 115
Mallorca, Mallorcan, 29, 200, 222
mampostería, 14, 15, 33, 34, 66–67, 81, 92, 93, 106, 110, 115, 117, 197
manager, 129, 168, 190
Manatí, 76, 78, 200, 234
manger, 31
manioc, 10
mansions, 35, 40, 127, 139
manufacture, manufacturing, 2, 45, 56, 168, 175, 237, 252
marginal, margins, 45, 56, 184; see also outskirts
María Teresa, 225
Martin Peña caño, 19, 57
masonry, 66, 74, 91, 92
mass-construction, mass-manufactured, 54, 61, 170
master, 18, 19, 28, 118, 120, 131
materials (construction), 1, 4, 9, 15, 26, 40, 41, 50, 54, 56, 64–67, 70, 72, 109, 127, 170, 181, 187, 204, 211, 215, 230, 237, 246, 248, 252

Mayaguez, 13, 28, 92, 136, 165, 233
mayordomo, 31
meanings, xxii, 1, 26, 63, 127, 192, 196, 197, 198, 207, 211, 221, 222, 230, 233, 234, 245, 256, 258, 259
mediopunto, 34, 74, 81, 87, 93, 98, 109, 136, 170, 216, 225, 238
Mediterranean, 33, 205
mementos, 218, 228, 239, 247
merchant, 127, 229, 141, 230
messages, xxiii, 195, 196, 198, 202, 203, 204, 205, 206, 207, 209, 211, 215, 218, 220, 223, 225, 231, 232, 233, 236, 240, 245, 250, 251, 253, 258, 266
metal roofing and siding, 45, 50, 57, 58, 66, 71, 90, 187, 216
Mexican, Mexico, 13, 48
migrants, migration, 27, 29, 30, 42, 61, 190, 200, 222
military, 19, 43, 190; fortifications, 13; out-post, 11; rule, 41
mill (sugar), 13, 16, 20
mirador, 133, 137, 151
Mission, 37, 163
Moca, 28, 99
modernized, 99, 222, 234
modifications to houses, 60, 99, 176, 188, 241, 246, 251, 255, 258, 266; see also remodel, transform
modular, 54, 170, 173, 175, 265
molding, 15, 25, 226
Mona, 2
Moorish, 12
mother-of-pearl, 34
mountain, mountainous, 2, 10, 11, 12, 21, 26, 27, 72, 117, 183
mozarabic, 93, see also arches
Mudejar, 48, 157, 172; see also arches
mulatto, 12, 15, 18, 264
Muñoz Marin, 42
Muñoz Rivera, 28

naboría, 10, 11, 12
Naguabo, 93; 156, 222, 228

Nechodoma, Antonin, 47, 154
neighbor, neighborhood, 26, 40, 127, 172, 180, 188, 192, 201, 203, 206, 209, 235, 237, 238, 244, 246, 249, 250, 255, 256, 258
New Orleans, 33, 36
New York, 190, 200
North America, North American, 18, 32, 35, 44, 45, 61, 141, 145, 154, 168, 204, 255

occupations, 45, 128, 129, 175, 190; see also residence pattern
Old San Juan, 25, 60, 110, 198, 233, 234; see also San Juan
one-room house, 180
O'Reylly, 27
ornament, ornamentation, xxii, 29, 32, 39, 40, 59, 69, 170, 175, 196, 202, 204, 206, 207, 211, 215, 225, 226, 228, 236, 237, 239, 241, 243, 248, 252, 255, 258, 260; see also exterior and interior ornamentation
outskirts, 15, 57, 184; see also marginal
owner: house, 31, 78, 90, 120, 129, 137, 139, 149, 170, 180, 184, 188, 230, 240, 242, 249; plantation, 127, 201; property, 40
owner-built, owner-constructed, 34, 54, 64, 70, 192
ownership, 59, 206, 255, 258

paint, painted, painting, 35, 56, 59, 70, 90, 109, 120, 151, 188, 197, 204, 205, 206, 211, 216, 218, 225, 226, 228, 237, 238, 239, 242, 244, 246, 249, 252, 253
palm, 4, 5, 8, 51
parapets, 48, 72, 76
parcela, 179, 180–81, 188, 190
pardos libres, 18
partial-second-story, 36, 133–39, 239–44
Patillas, 2
patio, 15, 23, 34, 47, 49, 52, 66, 72, 81, 92, 99, 109, 172, 209, 214, 253

pattern books. *See* handbooks
peasant, 13, 50, 57
pediments, 25
peon, peones, 17, 204, 233
persianas, 23
Philip II, 12, 15
photographs (family), 218, 220, 227, 239, 245
pilasters, 25, 34, 46, 48, 252
piracy, pirates, 12, 13, 26, 28, 198, 264
plan: city, town, 15, 201, 249; house, xxii, 47, 54, 63, 64, 65, 67, 68, 69, 73–74, 109, 111, 115, 120, 131, 133, 139, 141, 145, 151, 156, 157, 160, 165, 170, 180, 184, 212, 214, 253, 255
plantation, 19, 29, 40, 42; *see also* hacienda
plants, planting (farm, garden), 7, 30, 50, 203, 222, 246, 253
plaster, 48, 226
plastic, 56
plaza (square), 6, 15, 23, 26, 87, 137, 156, 201, 214, 230, 231
Ponce, 2, 26, 32, 46, 81, 85, 106, 111, 141, 163, 200
Ponce de León, 10, 14, 28
poor (people), 9, 15, 25, 26, 40, 45, 54, 56, 61, 180, 192, 198, 200, 201, 264
popular architecture, 64, 256
popularity: of architectural style or house type, 39, 49, 78, 134, 160, 190, 230, 231
population, 5, 10, 13, 15, 17, 19, 26, 27, 192, 201, 233, 234
portico, 106, 154
ports, 13, 198
Portuguese, 13, 17
post-and-beam, 65
post-and-lintel, 48
posts, 5, 7, 8, 9, 22, 26, 32, 51, 52, 58, 81, 84, 97, 175, 187; *see also zocos*
Prairie, 47, 145, 154–56, 159, 205, 230, 233
preservation (architectural), 60, 233, 234

pride, 39, 195, 200, 206, 211, 228, 240, 245, 246, 247
private, privacy, 74, 127, 141, 203, 211, 212, 214, 216, 217, 218, 225, 227, 241, 244, 253
professional, professions, 42, 44, 129, 166, 168, 175, 190, 200, 231, 233, 253
proletariat, 11, 28, 42, 44
property, 40, 87, 127, 166, 180, 181, 187, 201, 208, 211, 222, 223, 231, 247, 253, 255, 259
public: people, 212; interaction, 209, 211, 216, 217, 222, 233, 251; space, 203, 214, 225, 241, 244, 253
Pueblerino, 34, 39, 40, 49, 58, 60, 69, 111, 180
Puerto Real, 134

Queen Anne, 39, 131, 137, 139, 151, 205, 222

rafters, 8
rain, rainfall, 2, 22, 51
rancho, 52
reconstruct, reconstruction, 5, 58, 84
reforms (social), 27, 45, 54
refrigerator, 87, 175, 238
regidores, 12
region, 54, 61, 110; coastal, 52; identity with, 199–200; mountain, 22, 26; regional style, 29, 98
reinforced concrete, 45, 54, 145, 156, 157, 159, 170, 173, 175, 180, 190, 242
rejas (grilles), 15, 48, 56, 159, 211, 225, 238, 243, 247, 252, 260, 267
religion, religious, 15, 43, 215, 218, 227, 239, 245, 255
remodel, remodeling, 99, 149, 151, 170, 193, 242, 246, 255
residence pattern (social characteristics of residents), 128–31, 141, 168, 175, 188–92
respeto (respectability), xx, 70, 255

restoration, restore, 25, 60, 64, 98, 99, 109, 234
ribbon windows, 47, 49
ridge (roof), 8, 9, 51, 71, 72, 76, 164, 166
Rincón, 28
Rio Grande, 87
Rio Piedras, 111, 136
rivers, 2, 52
road, roadsides, 6, 52, 58, 120, 175, 203, 231
Rockefeller, 54
Romanesque, 36
roofs, roofing, 4, 5, 7, 15, 22, 33, 36, 37, 39, 45, 47, 48, 49, 50, 51, 57, 58, 66, 69, 71–72, 97, 98, 103, 118, 131, 141, 145, 148, 149, 151, 157, 166, 170, 172, 175, 183, 235, 238
rubble, 14, 23, 25, 26, 65; see also *mampostería*
ruined, ruins, 20, 42, 228, 234
rural: area, situation, 54, 61, 72, 110, 127, 173, 175, 197, 198, 201, 231, 244, 245; houses, 26, 40, 57, 61, 64; proletariat. See proletariat
rustication, 25

St. Croix, 18
sala, 51, 67, 68, 73, 74, 75, 78, 84, 91, 93, 109, 111, 115, 118, 120, 139, 145, 159, 163, 170, 183, 212, 214, 215, 217, 225, 226, 238, 245, 247, 253, 255
sala/comedor, 78, 81, 84, 86, 87, 90. 92, 93, 98, 99, 109, 127, 134, 156, 157, 159, 163, 170, 172, 241
San Cristobal, 13
San Francisco (hacienda), 127
San Germán, 12, 13, 15, 16, 30, 32, 60, 99, 139, 222, 234
San Juan, 2, 12, 13, 14, 15, 16, 23, 26, 29, 30, 33, 56, 57, 151, 160, 163, 164, 187, 200; see also Old San Juan
San Juan Bautista, 6
San Mateo de Cangrejos, 18

Santa Clara Abaja, 120
Santa Clara Arriba, 120
Santo Domingo, 2, 10
Santurce, 18
sapodilla, 15
schema, 67–69
schema one, 67, 69, 73, 74–78, 127, 129, 184, 193
schema three, 68, 69, 72, 74, 90–109, 110, 111, 127, 129, 131, 134, 137, 139, 148, 154, 156, 212
schema two, 67, 69, 72, 73, 74, 75, 78–90, 110, 111, 118, 127, 129, 131, 134, 141, 145, 148, 149, 154, 156, 157, 163, 188, 193, 212, 235, 236, 238, 242
sea, 6, 7, 15, 165, 197, 198
second houses, 176–79
second-story, 29, 58, 70, 111, 115, 120, 133, 209, 239
semiotic analysis, 197
servant, 87, 129, 214
settlement pattern, 10, 11, 19, 57, 246; *see also* arrabales
Seville, 12, 13
Sevillian tiles, 14
shelter, 15, 26, 60, 140, 212, 245, 259, 265
shotgun-type house, 36
shutters, 22; *see also* jalousies
siding, 50, 90, 99, 103, 109, 183, 235
signal, 196, 197, 203, 205, 206, 209, 214, 216, 218, 220, 221, 222, 223, 225, 227, 228, 231, 232, 233, 234, 237, 239, 240, 243, 245, 246, 247, 250, 251, 253, 255, 258
site, siting, 10, 19, 28, 54, 99, 120, 180, 197, 198, 201–3, 208, 222, 228, 234, 246
six-opening, 90
slave, 5, 11, 12, 13, 16, 17, 19, 20, 21, 27, 28, 30, 192, 198, 233; quarters, 20, 29; trade, 13, 17
smallpox, 11, 28
soberado, 22

social: control, 232; order, 27, 201, 260; system, 28
social characteristics, xxii, 63; *see also* residence pattern
social level, 5, 45, 56, 59, 61, 64, 127, 128, 129, 131, 168, 190, 192, 201, 202, 204, 207, 209, 217, 218, 250, 251, 258, 259; *see also* class
soffit, 15
solares, 12
soldiers, 11, 13, 18, 19, 27
sótano, 92
Spain, Spaniards, Spanish, 5, 9, 10, 11–16, 19, 26, 29, 40, 41, 44, 45, 48, 53, 60, 66, 91, 92, 99, 110, 129, 175
Spanish Colonial Revival, 47, 48, 49, 53, 145, 148, 157, 160, 163, 164, 172, 205, 223, 226, 230, 240, 258
Spanish government (colonial), 11, 12, 44
Spanish houses. See Colonial Spanish architecture
Spanish Renaissance, 15, 23, 90
Spanish tiles, 49, 56, 66, 111, 157, 226
spatial order, xxii, 5, 9, 67, 137, 202, 204, 207, 212, 222, 230, 231, 236, 244, 251
spatial organization, xxii, 98, 160, 196, 203–4, 221, 242; *see also* exterior and interior spatial organization
spindles, 48, 237
square. See plaza
squatter settlements. *See* arrabal
stair, stairway, steps, 29, 47, 69, 90, 92, 98, 106, 110, 115, 120, 131, 133, 134, 136, 137, 139, 145, 160, 163, 165, 166, 231
standardization, 59, 61, 170, 221, 251, 253
standards, 175, 211, 232, 233, 244, 250, 258
status (social), 11, 26, 40, 59, 60, 72, 127, 175, 190, 196, 201, 203, 207, 209, 211, 214, 215, 217, 218, 220, 222, 223, 226, 228, 234, 237, 238,

status (*continued*)
  239, 240, 243, 245, 246, 249, 250, 251, 255, 256, 258, 259
stone, 14, 15, 23, 26, 52, 60, 65, 192, 251
storage, 14, 15, 78, 86, 87, 90, 139, 214
store. See *tienda*
street, 6, 7, 15, 47, 49, 72, 92, 98, 99, 170, 175, 203, 209, 211, 223, 236, 246, 251
stringers, stringpieces, 8, 51
style, xxii, 1, 4–5, 26, 40, 52, 54, 59, 60, 61, 64, 70, 98, 99, 110, 127, 128, 131, 139, 145, 168, 172, 192, 195, 200, 204, 205, 221, 225, 231, 233, 236; see also particular styles, i.e., Criollo
suburban, 54, 159, 175, 200, 201, 223, 251
sugar, 12, 27, 28, 29, 30, 41, 230; companies, industry, 16, 17, 42, 165; mill, 13, 16; see also *trapiche*; plantation, 117, 118, 120, 127, 201; see also hacienda
swags, 46
symbol, symbolize, 4, 196, 207, 230, 234, 242

Taíno, 5–11, 15, 23, 50, 61, 198, 233; see also Indians; houses, 5–9, 22, 26; see also *bohío*
technical (knowledge), 15, 23, 64, 128, 180, 190, 196
technology (construction), 5, 8, 9, 11, 45, 56, 61, 64, 198, 256, 258
territorial unit, 211, 222, 223, 251
territoriality, 196, 203, 207, 208, 209, 211, 218, 221, 222, 223, 231, 232, 236, 237, 238, 240, 244, 245, 246, 247, 250, 251, 253, 267
thatch, thatched, 4, 5, 8, 9, 23, 51, 66, 235
three opening, 69, 78, 84, 87, 92, 93, 97, 108, 111, 120, 164
tienda (store), 111, 170, 173; see also house and tienda
tile, 15, 48, 49, 66, 71, 136, 145, 148, 154, 157, 172, 175, 215, 217, 239, 252; see also Spanish tile
tobacco, 10, 13, 27
tormentera, 52, 183
tower, 37, 133, 134, 239; house, 136, 137, 139; see also partial-second-story
town, 12, 25, 27, 28, 32, 40, 54, 56, 117, 127, 137, 176, 180, 198, 199, 200, 201, 202, 222, 230, 231, 246; houses, 21, 32–35, 127
transform, transformation, 84, 99, 103, 136, 145, 188, 193, 206, 232, 233, 235, 242, 251, 255; see also remodel
transoms, 34, 216
trapiche, 29, 41
travel, 27, 36, 128, 129, 141, 168, 176, 190; see also residence pattern
tren Jamaica, 41
trim, 61, 90, 93, 115, 120, 151, 205, 238
tropical, tropics, 1, 2, 26, 40, 61, 141, 187, 204, 205; see also climate
turret, 39, 131
two opening, 69, 74, 76, 78, 84, 165
two-house two-story, 111, 192
two-story houses, 25, 29, 109–27, 160, 173, 188, 222, 238
two-story one-family house and mansion, 131, 141, 145, 151, 160, 230

U.S. influence houses, 141–64, 168, 190, 204, 222–30, 232, 239–44, 258
United States influence: architectural, 39, 45, 50, 52, 54, 93, 115, 211; social and political, 41–45, 234
United States pine lumber, 66, 93
urban, 57, 58, 61, 84, 154, 197, 201; houses, 23, 26, 49, 61, 64, 127, 128, 145, 203; proletariat. See proletariat
urbanización, urbanizaciones, 54, 128, 175, 180, 198, 201, 202, 242, 265
urbanización house, 54, 56, 59, 61, 64, 72, 128, 168–73, 175, 176, 180, 188, 190, 192, 204, 208, 228, 246, 251–59, 260, 265

urbanization, 42, 46
Utuado, 10, 46

Valencia, 6, 7
Vega Baja, 28
Venezuela, 18, 27
ventilators, 93, 103, 115
veranda, 36, 47, 50, 70, 131, 166
vernacular houses, 5, 9, 15, 64, 70, 72, 74, 76, 78, 84, 92, 93, 99, 108, 111, 120, 127, 128, 129, 131, 133, 134, 136, 139, 141, 148, 149, 151, 154, 165, 170, 172, 175, 176, 179, 180, 188, 190, 192, 193, 204, 205, 207, 208, 230, 233, 234, 235–48, 250, 251, 253–55, 256, 258
Victorian architecture, 33, 36, 49, 61, 131
Vieques, 2, 199
villa, 12
village, 10, 20, 246

walkway, 81, 170, 179, 223
wall (boundary), 6, 52, 72, 81, 84, 90, 170, 198, 203, 209, 211, 214, 222, 223, 225, 231, 236, 251, 253, 255; see also fences
warehouse, 20, 22, 29, 31, 110, 118
water, 2, 12, 51, 58, 179, 184, 187, 246
welcome (messages of), 205, 207, 221, 222, 223, 231, 232, 236, 237, 239, 250; see also invitation
window, 9, 22, 23, 34, 39, 40, 45, 47, 51, 66, 69, 74, 81, 90, 103, 170, 172, 205, 211, 215, 216, 236, 253; see also glass
winds (prevailing, trade), 2, 197
wood houses, 15, 32, 34, 50, 51, 66, 67, 70, 72, 81, 91, 98, 106, 133, 151, 165, 205, 235, 242, 251
workers, 12, 28, 29, 30, 42, 45, 57, 141, 175, 176, 192, 233, 264; houses, 31, 42
Wright, Frank Lloyd, 46, 47, 150, 173
wrought-iron, 29, 33, 48, 70, 84, 97

yagua, 5, 14, 15, 22, 51, 65, 183, 235
yard, 23, 31, 81, 245, 255
Yauco, 32, 99

zaguán, 22, 81, 111, 115, 209, 265
zinc, 49, 50, 51, 66, 184, 244; see also metal roofing and siding
zocos, 22, 51, 72, 84, 120, 164, 175, 181, 183, 184, 188; see also posts